Bass Boss

Bass Boss

The Inspiring Story of Ray Scott and the Sport Fishing Industry He Created

ROBERT H. BOYLE

Whitetail Trail Press
Pintlala, Alabama

Whitetail Trail Press
Route One, Box 3006
Pintlala, AL 36043

Design by Randall Williams
Black Belt Publishing, Montgomery, Alabama

Printed in the United States of America
by Maple-Vail Book Manufacturing Group.

For my wonderful wife and best friend Susan,
who made this book possible,
and for great friend and early believer Don Butler,
who helped my dreams of B.A.S.S. come true.

—RAY SCOTT

Contents

Photographs follow pages 96 and 224.

ACKNOWLEDGMENTS

FIRST OF ALL, I must thank Ray and Susan Scott for their hospitality and for opening up their minds and hearts for what I declared had to be a "warts and all" biography. They held nothing back, and I owe a special debt to Susan for all the above-and-beyond time and effort that she gave to this book. My thanks to Big Wilson, Steve, and Little Wilson, and thanks also to Eddie Scott, the irrepressible Danny Scott, and Uncle Lloyd A. Scott for their memories of the family and Ray in the early days. Notable among the folks in Pintlala who went out of their way to assist this Yankee are Gary Burton, Beverly Williams, Lisa (Poundcake) Hargrove, the terrific trio of Jenny Olive, Vicki Bender, and Theone Carr, and let us not forget the late (dachshund) Butterbean, the greatest shoe cleaner on the planet.

I owe special gratitude to Sara Boyd Smedley who voluntarily took the trouble to write to me about the early days. My thanks to Dave Newton for his perceptive insights and comments and to Harold ("They're at it again") Sharp, Don Butler, Bob Cobb, and Rhodney Honeycutt for their reminiscences as well as their congenial company in both the States and Mexico. Thanks also to Earl Bentz, Roland Martin, Bill Dance, Archie Phillips, Gene Ciampi, Forrest L. Wood, Jack Wingate, Herman "The German" Tuck, Clark Brennan, Howell Raines, Seth Rosenbaum, Helen Sevier, Ann Lewis, Matt Vincent, Al Redding, Jerry and Debra Dean, Terry Oldham, and Johnny and Jeanie Morris, who not only put

9

up with a stranger but put him up as well on a truly dark and stormy night in Springfield, Missouri.

Back home, my thanks to Bill Tendy for his aid in many ways, and repeated tips of my hat to Carol Valentine for her never-ending help and for spurring me on with tales about the interest that this book holds for Mark Gilmore. I give thanks to Bill and Billy Schroeder, Eric Leiser, Paul Schmookler and Ingrid Sils, Nick Lyons, and John Thorn, all savants of publishing, and to Judith Bowman, booklady extraordinary, and Frank Volkmann, bookman extraordinary, who introduced me to bass fanatic Randy Backer who could not wait to read about Ray Scott. And always, my deepest thanks and love to Ria and to Damachka, *meine grosse liebling.*

ROBERT H. BOYLE

Bass Boss

INTRODUCTION

The Bass Boss

SATURDAY, MARCH 11, 1967. On insurance business in Jackson, Mississippi, Ray Scott took the day off to go fishing with a buddy, Lloyd Lewis, a postman. Spring was coming up the Gulf and the day was supposed to be sunny and warm, but the tail end of a blustery winter snuck down on White's Lake and sent icy rain stabbing through their clothes. After four hours of being soaked and chilled — made all the worse by no bass — Lewis pulled the cord on the eighteen-horsepower engine and headed the little outboard for the launch ramp.

Back at the Ramada Inn, Ray tried to wash the day's miseries out of his joints with a hot shower. Toweling himself down, he turned on the TV, flopped down on the bed, propped a couple of pillows under his head, and watched basketball players race up and down the court. The 1960s were truly the age of sports, he thought. Flick on the tube any weekend, and you could watch basketball, football, baseball, horse racing, auto racing, track , skiing, golf, tennis, bowling, even billiards. But never fishing. Never Ray Scott's favorite sport. Fishing, he realized, would never get anywhere with its lousy $2 derbies and too many cheating contestants.

Ray shot up straight. Never fishing? Why? Why? Hey, why not! Why not a real, honest professional bass tournament that would attract the right kind of fishermen!

13

"In a microsecond I saw it all," Ray recalls today about his 1967 epiphany. "I saw the lake I had just gotten blown off of. I saw a hundred bass fishermen competing, tournament-style. It just came to me. I knew it would work."

Lewis remembers that when he and Ray met that night for supper at Creshale's Restaurant, "He was on fire with this crazy idea of putting on a bass fishing tournament on some lake in northwest Arkansas and getting a hundred fishermen to pay a hundred bucks each to enter. Ray wasn't the same guy I'd fished with earlier that day. I thought he had gone nuts, but he was convinced that he could do it."

Not many men can lay claim to having discovered a new world, founded an empire, or created a new industry, but only ten months later Ray Scott made such a mark when he created B.A.S.S., the Bass Anglers Sportsman Society, an entity that not only begot great commercial success but became a national force for conservation.

I was not present at the precise moment of genesis when ammonia, methane, and electrical discharges sparked the B.A.S.S. brainstorm in Ray's mind, but somehow in the spring of 1969 I heard about Ray and his organization. At the time, I was a senior writer for *Sports Illustrated* in New York. I was also an eager fisherman, and among articles on boxing, baseball, the environment and writing and editing the Scorecard section of the magazine, I occasionally sandwiched in a piece on anglers and scientists involved with fish, be they bass, trout, stripers, bluefish or whatever lives in water, fresh, salt and in between.

The bass fishermen I wrote about ranged from Dr. George W. Bennett, head of the Aquatic Biology Section of the Illinois Natural History Survey, who had his own experimental largemouth lake and whose book *Management of Lakes and Ponds* belongs in every bass lover's library, to former heavyweight champ Floyd Patterson's eccentric manager, Cus D'Amato, a fanatical bass fisherman who once bought fifteen hundred Mepps spinners, his favorite lure, at Hardy's, the uppercrust London tackle shop, while in England for a title fight. Seeing the startled look on the salesman's face, Cus told him that he represented a club whose members only fished with Mepps spinners, because "otherwise the guy would have thought I was a nut."

Obviously this guy Ray Scott was not a scientist like George Bennett, but I wondered if he might not be some kind of an eccentric like Cus, albeit of the Southern school. The South does have its share of characters, and Yankees such as me often think in stereotypes. In any case, I was curious because I believed that bass fishing was the sleeping giant of angling in this country, and maybe Scott was just the man who could wake it to stride across the land.

BASS ARE IN every state except Alaska, but in the northern tier of states largemouth and smallmouth bass, the greatest of fish to millions of freshwater anglers, almost always got the short end of the rod from state fish and game agencies because a built-in bureaucracy that lived off trout hatcheries and stocked trout wouldn't pay attention to any other fish. I fished for trout on occasion, but if I mentioned bass, which I and many of my acquaintances fished for most of the time, I'd get a shrug of the shoulders, a contemptuous snort and the dismissal, "trash fish." In contrast, bass did not need a top-heavy bureaucracy to prosper. Just drop a handful of largemouths into a pond, or smallmouths in a deep rocky lake, and, bingo, the bass soon would be happily breeding and feeding, the population booming to fill the limits of the carrying capacity, all without fishing license holders or taxpayers having to underwrite the life styles of hatchery-happy bureaucrats like those feasting at the trout trough.

In addition, a rather snobbish cultural bias existed against bass, at least in the Northeast, where bass are relative newcomers. In fact, largemouths and smallmouths only gained entry to most of New York State, and eventually New England, after they swam through the Erie Canal which, upon completion in 1825, connected Lake Erie to the Hudson River.

A second encircling action took place in 1853 when General G. W. Shriver in Wheeling, West Virginia, "thinking the Potomac River admirably suited to the cultivation of bass," took twenty smallmouths from the Ohio River, put them in the water tank of a Baltimore and Ohio locomotive and let them go in a canal in Cumberland, Maryland, "from which they had free egress to the Potomac River and its tributaries."

An indication of the trout fisherman's distaste for bass is evident in the following account by the editor of the *American Turf Register and Sporting Magazine* in the March 1831 issue:

> The animal [largemouth bass] sometimes rises to 10 or 15 pounds. It will not take the fly, and is caught by live bait, fastened to the hook back of the dorsal fin, which ought to be played with a rod and reel, but never by hand. When a strong fish of this species strikes, he will give you fine play, and exercise all your skill to keep him from breaking you. He kills, however, much easier than the "monarch" [the brook trout] . . . there is no comparison, none at all, between sitting with your rod in a shallop, in one of the low, marshy lagoons of the south, surrounded by huge alligators sunning themselves lazily upon the blackened logs that float upon the turbid water, whose sluggish surface is not unfrequently rippled by the darting of the deadly moccasin hissing past you — and treading the bank of some beautiful, rippling brook in New England; gurgling and leaping in its living course to the ocean, with its cool retreat for its watery tenant, "under the shade of melancholy boughs," or amid the still water of an eddying pool. Here you watch your delicious prey [the brook trout], as he rises to the surface, elastic as a bubble, and just breaks the water with his fin, as he seizes the careless fly that sports within his range.

In *The Fishing Tourist* published in 1873, Charles Hallock, one of the leading anglers of the period, disparaged bass without naming them:

> Define me a *gentleman* and I will define you a "game" fish; "which the same" is known by the company he keeps, and recognized by his dress and address, features, habits, intelligence, haunts, food and manner of eating. The true game-fish, of which trout and salmon are

frequently the types, inhabit the fairest regions of nature's beautiful domain. They drink only from the purest fountains, and subsist upon the choicest food their pellucid streams supply. Not to say that all fish that inhabit clear and sparkling waters are game fish: for there are many such, of symmetrical form and delicate flavor, that take neither bait nor fly. But it is self-evident that no fish which inhabit foul or sluggish waters can be "game-fish." It is impossible from the very circumstances of their surroundings and associations. They may flash with tinsel and tawdry attire; they may strike with the brute force of a blacksmith, or exhibit the dexterity of a prize-fighter, but their low breeding and vulgar quality cannot be mistaken. Their haunts, their very food and manner of eating, betray their grossness.

Such opinions die hard. In fact, proper Bostonian Charles Eliot Goodspeed, after quoting the above passage in his 1939 book, *Angling in America*, gratuitously added that "these opinions are now held by most anglers."

In some quarters today, there is resentment not against bass fishing *per se,* even though it still may be regarded as *declassé,* but against bass tournaments. An expression of this came from Ted Williams — the outdoor writer, not the ball player — who, in a 1984 article for *Audubon* magazine, quoted his "favorite outdoor scribe" as saying, "I have the impression that the American sportsman is puzzled; he doesn't understand what is happening to him. Bigger and better gadgets are good for industry, so why not for outdoor recreation? It has not dawned on him that outdoor recreations are essentially primitive, atavistic; that their value is contrast-value; that excessive mechanization destroys contrasts by moving the factory to the woods or to the marsh. The sportsman has no leaders to tell him what is wrong. The sporting press no longer represents sport; it has turned billboard for the gadgeteer."

Williams, whose article was about fishing tournaments, including one held by B.A.S.S., added, "The scribe is Aldo Leopold, and he wrote all this in the 1940s. I scarcely dare imagine what he would write today."

To such comments, Ray replies, "Fishing is a very personal thing. A fisherman can be a fisherman interested in the challenge of light line rather than the prey, or he can be a meat hunter out to feed his family, and there's nothing wrong with that if he abides by the law. In tournaments, rules restrict the competitors to certain practices and certain limitations of time and tackle. A fisherman who doesn't like competition should not participate. You'll have an occasional person who complains about competition. Maybe it comes from jealousy after he sees all those competitors out there in fast boats with electronic gear and other gadgets, but the competitor who fishes for sport is far more likely to release his fish than the fellow complaining. And if by chance he does catch and release his fish, I daresay he learned it from me."

From research I had done at *Sports Illustrated* on the rise of sports in the United States, I knew that Ray's idea fit the times. It coincided with the boom in participation sports that had begun to build with the end of World II. In the immediate postwar years, consumers mainly bought automobiles and appliances, and when this demand, forestalled by the Depression and the war, was met, consumer spending took a new turn into what was called, in the jargon of the day, the "life-enriching industries" of sport, culture, and travel. Between 1946 and 1958, real and discretionary incomes rose by forty percent, and between 1946 and 1962, the National Sporting Goods Association reported that the annual sales of sporting goods tripled to $2.3 billion, and the number of Americans engaging in participatory sports had almost doubled, and the sports included some that had never before existed, such as skin diving, sky diving, and hot rodding.

The number of U.S. anglers tripled, from thirteen million to thirty-nine million between 1946 and 1968 when Ray Scott began B.A.S.S. Like it or not, government agencies such as the Tennessee Valley Authority, the United States Army Corps of Engineers, and the U.S. Bureau of Reclamation dammed river after river, driving out salmon, trout, and other native fish, and creating warm-water impoundments in which bass could thrive. Meanwhile technology was giving birth to the fiberglass boat, the fiberglass fishing rod, nylon line, and the plastic worm. On top of this, the arrival of the spin-casting reel and the spinning reel quickly permitted the novice to match casts with the bait-casting expert without having to unsnarl a backlash.

The spinning reel originated in Europe, but the spincast reel was the brainchild of a west Texas watchmaker named R. D. Hull who came up with the idea after watching a grocery clerk pull string from a spool to wrap a package. Hull realized that line coming off a fixed spool does not backlash as it tends to from a revolving spool, and so he took his brainchild to the Zero Hour Bomb Company in Tulsa. It was the right move at the right time because the company, which shortened its name to Zebco, was staring at an expiring patent for its oilfield explosive devices and had need of a new product.

The first twenty-five handmade Zebco Standard spincast reels came off the first-day production line in June 1949. The spincast took off, thanks in good part to wizard sales reps like George Goetz, who wore boxing gloves to show how easy it was to use the reel, and Bill Carter, who worked sports shows with an identically dressed chimpanzee casting beside him.

Outboard motors were also undergoing rapid development, particularly at Mercury, headquartered in Fond du Lac, Wisconsin. In the spring of 1947, Mercury came out with its famous "Lightning." Rated at ten horsepower, it outperformed competitive motors rated twice as powerful. Just two years later Mercury brought out "Thunderbolt," the industry's first four-in-line two-cycle engine. Advance followed advance. Indeed, just as Ray Scott and B.A.S.S. came on the scene in 1968, Mercury came out with a 125-horsepower motor. Interestingly, both Mercury and Zebco, which is the last of the major fishing tackle manufacturers left in the United States, are now part of Brunswick Corporation in Lake Forest, Illinois.

Given all this and more back in 1969, I thought to myself, "If this guy Scott is for real, if he's legit, his B.A.S.S. business is a story for *Sports Illustrated*." At the time fishing tournaments, or derbies as they were often called, were in bad odor because of cheating and last minute rule changing that would benefit one contestant and tick off all the others. As a result, none of the monthly outdoor magazines — *Field & Stream*,

Outdoor Life, and *Sports Afield* — were interested in an article about Ray Scott and his B.A.S.S. outfit, short for the Bass Anglers Sportsman Society.

So here I was, a bass fisherman who wrote for *Sports Illustrated*, a general sports magazine with a circulation of more than two million copies a week, picking up the phone to call Scott in Montgomery. I introduced myself and then for the next fifteen minutes — "well, shut mah mouf!" — I listened to a nonstop monologue delivered in a folksy drawl about the benefits of "fishin' fo' bass" from an utter stranger who allowed that he believed so much in what he was doing — "I can inspire people! I can make them dance!" — that he had recently quit his job as an insurance salesman.

I'm not sure I had ever heard anyone with the endurance of this ex-insurance salesman, but Scott was so convincing and so interesting that by the time the one-sided call ended, I had agreed to go to Hot Springs, Arkansas to cover the $7,000 All-American Invitational B.A.S.S. tournament on Lake Ouachita. As Rhodney Honeycutt, a friend of Ray's and a former pro fisherman who fished his first B.A.S.S. tournament at age fourteen, puts it, "Ray doesn't sell you anything. He just tells you what you bought." Ray's uncle Lloyd Scott says, "Ray's a salesman if there ever was one. He'll do you a favor and let you have it." And Elgin Ciampi says, "Ray could sell ice to an Eskimo, but it would be the best grade of ice in the world."

On September 24, 1969, *SI* staff photographer Tony Triolo and I arrived in Hot Springs. We found Scott, a tall, lanky man in a white cowboy hat, cavorting in the Crystal Springs Fishing Village Cafe. His name may have been Ray Scott, but with his cowboy hat, his long jaw and what has been called his "boxer's rumpled nose," he looked like the actor Randolph Scott after a fight. We shook hands, and for the next four days, I asked questions and listened as Ray, then thirty-six years old, sketched out his concept of B.A.S.S.

The tournament rules were strict, supervision was tight and cheating would not be tolerated. Anyone caught cheating would be thrown out for life. Personally, I was not wild about the idea of tournament fishing *per se* — I belonged to the old school that believed angling a contemplative sport — but I had to admit that I learned a lot talking to fishermen like Bill Dance, Don Butler, and Tom Mann, who were happy to share their insights into what made bass tick. Being at the tournament was equivalent to attending a seminar at a top university. That was Ray's twelfth tournament, and Dance's fourth victory.

Photographer Tony Triolo and I had both been in Hot Springs before, in 1962 when we did a story on the city, then wide open with illegal gambling and every vice that goes with it (and unbeknownst to us, the home of a high school student named Bill Clinton). After *SI* published the B.A.S.S. article, the mayor called my managing editor to ask how he could get twenty-five thousand reprints to send out.

Ray impressed me in a number of ways. He was honest, he was obviously sincere in what he was attempting to do, and he had a great sense of humor. With a family to support, he chucked a promising career in insurance to pursue his dream of putting bass fishing on the map as a paying proposition. In 1966, two years before B.A.S.S. began, I had cofounded the non-profit Hudson River Fishermen's Association to do battle with polluters, and by 1969, the association had three hundred members who paid $2.50 a year dues. In contrast, B.A.S.S., begun in January 1968, was a for-profit company that already had six thousand members, and I marveled at Ray's genius in coming up with the idea.

I believed in what Ray wanted to do and I liked him, and even though reporters are supposed to stay at a distance and not become involved, I told him, "Sign me up. Here's my ten bucks." He took it, and I said, "Ray, B.A.S.S. is bound to grow. What are you going to do when you have a hundred thousand signed up?"

Huge smile, teeth gleaming, cowboy hat tilted back, arms pumping up and down as if he had just kicked the last-second winning field goal for Auburn against Alabama, Ray exulted, "I'm gonna put all the money on the floor and waller nekkid in it!" The editors at *Sports Illustrated* cut the quote from the article, but anyone with any sense knew that Ray had started B.A.S.S. to make a profit.

Above and beyond joining the Bass Anglers Sportsman Society, I wanted to help any way I could. When Ray said that he was going to reprint Izaak Walton's *The Compleat Angler* to sell or use as a premium, I told him to forget it. It would not appeal to bubbas with bass on the brain. Instead he would do far better by reprinting Dr. James Henshall's classic, *The Book of the Black Bass*, originally published in 1881. Ray thereupon bought a copy from a bookseller I knew, Colonel Henry A. Siegel, the proprietor of the Angler's & Shooter's Bookshelf in Goshen, Connecticut, and reprinted the book in Kingsport, Tennessee. I also suggested to Ray that he get in touch with Elgin Ciampi, a friend of mine who had done a prize-winning underwater documentary film on bass called *Still Waters*. Ray did, and he used Gene Ciampi's film to recruit new members for B.A.S.S. on a cross-country seminar tour he made with Harold Sharp, Roland Martin, John Powell, and others.

Finally, when Ray mentioned problems caused by water pollution, I told him about the Federal Refuse Act of 1899 that the Hudson River Fishermen's Association was using to have polluters hauled into court and fined. Ray later used the act against polluters in Alabama, and he often began an anti-pollution speech before a luncheon group by flinging a streaming roll of toilet paper across the room. "On a real good pitch I get a rebound off the back wall," he said.

Then and now, be it at a weigh-in or speaking before a luncheon group, Ray is a superb entertainer. Dave Newton, a very savvy Georgia-born writer who was at the Las Vegas News Bureau before he went to work for B.A.S.S. for several years after the first Classic, says, "Ray's a terrific natural entertainer. He reads an audience as well as anyone I've ever seen. They say the success of a standup comedian is the ability to read the room and give them what they want. There is nobody in the outdoor field who reads a room the way Ray Scott does. He could have been a lot of things. He could have been an evangelist.

"Every town in the south has two or three characters like Ray. They're hyperactive, they live by their wits, they're always promoting something. The only difference between these characters and Ray is that Ray is a quantum level above in dreams, vision and accomplishments. Rough edges? Yes. Crude at times? Yes. His stories sometimes have tobacco juice running down the corners of the mouth. Say something before he thinks through it? Yes. But if he were different he wouldn't be Ray Scott. He would be somewhere selling life insurance and living his life in obscurity."

IF THERE ARE boundaries in life, they are there for Ray Scott to cross. A year after I met him, he came to New York to see me at my office at *Sports Illustrated*. He wanted to get on television. I didn't know what I could do to help, but when I turned on the set the next morning there was Ray on the "Today Show" talking to Joe Garagiolo, and when I tuned in at night, there was Ray on the tube with Dick Cavett. The man does have a way about him.

Besides starting B.A.S.S., which now has six hundred thousand members and is the largest fishing organization in the world, Ray had other ideas that have proved their worth. Among them: organized bass clubs, the outboard engine kill switch, catch-and-release, and the Wallop-Breaux Bill for funding of fisheries, which passed with help from his friend, then-Vice President George Bush, a life member of B.A.S.S.. Indeed, *Field & Stream* magazine named Ray, along with Theodore Roosevelt, Rachel Carson, and Aldo Leopold, among the twenty greatest outdoor Americans of the twentieth century.

Howell Raines, editor of the editorial page of *The New York Times* and the author of *Fly Fishing through the Midlife Crisis,* and a fellow Alabamian who has been critical of Ray, says, "I like Ray as a person. In one way, he's an American classic. He had one big idea. The success of professional bass fishing was important because it politicized an entire group of working-class sportsmen in America in two very important ways. It made them conscious of the importance of water pollution issues and of preservation of fish stocks in a way that they had not been before. And that became a very important force in the politics of conservation in this country."

In 1986, Ray sold B.A.S.S. to Helen Sevier and the Jemison Investment Company in Birmingham, Alabama. He continued to be the public persona of the company until August of 1998 when B.A.S.S. and

Ray broke off contract renewal negotiations. No problem for Ray. He is the man who woke the sleeping giant, the engine of a $106 billion sportfishing and boating industry, the "Bass Boss" who thirty years ago believed, "I can inspire people! I can make them dance!"

1

The Scotts of Montgomery

THE SKINNY TWELVE-year-old boy twisted in the damp sheets on a hot, sultry night in Montgomery, Alabama. Big ears framed his thin face. Mischievous green eyes peered into the darkness. The only blessed relief was from the new attic fan that brought some cooling air to the compact bedroom he shared with his brother Eddie.

He felt safe and secure with his two loving parents in their neat attractive white frame house in a working-class neighborhood. Life was good. The war was just over. His four uncles had made it home, although Uncle Paul was badly shot up in Italy.

It was an important moment for Ray Wilson Scott, Jr. It was that night he decided to be Ray Scott and only Ray Scott. Not like anyone else. Not like the popular Dewey Renfroe, five years his senior. No longer would he try to imitate the special way Dewey walked or the way he played fast pitch with that lightning, whirlwind windup. No, he would walk his own walk and talk his own talk. And could he talk! He had inherited the gift of gab from his father and boisterous uncles. At that moment, he gently slipped the bonds of adolescent conformity. Ray Scott emerged for better or for worse. And he never looked back.

He felt good. He never lingered over decisions. Tomorrow was Saturday and his fishing trip to Froggy Bottom was all planned. His poles were standing up in the corner and his tackle was neatly packed in a Tampa Nugget cigar box. The freshly dug worms were in a tomato can outside.

Contented, he closed his eyes. He sure liked to fish, especially for bass. As a matter of fact, only bass. He didn't know why. When it came to fishing, his father could take it or leave it. Brother Eddie was the same way. But not Ray. It was a passion he just couldn't explain.

RAY WILSON SCOTT, JR., was the first member of the Scott family to be born in Alabama and in a hospital. It was a hot August day, the 24th day of the month in the year 1933. He was the first born of Ray Wilson Scott, Sr., and Mattie Laura Ray Scott, known respectively as Bud and Matt.

Ray was born into a large extended family with lots of aunts, uncles, and cousins. His mother Matt had two brothers and a sister. All five of his Scott uncles lived in Montgomery: Uncle Marion, known as "Boo," Lloyd, Leo, Paul, and the youngest, Sam. A sister had been born stillborn and Elisha Boyd wandered off at the age of two and drowned in a nearby pond. His body was found by Bud who retrieved his brother by twisting a stick into the wet folds of Elisha's gown.

The Scotts' journey to the little house on Panama Street had not been easy. Ray's father was born in 1908 on a cattle farm in Glendale, Kentucky. In 1923 the Scotts went broke after their cows were shot by the government during an outbreak of hoof and mouth disease. The family received no compensation from the government.

So Leo Virgil Scott, Ray's grandfather, took his family and headed south. An old Kentucky friend, H. B. Stewart, gave him a job on his dairy farm in Catoma, ten miles west of Montgomery. Bud was fourteen years old and Sam only four months old. Their mother, Blanche Boyd Scott, set up housekeeping in a simple frame house. She died in 1930 after suffering severe abdominal pain. On the day of her death, despite her pain, she managed to do some baking and canning and never considered going to the hospital.

Bud graduated from Montgomery's Cloverdale High School while his sweetheart, Mattie Laura Ray, graduated from Sidney Lanier High School. Matt was an athletic, vivacious track and basketball star even though she was only five-four. Five-foot-nine-inch Bud had a distinctive appearance with his broad shoulders and his hair speckled with gray by the time he was twenty-one.

He married Matt, or "Babe" as he affectionately called her, on December 1, 1932, in the midst of the Great Depression, a month after the election of Franklin Delano Roosevelt as president. He was working for Young's Ice Cream — and glad to have a job.

Ray was born nine months later weighing in at nine pounds, eight ounces. His Grandmother Ray later told him, "Sugar, you didn't leave with your parents on their honeymoon but you sure traveled back with them."

Sixteen months after Ray's birth at Hubbard Hospital, Dr. Carney Lasley also delivered Ray's brother Edward Boyd. This birth came two days after Dr. Lasley gave Matt a large dose of castor oil to induce labor — he'd wanted to be certain to catch the train in time for Alabama's game against Stanford in the 1935 Rose Bowl. "I still have oil in my hair," says Eddie.

At first, Ray and his parents lived with Matt's widowed mother, Clara Belle Ray. Grandmother Ray was an extraordinary woman and a great influence on Ray's life and his blossoming self-esteem. He could do no wrong in her eyes. She just smiled at his antics and pulled more than a few of her own.

Clara Belle Duke Ray had been widowed in 1918 when her husband died of the Spanish Influenza which killed millions at the end of WWI. She was left destitute with three small children and one more on the way. Nevertheless she picked herself up and with innate entrepreneurial skills managed to take care of herself and her children. She never remarried. After selling her beauty parlor business in 1949 she settled in her paid-for home on Vonora Avenue. In her typical fashion, she rented out three parts of the house as small apartments. At the age of eighty-nine she checked herself into a nursing home and paid the bills. Clara Belle died at ninety-one. "She had no particular problems," says Ray. "She just wore out. But before she left, she got those 'old ladies' in the nursing home organized."

It was Grandmother Ray who told Ray there was Cherokee blood in

his veins. As a matter of fact, the family tree has been traced to one Sarah
Laughing Doe in South Carolina. Ray and other family members,
including his mother and grandmother, have distinctive high cheek
bones and Ray's skin tans easily to ruddy tones. Wife Susan teases him
about his "Indian eyes" which can easily pick out the white neck ring of
a kingfisher three hundred yards across a lake.

When Ray was a year old, his mother and father rented a one-
bedroom duplex at 214 Martha Street, an area that is now an historic
district of restored Victorian cottages. Besides Ray and Eddie who slept
in a bunk bed in the bedroom, their Uncle Leo slept on a Murphy bed in
the living room when he was home from the University of Alabama. Leo
played football at Alabama where he was a second-string end behind the
great Don Hutson. The other starting end was Bear Bryant. Leo's
football career was ended by a knee injury and he dropped out of college.

Bud and Matt were happy with their little family. Matt would sew
exquisitely detailed matching outfits for the boys, especially at Easter.
Church was an important part of Ray's and Eddie's life. When Bud got
married, he was not much of a churchgoer. However, Matt, a devout
Baptist since childhood, set such an example for him that he was
eventually saved and baptized at the age of forty.

At the time, Montgomery, the capital of the state and the first capital
of the Confederacy, had a population of only sixty-six thousand — it has
two hundred thousand today — yet it was to gain the reputation of
having served as home for more famous people than any city of compa-
rable size in the country. The roster of personages who have lived in the
city includes Zelda Fitzgerald, Nat King Cole, Hank Williams, Postmas-
ter General Winton Blount, Civil Rights Lawyer Morris Dees, Jefferson
Davis, Rosa Parks, Martin Luther King, Jr., Big Jim Folsom, George C.
Wallace, Federal Judge Frank Johnson, Toni Tennille of The Captain
and Tennille, Bart Starr, Ambassador Joe Rodgers, Marine Corps Commandant General Carl Muday, and of course Ray Wilson Scott, Jr.

The Depression made for extraordinarily hard times, and Montgomery suffered with the rest of the nation. Although fifteen million Americans were unemployed, Bud was an enterprising young man whose

motto and philosophy was "Nobody has any money but everybody has a nickel." With that in mind and thanks to his connections to Young's Ice Cream, in 1933 he started his own push cart and tricycle ice cream cart business.

BUD BOUGHT ICE cream sandwiches, popsicles, and "Big Boys" from Young's for two cents apiece and paid his salesmen a commission of a penny for every nickel sale. His push and tricycle carts eventually grew to a fleet of twenty-four as salesmen jingled their way throughout the city.

Years later, his father's ice cream business figured in an experience so moving that Ray can barely tell it now without his voice choking and tears welling in his eyes. The story reflects not only the despair of the Depression but the character of his father.

Ray had graduated from Auburn and moved back to Montgomery into a little brick home on Greenridge Road with his wife Eunice and son Wilson and daughter Jennifer. Son Steve would be born a year later.

"I always went fishing whenever I could," Ray recalls. "I woke up well before daylight one morning with a passion to go fishing at a special pond that I had in mind. I took off and stopped to get some bait at Blackie's Fish Bait House. "After I rang the bell, Blackie let me in through a gate in the side yard fence. I remember that he had an old funky undershirt on. In the sixty-watt light of the cricket, worm, and minnow emporium, I told him I wanted some worms and a few bobbers. I asked, 'How much is it?' And he told me. I reached for my billfold, but there wasn't a billfold there. I had forgotten it. There I was before daylight with no money. I said, 'I forgot my billfold. I can give you a counter check, or I can come back and pay you tomorrow. I can also go back home now and bring it back to you.'

"He squinted his eyes, and looked at me and said, 'What did you say your name was?' I said, 'Ray Scott.' He said, 'Is your daddy named Ray Scott?' I said, 'Yes, sir.' He said, 'Well, son, let me tell you a story. I came into this town in 1935 as a hobo on a train with my wife from Oklahoma. We were heading for Florida, we were broke, and she was sick with a fever. I put her in a Commerce Street rooming house and went looking for work. Anything to make a little money. I saw a man pushing a white ice cream cart. I followed the man with that ice cream cart all day, and finally he turned in on Martha Street. All the men with these carts were coming in to turn in their money. I hung around there until everybody was getting ready to leave. I went up there to this young fellow that was obviously the boss. I looked terrible. I told him I needed one of those jobs pushing a cart and he said he didn't have a job, every one was filled. I told him I needed one bad. He said he just didn't have one. I said, 'Mister, I have to have one. My wife is sick and running a high fever, and she is downtown in a little hotel room. We're hungry, I have to buy some medicine, and we got no money.' The man said, 'I wish I could help.' I turned and walked away. I got no more than fifteen feet away, and I heard a voice say, 'Mister, come here.' I turned around and went back and he said, 'Here,' and your daddy handed me $5. I hadn't seen $5 in two years, and he said to me, 'Go buy the wife some medicine and come back tomorrow. I'll have a job for you.'"

Blackie then said to Ray, "Son, anything you want in this store, get it."

In the late 1950s, *Reader's Digest* published a complimentary article, "Blackie, The Fish Bait King of King Street Hill." Ray says, "I've often wondered what Blackie would have done if Dad hadn't given him that job pushing that cart. Blackie ended up buying about every house on the block and filled them with crickets that he wholesaled around the South."

In 1937 Bud opened the Catoma Street Cafe in downtown Montgomery, a hole-in-the wall eatery in a two-story building a block north of the venerable Jefferson Davis Hotel. Bud's widowed father — Grandpap to Ray — and all five of Bud's brothers often came by to eat. Their food was on the house. However, Bud, a lifelong teetotaler, made his father pay for beer.

The other ground floor tenants were Mr. Gresham, a shoemaker, and a one-legged barber named Hoochy Pap, while upstairs the mother of Hank Williams ran a rooming house on the second floor. The performer lived there as a teenager. Ray, who was ten years younger than Williams, vaguely remembers the thin young man carrying a guitar and wearing a cowboy hat and cowboy clothes. The Scotts would joke about his western garb, an oddity in Montgomery.

Ray remembers his Grandpap Scott as a jovial man, a kidder. "In fact," says Eddie, "Ray is very much like him." One day in November of 1938, Grandpap got off a Dixieland Dairy truck after making his route and shuffled into the Catoma Street Cafe. He was dragging one leg behind him and unable to speak clearly.

Although Grandpap lived only two blocks away on Goldthwaite Street with Bud's unmarried brothers Paul, Lloyd, and Sam, Bud brought him to the little duplex. He gently put him on the Murphy bed and called the doctor. After examining the elder Scott, the doctor pronounced that he had suffered a stroke and he doubted he would live through the night.

"Eddie and I came out from the bedroom that night to see him," recalls Ray. "I remember standing by the Murphy bed where he lay. When we woke up in the morning, I asked Dad, 'What about Grandpap?' Dad cried and said that Grandpap had died. The whole family attended the burial in Glendale, Kentucky."

With his father gone, Bud was now patriarch of the family at the ripe old age of twenty-nine. His hair was now silver-white. He took in Paul and Sam. Paul was eleven years older than Ray and Sam only nine years older. Ray and Eddie looked upon them more as older brothers than uncles.

"There were seven people in that one-bedroom apartment," says Ray "but I don't remember feeling crowded. We were happy. There were so many pranks, so much joking. As the very first nephew I was spoiled rotten. I had a ready audience for all my antics. I was a cocky little fellow, walking around with my baby bottle stuck in the back pocket of my overalls till I was three years old. I really got teased about that."

In September of 1939, just as Nazi Germany invaded Poland to start World War II, Ray entered first grade at the Cottage Hill School just a block away from the Martha Street house. Barely six, he was the youngest child in the school. His teacher had the first name of Ruth and for the children, an unpronounceable last name. Hence, she was known simply as "Miss Ruth."

At the first PTA meeting, Matt asked how little Ray was coming along. Miss Ruth replied, "Mrs. Scott, he is doing fine, but he talks a whole lot and is determined to run this class, and I am determined he is not." Even so, Miss Ruth picked him to play George Washington in a class play, and he proudly wore a white wig and a uniform that his mother made for him.

At the last PTA meeting of the year, Matt again asked, "How is Ray doing?"

Miss Ruth answered, "Mrs. Scott, you remember I told you at the first of the year Ray was trying to run the class. Well, he is *still* trying to run the class."

Despite his determination to run the class, Ray, doubtless to the astonishment of anyone who has ever seen and heard him in action as an adult, was a slow learner in school because he is somewhat dyslexic. A very perceptive and pragmatic woman, his mother went through his homework with him and then hired a tutor to help him.

She saw nothing but greatness and talent in Ray. Because he was forever talking, she told him that he should be a lawyer when he grew up. A few years later she took him to an after-school class on Mulberry Street called "Expressions," where he received his first lessons in showmanship. Teachers had him memorize and recite poems, taught him how to use his voice, gesture expressively with his hands and move his body, all of which Ray calls "a natural for me."

When Eddie was old enough, his mother paid for piano lessons for both boys; and she did the same with Danny who was born in 1945, twelve years after Ray. Ray lasted for four lessons before softball interfered, ending his musical career except for a brief time in junior high school when bandmaster George Printz allowed him to pound the bass drum.

When Ray's first year in school ended, his parents bought a lot on unpaved North Panama Street in the new Capitol Heights section. They paid the Bear Lumber Company $3,500 to build a three-bedroom, one bathroom wood-frame house and a separate one-car garage. This house, 319 North Panama Street, where Ray, Eddie, and Danny grew up, had a front yard and a spacious back yard with a big pear tree that the boys often climbed.

While Bear Lumber was just starting on the house in the summer of 1940, Bud came home one day to the duplex on Martha Street and told Matt, "Get your clothes and the kids' clothes packed up. We're about to go somewhere." She asked, "Where are we going?" He repeatedly refused to say.

"My dad was up to one of his little tricks," Ray says. "We stuffed ourselves in the 1939 Chevy, and he headed down the road. After we got out of town, Dad announced that we were headed for Panama City, Florida. Wow! Panama City! Florida! Playing on the beach! We stayed there four or five days and had a great vacation. That was probably the first place I ever caught a fish, including the little hardtails that my father made into a joke. They were baitfish, and my father would hook one on and make us think that we'd caught it."

But something clicked for young Ray. There was something exciting and satisfying about this process of fishing. It was kind of like an Easter egg hunt. There was the same anticipation.

That same summer Ray learned a great lesson when his uncle, Cecil Ray, Matt's brother, let him borrow his rod and reel to practice bait casting. After Uncle Cecil watched the child for a spell, he gently took the rod out of Ray's right hand and put it in his left hand.

"As long as you keep the rod in your left hand, I'll let you fish with it," Uncle Cecil said. "I know it feels awkward now, but if you learn to cast with your left hand, you'll catch more fish because you won't be wasting time changing hands. A left-handed caster will wind up with a hundred more casts a day than a right-handed caster, and that's a hundred more chances you'll have to catch fish." Ever since, Ray has cast with his left hand, though he uses his right hand for everything else.

Ray's love of fishing became a constant in his life. When he was in the fourth grade he and a buddy used to bike down to Three Mile Branch, where they caught bream. Bream, in fact, were the first freshwater fish Ray caught, and he would bring them back home on a string where Matt would patiently clean and cook them, coated in meal and fried to a perfect golden brown.

Later on, when Ray cut his fingers badly in an accident, she drove him to the creek in the family's car, the poles sticking out the back window. "My mother fished with me," Ray says. "She was really special."

A few years after Uncle Cecil taught him to cast with his left hand, his parents became friends with the K. C. Knight family who lived across the street and belonged to the Bridge Creek Fishing Club on a two-hundred acre lake north of Prattville. The Scotts became members, and Ray recalls catching small bass and bream with live bait near the old gristmill. Ray was a skinny Huck Finn who loved to wander off with a cane pole and a can of freshly dug worms or fresh-captured crickets.

When Ray began second grade in September 1940, the North Panama Street house still wasn't finished. But knowing that it soon would be, Matt drove him across town and enrolled him in the Capitol Heights Elementary School, only three blocks from their home-to-be. "My second grade teacher was Mrs. Cassidy," says Ray, "and she passed me along just to get rid of me."

2

Early Entrepreneur

SPRING AND SUMMER of 1940 were a busy time for the Scott family. Anxious about financial security, Matt persuaded Bud to sell the Catoma Street Cafe and go to work for the Post Office as a clerk in the railway mail service. For twenty years, Bud was to have two days on and four off while he worked the mail car back and forth between Montgomery and Waycross, Georgia. He would arrive in Waycross in the early evening, eat at the Green Frog Restaurant, spend the night at the YMCA, and return to Montgomery in the morning. At stops along the way, he was often given fruits and vegetables in season. At home the boys eagerly awaited his return.

Ray continued school at Capitol Heights. He remembered his third grade teacher, Mrs. Sue Bickerstaff, as "a good looking lady" who passed him along even though she told Matt that the boy was "distracted."

Distracted? Yes, and for good reason. Ray was very thin, with legs so skinny that he spent half his time pulling his knickers up to his knees. Eddie was much the same; he got the nickname of "Britches" because his pants were always falling down.

Wanting to see Ray gain weight, Matt kept urging him to eat. And he obliged, in his own way. Two weeks into the third grade, he asked his mother to make him three sandwiches to take to school for lunch. A week later he asked for five.

Within three weeks he had worked his way up to eleven sandwiches.

His mother happily complied, making a variety of sandwiches, starting with peanut butter and jelly, his absolute favorite, followed by banana, peanut butter and mayonnaise, and bologna and pineapple with mustard and mayonnaise.

"When do you eat them, Sugar Buddy?" Matt asked, using her pet name for Ray, one that family members still use today.

"On the way to school, Mother, at recess, and at lunch time," he answered.

Yet despite the bundle of sandwiches he lugged to school each day, little Sugar Buddy was gaining no weight.

At a PTA meeting, Matt asked Mrs. Bickerstaff, "How is Ray Junior doing?"

"He's doing all right," said Mrs. Bickerstaff. "But his business is his biggest distraction."

"His business?"

"Yes," said Mrs. Bickerstaff, "he has a sandwich concession. He sells sandwiches for five cents apiece."

The inspiration for the sandwich concession was May Hepburn, a girl who just loved to eat. And she came to school each day with at least a quarter. Ray's aim was to get as much of May's money as possible. He built up his business satisfying her appetite, especially with peanut butter and jelly sandwiches.

He used another ploy to advantage with the other kids. The school lunch cost fifteen cents, but after he sold a youngster a sandwich for five cents, he would say, "Now that you don't have enough money for lunch, why don't you buy two more sandwiches from me for ten cents?"

Immediately after that PTA meeting, external market forces ended Ray's initial foray into capitalism. From then on his mother limited him to two sandwiches a day. Ray says, "Mother was smart, but she would have been a lot smarter if she sat down and made a deal with me on how I could sell sandwiches."

At home, the Scott family collected tin cans, paper, and old rubber for the war effort. Bud also dug a thirty by sixty foot "victory garden" in the backyard.

With food rationing in effect, Bud bought a hundred yellow baby chicks and put them in a cage in the garage with an electric light to keep them warm. Ray and Eddie fed them growing mash and soon they were of such a size that Bud had to build a coop outside.

The chickens kept growing and soon the coop was hardly big enough to hold them. When they reached a pound and a half Bud began wringing their necks. Matt and the boys plucked and cleaned them and then she battered and fried them in true Southern style.

"So we had chicken for dinner, some of the best chicken I ever ate," Ray recalls. "Then the next afternoon at lunch we had chicken again. I must have eaten four or five drumsticks. The next day when Dad came home from work, Mother put on some more chickens. By now Dad was wringing their necks pretty regular, so in five days we had chicken at least once or twice a day.

"At the end of the first week, Dad figured that the chickens were eating up more feed than he could buy, so he decided we needed to eat even more chickens. Eddie and I got up to go to school one morning, and we came in ready for breakfast. Fried chicken! I was just about to gag on chicken; and I made the bad mistake of making the remark, 'Great goodness alive, we ain't having chicken again, are we?' Boy, when I said that, Dad reared back; and if I hadn't ducked he would probably have knocked me out of my chair.

"I learned a lesson there. You don't complain about chickens when you have a war going on . . . and a yard full of chickens that are eating you out of house and home."

Ray got some whippings — probably, he admits, never as many as he deserved — but one was particularly memorable because it dealt with the prized victory garden. Cousin Happy Scott, whose father Boo was away in the Army, came over one balmy April afternoon to play with Ray and Eddie. Bud, who had meticulously prepared the garden for planting, was expected home that evening when the mail train returned to Montgomery. The three boys, barefoot and in shorts, went out to the backyard to play catch.

A warm rain started falling. That made no difference to the boys. In high spirits they continued to throw the baseball around. Then one overthrew the ball and it landed in the pristine garden. "I'll get it!" Eddie shouted, and just as he did the rain began to pour down. He teetered-tottered into the garden to get the ball, and the ground felt warm and gooshy, like oatmeal between his toes. He picked up the ball and as he raised up a muddied bare foot to show Ray and Happy, he said, "This feels goooooddd."

The rain turned torrential, but that only made playing catch more fun. Again the ball landed back in the garden, and Ray and Eddie chased after it. Ray slid ahead through the mud to grab it, and Eddie jumped on top of him to wrest it away. They were rolling around laughing when Happy charged through the slop to join them, and an impromptu mud 'rassling match was underway.

The three finally got up, sloshed through the mud, and washed themselves off with the garden hose. The garden was a mess, but there was nothing they could do about it.

It was dark when Bud came home. They all sat down to supper and Ray, Eddie, and Happy, who stayed over, went to bed. When Bud got up the next morning, he went to the bathroom in the back of the house that overlooked the garden. The boys were still half asleep when they heard a roar "that sounded like something you'd hear in a zoo or the circus," says Ray. "It was the most awful sound." The hair stood up on the back of his neck. Eddie kicked the sheets back, sat up like a shot, and asked, "What was that?"

"I think Dad has seen the garden," Ray said. Bud yanked the bedroom door open and strode in, his face red and his eyes ready to pop from their sockets. "What have y'all done?" he yelled at the three boys.

No one said a word. He stormed outside and by the time he came back to the bedroom after inspecting the garden, he was seething.

"Let's go to the garage," he said.

That meant only one thing — a whipping. He never whipped them in the house.

In the garage, Bud took off his belt and grabbed Ray first. He started hollering before Bud could whip him. Eddie, who knew he was next, stood holding on to himself, trying not to wet his pants. Happy, scrunched down in a corner next to the door, had already wet his.

Bud gave a yowling Ray ten good licks, and then shoved him to one side while he reached for Eddie. He grabbed a squirming Eddie and marched him around the garage, whacking his fanny. Then it was Happy's turn. Huddled in the corner in his wet pants, Happy was as white as milk. Dad looked at him, shook his head and said, "Boy, don't you ever do that again." And with that he turned away and walked out of the garage. It wasn't right for an uncle to whip his nephew.

"Dad didn't whip us much," Ray says. "He was good, he was patient and he'd give you all the slack in the world."

Although Bud applied the occasional spanking, Matt was the primary law enforcer. She was a very perceptive mother, especially when it came to Ray. When he was seven or eight, he and his friends would pilfer cigarettes from carpenters and workmen laboring on new houses nearby in the growing neighborhood.

After he smoked, Ray would grab a handful of onions from the garden and eat them. Each time, when he returned to the house, his mother would say, "Ray Junior, you've been smoking," and he'd get a switching. Years later he would ask his mother how she knew he'd been smoking. Matt replied, "I smelled the onions. You didn't like onions."

Another punishment Matt tried for the never-repentant Ray was to confine him under the bed. Sometimes, on his back in the cool dark, he would fall asleep. Sometimes he would play with the wires of the springs. Ping. Ping. Different coils would make different sounds. "What are you doing?" asked Matt. "I'm playing music, Mother. It's fun." Matt would haul him out in exasperation.

As children, Ray and Eddie sometimes teamed up to play practical jokes, with Ray as the instigator. Their house was the gathering spot for all the rest of the lively Scotts who lived nearby. One night Ray and Eddie were in the bedroom next to the living room where their parents were talking to Aunt Boo, Uncle Boo's wife, Uncle Sam, and other family members. It was summertime and all the windows were open to catch any cooling air, when Ray got a notion to scare them.

He quietly unfastened the bedroom window screen. Then, while Eddie held him by the legs, he leaned forward out the window as far as he could with a long back scratcher in hand and scratched the living room window screen. Quickly they jumped back into bed and pretended to be asleep. The two boys heard Aunt Boo, who was sitting in the rocker next to the window, "come half unglued," and the men began babbling excitedly.

After a while, everyone calmed down and conversation resumed. Time for Ray to strike again as Eddie again held him by the legs. Scratch, scratch on the window screen. There was a shriek from Aunt Boo and shouts of "There it is again!" A quick jump back into bed as feet stomped down the hall. It was Bud. He stopped right by the hall closet where he kept his shotgun. The boys heard him open the breech of his sixteen-gauge Winchester pump, load it and stomp back to the living room, out the front door to the boys' side of the house, ready to blast whatever or whoever was responsible. End of story, at least then, because as Ray says, "We didn't dare tell that story for many, many years."

To say that Ray still enjoys practical jokes would be an understatement — he revels in them. Several years ago when his good friend Forrest L. Wood suffered a heart attack, Ray did not send the customary flowers to the hospital. He called Wallace Lea, a veteran fishing pro who lives near Wood, and arranged to have doughnut-loving Forrest receive two dozen glazed Krispy Kreme doughnuts every day for a week.

These days Ray often teams up with his brother Danny, a born cut-up who might be more outrageous than Ray. Danny is not above inserting an utterly grotesque set of projecting false teeth in his mouth and, with a deadpan expression and in a voice reminiscent of Mortimer Snerd's, striking up a conversation with stupefied strangers. Even worse, but to Ray's knee-slapping joy, Danny will simply sit down next to a stranger in a hotel lobby and stare intently at him without saying a word.

Danny resembles Ray so much that when Ray wanted a respite at the 1996 BASS Masters Classic, he had Danny don his white cowboy hat and act as a decoy. True to form, baby brother happily signed "Ray Scott" autographs for dozens of fans. Later Ray apologized to those he could and Danny's pen-wielding was over.

Though eleven years younger, Danny is a testimony to genetic transfer being far more influential than environmental effect — after all Danny was only six when Ray left home.

PRANKS AND JOKES aside, Ray was only eight when he got his first real job. Able-bodied men were going off to World War II and help was becoming hard to find. He got the job thanks to a rivalry between two small grocery stores, Morningview and Holt's on Mount Meigs Road. It was well before the advent of supermarkets, and these two stores in side-by-side buildings even shared a common interior wall that only intensi-fied the rivalry. Ray started hanging around Morningview, and after several days the owners agreed to pay him a dollar to work all day dusting and straightening the goods on the shelves. He performed with such vigor and enthusiasm that after two Saturdays, the owners decided to try him as a bicycle delivery boy. The store bicycle had a small front wheel, overhung by a huge grocery basket, and a standard back wheel.

"They loaded that basket up with twenty pounds of chicken feed and a couple of bags of groceries," Ray recalls. "I couldn't get going by myself. I was big enough, but that load was heavy. The owners finally got me going by pushing me while I started pedaling. Well, after that start I didn't dare stop because I knew that if I did I would never get going again. So I pedaled the whole way and crashed right in front of the house where I made my delivery."

Back in school, Mrs. Culver, Ray's fourth grade teacher, passed him along. But he met his match in his fifth grade teacher, Miss Pylant, "a stiff-necked old maid with a perpetual scowl." Fifth grade teachers did not give grades of A, B, C, D or F, but instead wrote letters to parents on how their child was doing.

"I couldn't argue with A, B, C, D or F," Ray says, "but I thought that I could argue with any letter sent home because that was just Miss Pylant's opinion. I got along with everybody else in school, but I did not get along well at all with her. Among other things, she was consumed by photography. We all had to learn how to develop photographs and enlarge them. Our cloakroom was the photo lab. My mother didn't like this because she thought it was a waste of time.

"Miss Pylant waited until the last 'letter' to proclaim my passing on to the sixth grade. I gave a great big sigh of relief, and as I walked out of the classroom the last day of school, I turned to look at her and stuck my tongue out, which was the most offensive thing I knew to do. She squinted her eyes at me as if to say, 'Just wait, you little scamp.'"

An accident in the summer of 1944 left Ray marked for life. Mr. Delmar Jackson, a next-door neighbor, owned the Del Mar Dairy, and Ray asked if he could help with deliveries. Mr. Jackson had a thirteen-year-old black boy already helping on weekends, but he figured that if he hired Ray he could double the speed of deliveries by having Ray jump off the right side of the truck to take care of customers on that side of the street while the other youngster handled those on the left side.

The pay was a magnificent $2 a day. One morning after a soggy rain, Ray hopped off the truck with two bottles of milk in his hands and trotted up the walkway to a house. He slipped on a wet spot and went down. The bottles broke, and glass sliced his ring and middle fingers right through to the bones, all but severing them from his right hand. At first, he did not feel any pain, but a gusher of blood spurted almost a foot in the air from the dangling fingers.

Horrified by the sight, the milk man, twenty-six-year-old Lester Gunby, scooped Ray up in his arms, put him in the truck and took him to the nearby Giles Drug Store on Lower Wetumpka Road in north Montgomery. Ray was unable to close his fingers. They dangled helplessly. Completely unable to help, the druggist told the milkman to rush the boy to St. Margaret's Hospital. By the time he did, Gunby feared that Ray might die from the loss of blood. Doctor John Blue stopped the bleeding and stitched the two fingers back in place.

A week later infection set in and the fingers became painful and yellow and swollen with pus that made them twice their normal size. Doctor Blue soaked them in a salt solution, and the swelling finally declined; but when the infection was over, Ray was unable to bend his fingers. They were stiff as sticks, particularly the ring finger.

As with any youngster, the bones in his fingers had continued to grow, but they had fused out of line. Doctor Blue said that Ray would have to be hospitalized and the bones broken and reset, otherwise the fingers would be permanently deformed and the hand partially useless.

Ray remembers going back to the hospital, and to his horror, having a mask put over his face, almost smothering him with ether to put him to sleep. The first operation did little good, and he had to undergo a second one.

"On both occasions I was raising cain when they went to put me to sleep. They had to have three people to hold me down," he recalls. "The doctor broke the joint of the ring finger twice, but it has stayed stiff until this day; and I can't do anything with it except to wiggle it. I have no control over any part of the joints. I can bend my middle finger a bit, but I cannot bend the last joint. I've had to learn to live and fish with these little problems."

Returning to school for the sixth grade, Ray discovered to his dismay that the principal had adopted a new practice, "tracking." This meant that starting that year, teachers would be moved up a grade to be with their students from the previous year.

The minute Ray walked through the classroom door, old Miss Pylant squinted her eyes at him and cackled, "Well, well, we're back again."

Somehow or other he managed to learn the multiplication tables and other essentials. He claims he even became a good photographer. Best of all, he finally passed the sixth grade.

That summer Ray mowed lawns and since Dad and Uncle Paul had the concession rights, he also sold peanuts at Cramton Bowl stadium, the home of the Rebels Double-A baseball team and the site to this day of the annual Blue-Gray football game. He had already developed his own "peanut philosophy." He didn't count his money until the game was over. He was too busy selling peanuts — and making sure they were *hot* — to waste time counting money. With his snappy manner and friendly smile, many customers told him to "keep the change." In later years in the insurance business, he would rather make sales than spend time to check over his commission reports in agonizing detail as some of his co-workers did.

When he wasn't making money at a job, he had his own way of finding cash when needed. On Saturday, when no one was at the playground at Capitol Heights Elementary school, he would search the grass for coins that had slipped out of the pockets of kids playing and rolling around. "You could have a heck of a time with twenty-five cents in those days," he says. "It was only a nickel for bus fare to town, ten cents for the movie, a nickel for popcorn and another nickel for the bus fare home. I can remember several occasions when I desperately needed a quarter; and I would visit the playground, my secret little treasure chest."

As if to make up for the cut fingers, Mr. Jackson, the dairyman, called Ray into his office and asked, "How would you like to make some money?" Ray said he sure would like to.

"Well," Mr. Jackson said, "I have a stack of accounts here that won't pay for their milk. I have done everything to get paid, but I have not been able to collect and neither have the route men. If you can collect any of this money, I will give you half of what you collect." Ray's eyes bugged out as he looked at the accounts. Some customers owed $2, some $4, and several owed almost $10.

In five minutes, he was off on his bicycle. His approach was already worked out in his mind. Knocking on the first door, he said, "I am calling on behalf of Del Mar Dairy. You owe them $6.38 and they asked me to come by and ask you to pay for it before they turn you over to a collection agency."

Ray recalls, "Here I am, a kid with a bicycle parked out in front of their house, delivering this message. Del Mar Dairy had exhausted every effort in getting paid, and then some skinny little kid comes by and lets them know they're about to be turned over to a mean collection agency. It was amazing how many people paid me — about twenty-five percent. Not a high percentage to be sure, but still amazing because the dairy had not been able to collect a cent. I made about $30 with that job that lasted about a month."

AS RAY APPROACHED adolescence, his interests and his energies exploded, especially after that August night when he decided he wasn't going to try to be like anyone else. He was happy just to be Ray Scott. Fishing, sports, jobs, and a new awareness of girls took easy precedence over schoolwork. The warning signs were evident in sixth grade which had been a struggle to say the least.

Although Ray shrugs off his mediocre academic performance, his parents were concerned enough to enroll him in the Starke University School — a local military school for boys that had enjoyed an especially illustrious history in the thirties and forties with such graduates as future United States Senator Lister Hill and numerous future doctors and lawyers.

Despite a tight budget, Bud and Matt sacrificed to provide the tuition money for their eldest son. Matt's income from her home beauty parlor helped. Ray's studies improved at the military school and he passed the seventh grade with a good "C" average.

The following fall he returned to public school — Capitol Heights — and again his interests returned to the extracurricular.

He got Eddie and a number of friends to agree to form a football team to play in a YMCA program. Ray then hopped on his bike and rode all over downtown Montgomery looking for a store or a business that would sponsor the new team. At every stop he'd make his sales pitch: in exchange for giving the team thirteen numbered jerseys, the sponsor would have his name proudly and prominently displayed on the front.

Turned down repeatedly, he finally struck pay dirt with Les Weinstein, the owner of City Pawn Shop. Mr. Weinstein patiently heard Ray's pitch and then picked up the phone and called the Pake Stevenson sporting goods store. He said, "I'm sending a young fellow by the name of Ray Scott to you. Let him have thirteen jerseys and put my City Pawn Shop name on the front and numbers on the back." Ray was elated.

That afternoon Ray jumped off his bike in Oak Park for the first practice and heralded the good news to his teammates. There were cheers all around, and it was agreed that since Ray had gotten the sponsor, he could pick the position he wanted to play. Ray didn't hesitate. "I'll be the quarterback," he said, and as a result, fellow team member Bart Starr — the future Green Bay Packer quarterback and Hall of Famer — played guard. Rolling his eyes heavenward, Ray says, with a sigh, "Those were the days."

Throughout their middle school years, Ray and Eddie, as usual, had jobs. At Dixieland Dairy on Highland Avenue they earned forty cents an hour concocting banana splits, sundaes, and milk shakes at the fountain and cooking hamburgers and hot dogs in the short-order kitchen. They also waited inside on tables and gave curb service outside.

"I'd serve the curbside order on a window tray," Ray says. "And I learned that the more you tended to people's needs, the more generous the tip. Without being taught, I also learned that if I put the change on the tray instead of handing it to them, they were more likely to leave some of it for me as a tip."

Unfortunately, Ray flunked the eighth grade at Capitol Heights and had to repeat it. He had discovered girls and soap box derby racing.

The summer after he passed the second time around, he played the outfield and caught for the Del Mar Dairy baseball team coached by Kyle Renfroe, coach and athletic director at Capitol Heights Junior High. After the summer ended, Renfroe was upset when Ray did not appear at the school. Instead the young Scott had returned to Starke University School. Earl Willis, newly hired to coach Starke's junior high football team, had recruited him. "You'll get everything free — uniform, books meals, and tuition," Willis promised. "All you have to do is play football."

Ray agreed, but on one condition. "What's that?" asked an astounded Willis, not really prepared to negotiate terms with a thirteen-year-old.

"Well," said Ray, "I know another fellow who is a great football player by the name of Guy Thigpen. He's built like a fireplug and he's strong and fast."

"Really," said Willis.

"Yes, sir, really," said Ray, and Willis signed up Guy Thigpen who joined the team at Starke. Thigpen went on to become a high school All-American halfback. Ray played left end on the junior team and then center, linebacker, end, and finally halfback in his senior year. He was named on the *Montgomery Advertiser* All City football team.

Ray thrived at military school and made acceptable grades. Even though he tried to beat the system at every turn, the discipline and structure focused his energies.

But he was still more interested in making money. "I think Ray inherited his father's zest for business," says Sara Boyd, later Smedley, his girl friend while a senior at Starke. "His father was really an entrepreneur; and if you follow his life from the time he was a young child, Ray followed in his father's footsteps.

"My first impression of Ray was of a young man who loved life. He had a knack, even in high school, of selling ideas and making everyone want to participate. He was very hard-working and gave all he had to each thing he was involved in. He was a good and loyal friend who cared — and still does — about his friends."

While at Starke, Ray worked three years for the A&P Grocery store on Madison Avenue for forty cents an hour, and again he proved himself quick to understand the mind of the customer.

"Just like any bagboy I stuffed groceries, but I quickly learned to ask to help any lady who had more than one bag to take to her car. If I did it with enough snap, crackle and pop, I might get a ten- to fifteen-cent tip. I worked on Friday afternoon and all day Saturday until quitting time, which was usually about 8:30 or 9 o'clock.

"When I came back the next year, the manager put me in the meat market. That was back in the days before you'd buy the meat already packaged. Then a customer said, 'I want two pounds of hamburger,' or 'five pork chops,' or 'a half a pound of sliced ham.' And we'd always try to give customers more than they wanted because we were told to keep the volume up. When a customer asked for two pounds of hamburger, say at fifty cents a pound, I'd scoop the hamburger out of the tray and make the order at least a half pound heavier. I'd ask, 'Will $1.25 be all right?' And the customer would say, 'Yes, that will be all right.'"

The meat department manager was P. Y. Shirley, a short, bald man who, out of necessity, kept a very sharp eye from the rear of the store.

"He'd be talking to you at the very same time he'd be looking up and down all the aisles leading to the front of the store. I remember one day when he said, 'Hey, Ray, look up yonder. There is old Claire,' or whatever the lady's name was. She was a big, buxom lady and wore an apron with great big pockets. P. Y. said, 'Look at her. She is fixing to steal some eggs.' I squinted my eyes and looked up the aisle, and sure enough she was standing up where the eggs were. In those days you could buy loose eggs. She was standing up there looking in one direction, while she was reaching over with her hand to get eggs and slipping them into a pocket in her apron. She must have put in at least six to eight eggs when P. Y. said, 'Watch this.' He walked out from behind the meat counter out into the main store and down the aisle where that buxom lady was standing and said, 'How are you doing?' And with that, he kind of accidentally bumped against her with his hip and cracked those eggs; and they began running down through the seams on her apron. P. Y. just walked away without having to say another word."

Busy as Ray was, he always found time for fishing with school and neighborhood buddies like Guy Thigpen, Dan Nolen, and Roy Hines. Sometimes even his fishing got him in trouble. As a sixteen-year-old ninth grader at Starke, he had been granted rare permission to use the family car to take a date to the school's Christmas Ball. His mother was delighted at the prospect of Ray going in his full dress uniform to the Montgomery Country Club with a nice young girl.

Unknown to her, Ray had never made a date. Instead, he phoned three buddies and made plans for a night fishing trip at Lake Jordan about twenty miles away.

Ray appeared the night of the party, in full uniform, adorned with brass, medals and braid. Before he left the house, however, he had opened his bedroom window and carefully set his fishing togs outside in a flower box to be retrieved as soon as he left the house. Matt proudly kissed him good-bye.

When he returned home after midnight, again fully dressed in his uniform, he tiptoed down the dark hall to his bedroom and his mother called out.

"Ray, how was the dance?"

"It was great, Mother."

"Was the music good?"

"Yes, ma'am."

"Did you dance much?"

"Yes, ma'am."

"Ray junior, I found your window unlatched and I knew something was going on. I called the country club six times this evening and you weren't there. Where have you been?"

"There I stood in the dark hall," says Ray "all dressed up in my uniform." I told her, "I was teasing, Mom. I didn't go to the dance. I went fishing at Lake Jordan."

She replied, "We'll talk about it tomorrow morning."

"I went to bed," recalls Ray, "a condemned man waiting for the light of day. I knew I was too big to whip, so I didn't know what to expect. Dad was gone. The next morning at breakfast I was informed the *only* time I would be riding in the 1939 Chevy for the next ninety days would be as a *passenger* on the way to *church*."

When he was sixteen, he formed his first fishing club, the Bluegill Fishing Society, with Danny Nolen, Edwin Blalock, John Hubert Hall, and Curtis Jackson Jones, Jr. Blalock once smuggled his grandfather's prize casting rod out of the house to go fishing. He put it down by a pond, and returned to find that hogs had eaten the cork handle.

All the members of the Bluegill Fishing Society would go off on short out-of-town trips in the 1939 Chevy that Ray and Eddie inherited from their dad after he moved up to a used Packard. Ray charged everyone who joined the Bluegill Fishing Society a quarter. Imagine that.

3

Drifting

AFTER HIGH SCHOOL graduation from Starke University School, Ray didn't know exactly where he was going. He would describe himself as "a lost ball in high weeds." He did know he would like to go to college and his parents encouraged him.

His first choice was Auburn, known then as Alabama Polytechnic Institute. Ray's father had been a fervent fan since 1929 when he went north with his future brother-in-law Cecil Ray to see Auburn play at Wisconsin. "Dad *loved* Auburn," says brother Eddie. "As a little boy, I remember him telling me all about Auburn. A week later he told me about Jesus."

The only way Ray could afford Auburn was with a football scholarship. He tried out, but at 175 pounds he lacked the heft the school wanted.

Then he thought perhaps the Lord was calling him to be a preacher. "I felt that in my heart, but I wasn't completely sure," he says. When his pastor, Louis Armstrong, at Morningview Baptist Church, heard that Ray was considering the ministry, he offered to help get him into his alma mater, Howard College in Birmingham, an excellent small Southern Baptist school now called Samford University.

Ray had always had an evangelistic spirit. "If I was on to something good I just wanted to share it with everyone," says Ray. "I'm still that way. It was that spirit that kept me going with B.A.S.S. I still love to invite people to come to my church."

Ray was accepted into Howard College. Within two days after his arrival he was approached by a fellow student from Montgomery, Ed St. John, a member of the Howard tennis team. He asked if Ray would be interested in playing football for Howard. Ray said he would and St. John said that if he did well, he'd be sure to get an athletic scholarship. Coach Earl Gartman was impressed with Ray's tryout and gave him a scholarship that paid for his tuition, room and board and books — everything but his meals. Ray took care of those by hopping tables at Andrews, a popular student restaurant, where he got his meals free.

A senior named Bobby Bowden, later the successful coach at Florida State University, was the Howard quarterback and Ray played right half and defensive back. It wasn't a big team. Bowden weighed 160 pounds and Ray 189. The two heaviest men on the team came in at 220, and one of them was Ray's roommate Talmadge Smith, later to be the co-pastor at Hank Williams's funeral. Despite the lack of beef, the season was a winning one. Howard's first game was against the University of the South, and Ray immediately made a mark with a hard but fair tackle that knocked the opposing star receiver out of the game. His abilities on the football field and his outgoing personality won him election as the vice president of the freshman class.

In the spring Ray ran track: the hurdles and the hundred-yard dash. In a meet with the University of the South at its home track in Sewanee, Tennnessee, he ran the hundred in a flat ten seconds. "Not fast by modern times," he says. "I don't know if I had a tailwind or what, but I was the first Howard sprinter to do the hundred in ten seconds. And by the way, I never did it again."

But that freshman year would not be all roses and smiles as Ray quickly discovered in his English composition class. He may have been a smooth talker, but he was far from a smooth writer. He had learned some of the bare essentials of grammar at Starke, but he had never had a class in English composition.

Ray sensed trouble the first day he attended Mrs. Lizette Van

Gelder's class in freshman English. He found her "a kind of quiet but snooty lady with a big ball of hair wadded up on the back of her head with some long pins stuck in it." But she knew what she demanded of her students.

"Everyone take your notebooks. We are going to write a theme," he remembers her saying. *A theme? What was a theme?*

Mrs. Van Gelder added, "The subject is 'My Most Memorable Experience for the Summer of 1952.'"

Subject? Wasn't a subject the subject of a verb? How could anyone write about that? And what was a theme? thought the man who would be the first editor of *Bassmaster Magazine*.

Ray stared at Mrs. Van Gelder waiting for an explanation. Mrs. Van Gelder did not explain. Mrs. Van Gelder sat down at her desk in front of the class and started piddling with some papers.

Ray leaned over and very quietly and very urgently whispered to the boy in the adjoining desk, "What's a theme?"

"Shh," he whispered back. "You better get to writing, you ain't got but a hour."

Ray did not know what to do or where to start, but in desperation he began scribbling some experience on the paper in front of him. Several days later, Mrs. Van Gelder returned the papers to the class, and Ray looked at his. It had so many red marks he had difficulty seeing what he had written. Mrs. Van Gelder had underscored words here and there, circled this word and that word, and written in the margins. Ray looked at the top of the paper for a grade. There was a big "E." He looked at it closely. It was an E, not an F, and that was encouraging because F meant Fail. *E, mmmmm, maybe E meant Excellent. Or maybe even extraordinary.*

The class did three more themes, and Mrs. Van Gelder gave Ray three more E's. Then Mrs. Van Gelder gave him a fourth E. After class he went up to her desk and said, "Mrs. Van Gelder, I have been noticing all my grades have been E's. What exactly is an E?" Mrs. Van Gelder looked up at him and said, "Mr. Scott, an E means that you are going to have the *Experience* of doing this course again. The E is also to *Encourage* you to stay in this class and help prepare yourself for your return."

"Actually," says Ray, "Mrs. Van Gelder was an excellent teacher and I learned in spite of myself. She was a highly respected teacher and has a chair named for her at the college."

When Ray repeated the class in the spring semester, he had a male teacher who was a bit easier; and this time he slid by with a D. He got C's in his other courses. The most important lesson he learned, however, was that the Good Lord wasn't calling him — he was not destined to be a preacher. "I don't know whether it was living with Talmadge Smith and all those young student preachers, but it became very clear to me that that was not my calling. I didn't know what my calling was, but preaching I knew it wasn't." His view of the matter was substantiated when he barely escaped flunking his class on the Old Testament.

"I just didn't know what I was doing in college," Ray admits, "but I didn't particularly worry about it. Of course football was there, track was there and my friends were there; but I didn't have any real focus on preparing myself for accounting, pharmacy or for any profession. I was wandering in the wilderness."

WHEN RAY WENT home for the summer, he and Eddie, who was still in high school, got jobs with the Bear Lumber Company, thanks to Herman Dean, a foreman they knew. Bear Lumber did contracting in the Montgomery area and the two boys started out in June digging ditches near Maxwell Field. It was just the sort of physical labor that Ray needed to keep in shape for football. At the end of July, Bear Lumber transferred Ray and Eddie to work at Ray's old school, Capitol Heights Junior High, only two blocks from their home on North Panama Street. The company was building extensions at both ends of the school.

"Bear Lumber needed someone who could do steeplejack type work," Ray says, "and I was awfully strong, agile, and lean — in just great shape." Right after lunch on July 31, he was told to dismantle a three-story stacked steel scaffold alongside the rear of the school. He climbed up to the top of the scaffold through the shaft in the middle, trailing a rope behind him. When he got to the top above the third floor windows, he sat down on a two-by-ten board laid across the scaffold, his legs hanging straight down through the shaft. He began to work. The first section of scaffolding that he was to take down had obviously been bent at the connection and he had difficulty taking it apart.

"Every time I would pull up one side the other would go down," Ray says. "Frustrated and impatient, I dropped the end of the rope down to a black fellow working on the ground and asked him tie on a ten-pound sledge hammer. He tied on the hammer and I pulled it up. I straddled the two-by-ten and started bumping the section underneath with the hammer to get it to come loose. I would get it up on one side, and it would go down on the other. I thought what I really needed to do to get the section loose was to give it a big whack with the hammer. So I started swinging the sledge hammer like a pendulum, preparing to whack the bottom of the section. My swing was short and I missed my target and that hammer went flying by it. The momentum that I had built up caused the two-by-ten that I was on to lurch forward and fall. The ten-pound sledge hammer and I headed for the ground."

Ray doesn't remember hitting the ground, but he was told that he landed feet first, and then fell backwards, just before the hammer landed. The hammer was slower in falling because it bounced off the sides of the shaft on the way down. When it did land, the head of the hammer struck Ray's jaw. It burst the jaw like a ripe tomato, knocked out one tooth, bent another straight back, and drove his upper teeth through his lower lip. He was knocked out cold with a concussion. As earlier with his severed fingers, this was another instance in which he could have bled to death, but the construction workers called an ambulance that rushed him to the hospital in time. To this day, the scars are evident on Ray's chin. Between his much broken nose (football) and the chin scars, he looks like a well-worn prize fighter.

Ray was released after four days, a week before he was to report back to Howard College for his second year. There was no way that he could play football, but he went back. Although his friends were there and college authorities assured him that he would retain his scholarship, the fact that he could not play disheartened him; and he decided to drop out for a year. Back home in Montgomery, he had an idea about what he wanted to do. When he was fourteen, his Sunday school teacher at Morningview Baptist Church was Jim Malloy, a young man in his mid-twenties. Ray says, "Jim Malloy really set an example in his general demeanor and his dress. He was a real slick dude, a real go-getter. He was also an insurance man and because of my admiration for him, I decided to look for a job in the insurance field."

RAY SPENT A fruitless September looking for a job. The insurance people were polite, but they considered him too young to be an agent. There wasn't a market for people his own age and he didn't know the people who had the money to buy policies. He talked to a half dozen insurance companies including Vulcan Life Insurance, a new company out of Birmingham. The response was the same as it had been from the other companies, "Don't call us. We'll call you." He waited around home for calls, but the phone never rang. One Thursday afternoon in October he told his dad, "If I don't hear something from one of these companies by tomorrow, I'm going to Sears Roebuck and try and get me a job working in the sporting goods department." Dad was patient and said, "Whatever you do is fine, son."

No sooner had Ray spoken than the phone rang. It was Bill Thackston with Vulcan Life and he asked, "Do you still want a job in the insurance business." Ray said, "I surely do."

Thackston said, "I've got one for you. As a debit insurance agent."

The job paid $60 a week plus an expense account of $5 a week. It was in Phenix City, Alabama, ninety miles due east of Montgomery, just across the Chattahoochee River from Columbus, Georgia. Bud, with Uncle Paul's help, lent Ray $500 to buy a 1948 Plymouth. Early the next Monday morning he was off to Phenix City, his mother's birthplace and where her father Ed Ray had died in the 1918 influenza epidemic.

At the time, Phenix City — right at the doorstep of Fort Benning, the big army base — was the underworld gambling and prostitution capital of the South, if not the entire country. "Combat zones weren't as dangerous," Ray recalls. "Jails had higher class. The back streets where I worked were too bad for rats."

The job called for Ray to go door-to-door collecting insurance premiums on funeral policies, totally in black neighborhoods. The policies didn't pay off in cash, but they did make sure that the deceased would have a proper funeral with embalming, a good casket and shroud, a full funeral, hearse, grave cover, fake grass, and chairs. Policy owners kept Vulcan receipt books in the house to note when they paid. Premiums were fifteen to twenty-five cents a week. For only another five cents or so, the insured could have a full-color picture of Jesus installed on the top inside lid of the casket.

Ray was expected to bring in about $200 a week, and, he adds, "Lord help you if a policy lapsed. The company wanted you to write another policy as quickly as possible to replace it. If you got careless and a customer wound up four weeks in arrears, the premiums came out of your pocket."

To make matters worse, slick salesmen for a brand-new company, White Angel Insurance, swooped down on Phenix City and Ray's customers began to cancel their Vulcan policies. Vulcan Life took its name from the statue of Vulcan, the Roman god of metal working, that overlooked Birmingham and its steel mills. White Angel salesmen slyly spread the word that Vulcan was a Satanic figure who embodied evil and was a curse to the home of any unfortunate policy holder.

Ray fought back. One morning he went to see a gentle lady named Mary. When he reached for the receipt book inside her doorway, it was gone. Ray: "You've taken up with the White Angels, haven't you, Mary?

No answer.

Ray: "I don't really care because I don't make any money off your premium. You've just saved me a trip here every week. But I've got to tell you that you did wrong and I hope you won't regret it. Do you really know the White Angels?"

Mary: "They say they're good."

Ray: "Do you know where Sylacauga is?"

Mary: "Yes, sir, I believe I do."

Ray: "I'm sure you heard about what happened to those twin boys there?"

Mary: "No, sir, I don't think so."

Ray: "It was a terrible thing, Mary. Those twins had our Vulcan insurance, but their momma dropped it. Took the White Angel policy instead. Those boys were just seventeen years old when the ditch where they were working caved in and killed 'em. Covered 'em up. Our company no longer had the insurance on them, but they were still our friends. And we were certainly sorry to hear what happened. They had a double funeral. And the pallbearers marched out of that little church and up a winding path to a graveyard on the hill. They had real pretty caskets, just like the ones I'm sure they promised you. But as they were making their way up to the grave, a pallbearer stumbled over a root and jarred the first casket. And when he did, the bottom on that casket flopped open, and that poor boy slid out onto the ground. A trap door. It was an awfully pretty casket, Mary. Real pretty. But no telling how many times it had been used."

Mary threw the White Angels policy in the fireplace and renewed with Vulcan.

Success story? No, a blatant lie. Ray says, "I told that bald-faced lie to poor, unfortunate people each week so that I could collect my lousy ten, fifteen, or twenty cents from them. I was no better than the White Angels. I was nineteen and trying to survive in a street fight. I was really more interested in collecting the premiums than I was in the welfare of my customers.

"Facing that fact hurt, but I was wrong; and I vowed never to do such a thing again. I learned that truth is the greatest ally anyone can have. So I crawled out of the gutter, gassed up my Plymouth and put Phenix City behind me. I loved people, I still wanted to be a salesman, but I told myself that I would never be caught selling insurance again unless hell froze over. Insurance ultimately lured me back into its fold, but I was determined not to be a fighter who could only win by delivering low blows."

4

On Course

UNCLE SAM TOOK care of Ray's future for the next two years. In May of 1954 he was drafted into the United States Army. Ray took his basic training at Camp Gordon, Georgia. He was unfazed by the rigors of boot camp partly because of his military school experience and partly because he was fascinated by the trauma and drama unfolding around him. He spent some of his time consoling a fellow Montgomerian, Walker Hobbie, who was very homesick and dejected by the abrasive and abusive treatment he was receiving at the hands of the drill sergeants.

One blazing day in July, with no special training scheduled, Ray's company was ordered to pick up every rock and pebble in the barracks area. As the GI's fanned across the red Georgia clay in obvious "busy work," Ray motioned Walker into the relative cool of the latrine and they spent two hours sitting on the toilet seats chatting.

Walker would become a long-serving and popular probate judge in Montgomery till his death. He kept his very first political contribution — a five-dollar bill from Ray Scott — under glass on his desk. He would later personally issue Ray and Susan's marriage license — the second marriage for both — and grant him formal adoption of Susan's son from her previous marriage.

After basic training, Ray was sent to quartermaster school at Fort Lee, Virginia, to become a supply records specialist. He learned how to type, but his top speed in competition was about twelve words a minute. He expected to be sent to Korea after graduation, but he met a member of the Airborne Quartermasters stationed at Fort Lee, who suggested that Ray become a paratrooper. He told him, "If you do commit to becoming a paratrooper, you'll be sent to Fort Campbell in Kentucky and you'll learn how to jump out of airplanes. Then they'll send you back here to teach other people how to jump out of airplanes with quartermaster supplies."

"I thought jumping out of airplanes would be better than going over to Korea," Ray says, and three weeks before graduation he talked two of his buddies into volunteering for Airborne. The trio went to see the lieutenant in charge of transfer requests. He grumbled, but said he would see what he could do. The days went quickly by with no word. Five days before graduation, Ray saw the lieutenant who admitted that they were out of luck because he had been late in submitting the transfer requests. Ray was sure he'd be sent to Korea.

At graduation, Private Scott received an envelope containing orders for his next station. Fully expecting Korea, he was jubilant to find that he was to proceed to Fort McClellan, Alabama, about 120 miles from Montgomery. And he still had his 1948 Plymouth! Later, in March of 1955, he was assigned to the Second Armored Division in Germany, General George Patton's "Hell on Wheels" Division in World War II. He joined the 502nd Replacement Company in what was still occupied West Germany.

Ray was relieved to arrive safely on German soil after spending ten days on a heaving troop ship in late March in the North Atlantic. The seasick soldiers slept below four-deep on canvas racks. "One poor guy never got out of bed the whole time," says Ray. "We brought him crackers to eat."

Germany was good duty. Ray traveled every opportunity he could and managed to get around most of Western Europe, including a bone-chilling eleven-day trip to London where he was stranded by the military "hop" system of air transport. In Germany, he loved to go into the little villages and get a beef filet, potatoes, salad, and delicious local wine for less than $3.

He especially enjoyed the company of the diverse young men in his company. "They were an extraordinary bunch," recalls Ray. "Many were graduates of prestigious colleges in the northeast. I decided these Yankees were O.K." Among them was Paul Spong, a talented musician who went on to be a musical director for the Joffrey Ballet in New York. Spong says, "Ray could charm a bud off a tree. He could get you to do anything he wanted and you would enjoy doing it. I always thought he would be a preacher, even though he told me he had already decided against that."

At his home base he answered the captain's call for football players after the base team got whipped by 42 - 0. Ray played halfback in the next game and scored the only touchdown to give his team the victory. Two days later the captain promoted him to private first class. He never scored another touchdown, but ninety-one days later the captain promoted him to corporal.

Talking with an army buddy one day, says Ray, "It finally dawned on me what I was going to do with my life. Until that moment I was clueless. Then it clicked — I was going to be a salesman. I didn't know what kind of salesman and it didn't seem to be important, but I was going to be a salesman. I thought, I don't have to worry anymore, I'll be a salesman. About a day later I started thinking about it some more and wondered, what am I going to sell? So I worried about that and had a few semi-sleepless nights. Then again, another awareness came into mind. I could sell anything! I just had to know and be enthused about my product, and I could make money selling it. My next main objective was to get back in college."

ON A FRIDAY in March of 1956 Ray was formally discharged from the Army. On the following Monday he went through late registration at Auburn and on Tuesday he was in class as a business administration major.

By happy coincidence, his old neighborhood buddy, Danny Nolen, fresh out of the Marine Corps, was also starting at Auburn. They roomed together, each paying $12.50 a month to share a room in a small two-bedroom apartment.

The young men did not know anyone, women in particular, among the five thousand students on campus. Classes were too hurried for anyone to socialize. But it didn't take the enterprising Ray long to come up with a system. The University had a directory of all students with pertinent information including phone numbers. Ray would peruse the directory and find a name that caught his fancy. He would call the number and ask the girl if they had met before on campus. Then they'd chat for a while. If she sounded nice, Ray would invite her out — sight unseen — on a double date with his buddy Dan. Did she have a friend for Dan? And the two ex-GI's got in circulation on the campus. Dan hit the jackpot with Ray's system. He met his future wife, Jane Sulzby, on one of Ray's blind double dates.

Shortly after arriving on campus, Ray came across the Green House, a boarding house owned and run by a Mrs. Seagraves, in a pre-Civil War building. Ray stopped for a family-style lunch there and liked what he saw. He presented himself to Mrs. Seagraves and said, "Mrs. Seagraves, I would like to go to work for you as your public relations man."

"And just what do you propose to do, young man?" she asked, looking kindly but skeptically at this lanky, young stranger with an easy gift of gab.

"Well, Mrs. Seagraves," said Ray, "I propose to put pictures of the Auburn football players all over the walls around the dining room and then hang a sign out over the front step that says, 'Through this door walk the best-fed Tigers in Auburn.'"

"My goodness gracious, Mr. Scott, how you do talk," said Mrs. Seagraves. "I think that's a lovely idea. Now just what do I have to do to get you to do this?"

"All my meals free, Mrs. Seagraves," said Ray, with a gracious bow; and she immediately agreed to the deal.

As an inducement, Ray gave free "introductory" meal tickets to freshmen and within a week Mrs. Seagraves had a full house of diners. The "oohs" and "ahs" and the satisfied belches that burst forth from the Green House were not lost on local merchants. About a week later, Ray got a call from George Johnston, owner of the Johnston-Malone Bookstore, asking him to drop by. Ray did and Johnston offered him a job sitting in the window with a PA system and yakking through a microphone to draw students into the store.

"What do you pay?"

"Fifty cents an hour."

"I can't do it for that."

"Seventy-five cents an hour," said Johnston, and Ray agreed.

His reputation as a talker spread. A merchant named Olin L. Hill asked Ray to work in his clothing store. He took Ray way into the back of the store and whispered, "Fifty cents an hour." "Mr. Hill, I can't work for that," Ray said. "I need a dollar an hour and I'll be the best salesman you ever had." Hill peeked around and then said, "Okay, but don't tell anybody."

Ray didn't have to use his directory dating system too long. In mid May he parked his old 1948 Plymouth next to a black-and-white two-door 1956 Chevrolet at a drive-in restaurant. The other driver was Eunice Hiott; she was with a girlfriend and Ray was with Danny.

Ray and Eunice talked briefly. She was a physical education teacher at Auburn and already had her masters degree from Columbia University teacher's college in New York City. Her hometown was Pickens, South Carolina. Not long after the drive-in meeting, they met again through mutual friends and Ray got to know this tall, dark-haired girl better and he liked what he saw. Ray loved tall women and she was five feet ten inches. She was also quiet, reserved, intelligent, and a great cook. Ray was pretty sure he had found *The One*. They started dating. "We had so many inexpensive Coke dates, I thought I'd become diabetic," says Ray.

Between summer and fall quarter, Ray went home and sold his Plymouth for $200. Then he and his mother went downtown to pick out an engagement ring for Eunice — a nice diamond solitaire. He hitchhiked back to Auburn with the diamond ring in his pocket and rendezvoused with Eunice and a married couple to go to Florida on a short break between school quarters. Ray and Eunice were on the beach late one morning with the ring safely tucked in Ray's bathing trunks. He didn't ask, "Would you marry me?" Instead, he slipped the ring on the finger and closed the sale: "Do you want to get married in early or late December?" They married during the holidays on December 28 in Eunice's hometown.

Eunice continued teaching in a local high school, but she had to quit when she was six months pregnant with their first child, Ray Wilson III, who was born March 31, 1958. Ray and Eunice and baby Wilson lived in a furnished one-bedroom apartment on Genelda Avenue. They were living on the GI bill — $160 a month for a family — and whatever else Ray brought in from his dizzying array of part-time jobs. His dad faithfully sent $30 a month from an educational policy he had bought when Ray was born. Eunice's mother also helped out, slipping money occasionally into her letters from home. "We got along fine," says Ray.

Ray still loved to fish, often "visiting" the university's test ponds, part of its well-known fisheries program. And of course there were other lakes and ponds in the county. Only now, the fish were more likely to be supper.

He became a buddy of another ardent fisherman and student, Archie Phillips, who was deep into taxidermy. "Archie lived a block away from us," Ray says, "and a blind man could find Archie's house by following the smell of formaldehyde." Ray esteems Archie as a truly multifaceted man. In addition to being a top angler and an outstanding, nationally renowned taxidermist, he is also an author, a pilot, a scuba diver, a spear fisherman, outdoor TV host, hunter, and a student of history and archeology. A decade later Archie would help Ray get prospective members for his fledgling B.A.S.S. organization.

In 1959, Ray's senior year, he had job interviews with several companies. Jobs were not that easy to get at the time, but he landed a plum of an offer from Procter & Gamble: $375 a month plus a car, as a salesman in the food division. After subsisting on the GI Bill, he thought he had it made. But a career with Procter and Gamble was not to be.

He, Eunice, and nine-month-old Wilson were in their upstairs one-bedroom apartment one afternoon during the Christmas break when two men knocked on the door. They were an agent and a trainee from the Penn Mutual Insurance Company. The agent told Ray that his friend

Dan Nolen had suggested that he talk to him about buying a $10,000 life insurance policy.

"No, thanks," Ray said. "I already have $10,000 in GI insurance, and I don't need any more."

"Let me show you, Mr. Scott, if you don't mind," the agent said.

The Scotts' black and white TV set was broken at the time. "Go ahead," said Ray, "I've got nothing else to do."

By the time the agent finished his sales pitch, Ray was awash with excitement. The $10,000 policy sounded like a great deal. If he lived to be sixty-five, he'd get back all the money he'd put into the policy and a big profit as well. Even if he dropped dead the day after buying the policy, Eunice would get the $10,000 death benefit. And if he got hurt or became sick, the policy would pay the premiums after six months of disability. He could also borrow against the policy; and if he decided that he no longer wanted to keep the policy, he could cash it in. And the $10,000 jackpot would only cost him $200 a year in premiums or "savings."

"You mean I have everything to gain and nothing to lose?" he asked.

"That's right."

"And you get paid to do this?" Ray asked.

"That's right."

"And how much do you make on one of these $200 policies?"

The agent hesitated and then said, "About $100."

"You mean if I sign up right now, you make $100?"

"Right," said the agent. "You want to buy?"

"No," said Ray, "but I sure want to meet your boss."

Thanks to the Auburn student placement office, Ray ended up talking to Joe Sutherland, the assistant manager of the Montgomery office of Mutual of New York, (MONY). After Sutherland told Ray that he could start selling after graduation in March, he turned down the offer from Procter & Gamble.

ACTUALLY IT WAS no trick getting a job with an insurance company, even with MONY, the oldest mutual insurance company in the United

States, because would-be salesmen passed through by the battalion. The great majority of them didn't take to the work — it took a never-say-die go-getter to do the job — and most quit or melted away after a short time. Thus, there was always a need for fresh bodies.

His last college quarter resumed after New Year's. Ray was talking to Bob Folsom, the nephew of Governor "Big Jim" Folsom, while waiting for an economics class to start. Ray allowed that he was going into the insurance business when he graduated in March. Folsom, who was graduating at the same time, remarked that he was just about to buy a life insurance policy from a Lincoln National agent. In fact, the agent was waiting for him at his fraternity house after the class was over.

"Don't do anything until you graduate," Ray said. "I'll take care of you."

"But I'm going to work in Oklahoma right after I graduate," Folsom said.

"Don't buy anything till I talk to you," said Ray, who phoned Joe Sutherland as soon as he could after class. He told Sutherland, "Send me an application blank for a life insurance policy."

"I can't," Sutherland said. "You're not licensed. You have to go to a one-week school after you graduate on March 15th." After the call, however, Sutherland spoke to Fred Hardy, the manager, and they agreed if this kid Scott was that hot, they could find a loophole so he could sell. The next day Sutherland called Ray and sent him an application blank and a rate book. "I sold another guy even before I sold Folsom," Ray says. "As a matter of fact, I sold $93,000 worth of life insurance before I graduated six weeks later."

Even so, as he looks back on those days — and this was before he absorbed the philosophy of Ralph K. Lindop, the man who was to change his life — Ray says, "My sales technique was ragged but enthusiastic. It was a reflection of my own personality."

One day Joe Sutherland drove over from Montgomery to accompany Ray on a sales call. Ray made the call, made the sale, and got the money. They climbed back into the car. Sutherland was quiet. After Ray drove several blocks, Sutherland finally said, "Pull over and turn the motor off."

Ray pulled over and stopped.

Sutherland turned to Ray, took a deep breath, shook his head and said, "You did not handle that right. You started out with the close and ended up with the introduction — and yet somehow you sold him." Sutherland shook his head again, took another deep breath and added, "Whatever it is you're doing, keep doing it."

Upon graduation, Ray spent a week in Montgomery attending MONY's insurance school. "It was all about how to make sales, how to read mortality tables, how to properly use the phone, and how to do this and that," he says. "And they had all these sales brochures about everything. My head was exploding with knowledge when I went back to Auburn to sell insurance. The first thirty days I did not sell one policy — not one. I became totally distraught. I was depressed. I thought I knew everything. After all, I had been to the insurance school. I was telling every prospect everything I knew. But I was just telling, not selling. My mind and mouth were pouring out gibberish. I took all the brochures out to the backyard and made the biggest fire you ever saw. When it was all over, all I had left was a rate book, a stack of application blanks, and a legal pad; and I went to war.

"In a file in the Student Union building, every student was listed alphabetically by name from Abbott to Zypher, along with personal information including local address, phone number, hometown, major study, and graduation date. Every other insurance salesman in Auburn was looking through those names starting with the A's. I went to the Z's and worked back. I had very little competition until I met the other salesmen around the R's.

"My average prospect was twenty-two years old. I was dealing with young men who were not going to die. They were protected by the 'impenetrable shield of youth.' So I would sell a savings plan. I'd tell them, 'I think life insurance is one of the greatest creations in the world. You can create an estate with a stroke of the pen.' But I couldn't sell a death policy. So I would sell a savings plan. It was an investment. Death was an accessory to the savings plan. I'd tell them that three things were going to happen: you'll live to be sixty-five, you'll die, or you'll get disabled. There's a waiver of premiums if you become disabled for six months. If you live to sixty-five, you'll get all your money back, plus a nice profit. If you die before sixty-five, your family gets $10,000. And if you want to borrow along the way, you can borrow at modest interest rates."

To help put over sales, Ray made an arrangement with the First National Bank of Montgomery. This allowed him to tell a cash-short senior who did not have the initial payments, "You pay the bank back after you graduate. The interest rate is only six percent and this 'relationship' form will help you establish your credit. I'll just fill it out for you. Let me tell you what all this small print says. It says that if you don't pay on time, the bank will have you put in jail. You can read it if you want to."

Adds Ray, "I would smile, he would smile, and he'd sign. What he didn't know was that I was a co-signer on the note. But I never had one failure or one slow pay."

After working a year in Auburn, MONY moved Ray, Eunice, Wilson, and new daughter Jennifer to Montgomery where Ray became the assistant agency manager. He bought a neat little brick house for $15,000 with a down payment of $1,200 and a monthly payment of $101. He was on top of the world. But he did not get a glimpse into his potential until the fall of 1961 when he met a man he absolutely had no interest in meeting.

5

Wheel of Fortune

RAY QUICKLY LEARNED a fact of life in the insurance business: Men and women fail as commission salespeople at an extraordinary rate. He saw those who hung on merely to survive, but never to taste the glory and greatness of their potential. It was obvious to Ray that they failed first because they could not find someone with a need for their product, and they failed second because if they did find someone, they could not get the prospect to listen objectively to the sales presentation.

The turning point in Ray's business life came unexpectedly in the fall of 1961 when he met Ralph K. Lindop. "I would have succeeded in life if I'd never met Lindop," Ray says, "but by embracing the power of his sales and prospecting philosophy, there was no mountain too high for me to climb. Before, I had been a somewhat successful salesman, but I was succeeding by sheer brute force of personality. By unconditionally embracing Lindop's philosophy, I took on a boldness, power, and strength that's incomparable. I felt it in the pit of my soul."

For Ray the encounter was somewhat like the blinding moment on the road to Damascus when Saul suddenly became Paul.

Mutual of New York had 170 agencies throughout the country and the Montgomery agency was one of only five that Lindop was visiting to reintroduce disability income insurance to the sales force. The time had arrived for disability income insurance — a loser during the Depression

— to make a comeback. But why was Montgomery, which ranked seventieth from the top of the 170 agencies, picked? As fate would have it, Lindop, who had been born and raised in nearby Selma, Alabama, wanted to visit his aging mother.

The irony is that neither Ray nor anyone else in the agency had any interest in listening to Lindop when he showed up at nine on a Tuesday morning at the Whitley Hotel. "We weren't excited about seeing Lindop," Ray says. "He was just another name nobody knew, just another of those clowns that the home office insisted on sending down to unveil a new product or sales technique for us. Such sessions weren't uncommon, and most were boring."

Of medium build, gray-haired, and in his fifties, Lindop had piercing eyes, a confident manner, and a commanding speaking style spiced with a country boy vocabulary. He strode into the room trailed by a disciple, Jim Conti, toting two oversized briefcases containing Lindop's equivalent of two stone tablets. Within an hour after Lindop began expounding his sales philosophy with the fervor and intensity of an old-time circuit-riding preacher, Ray felt himself on fire. "In a sense Lindop was preaching salvation for salesmen," says Ray. "All we had to do was listen and believe. None of us had cared about listening at first, but I became committed to his words and accepted them as the gospel."

A graduate of the University of Chicago and trained as a lawyer, Lindop went to work during the Depression when jobs were hard to get as a claims buster for the Prudential Insurance Company. Prudential had been selling disability income policies that would provide buyers with an income if they became sick or hurt and unable to work. However, the policies were renewable annually only at the option of the company. Policyholders were not really buyers, but renters; and in those tough economic times when a job could end tomorrow, a high percentage began making fraudulent claims before their policy expired. People wouldn't fake death to collect on their life insurance policy, but they certainly would — and did — fake a bad back or another ailment to collect disability payments. It was Lindop's job to contest the numerous claims believed to be fraudulent.

Lindop did well. But convinced that he could make more money selling insurance rather than fighting claims, he asked Prudential to let him sell. Prudential rejected his request because at that time the company did not permit any employee to make more than $9,999 a year and he could easily exceed that amount. As a result, he started moonlighting on weekends as a salesman for Monarch Insurance. He did well by selling non-cancelable, guaranteed renewable disability income insurance, as well as some life insurance, mainly to professional people who were pretty good risks.

In time, Lindop left Prudential to establish Monarch's agency in lower Manhattan. With a staff of forty full-time agents he became so successful that he sought to take over the company in a stock proxy fight. He lost the fight, but Mutual of New York immediately took him on. Like Prudential, MONY had taken a beating with fraudulent disability claims during the Depression. Given Lindop's record at Monarch, he was just the man who could make this aspect of MONY's business profitable. Perhaps even more importantly — and this is what set Ray on fire — Lindop had developed, honed, refined and simplified a sales and prospecting philosophy that had wide application above and beyond selling disability income insurance.

At the meeting in the Whitley Hotel, Lindop drew a cogwheel circle on a blackboard and divided it into four equal parts labeled "Sale," "Delivery Process," "Prospecting," and "Definitizing Appointment." He then drew an adjoining smaller cogwheel labeled "Continuing Service."

Lindop called the combination the Cycle of Success. Ray renamed it the Wheel of Fortune and it became his prime tool not only to sell insurance but to start B.A.S.S. It may strike some as simplistic, even hokey, but it works. Ray firmly believes the Wheel of Fortune can be effective in any business or any endeavor in which a sales person has to make his or her own market.

STEP ONE WAS THE SALES STORY. "To Lindop," Rays says, "a sales talk was not merely explaining the facts about a policy or a product. For instance, when selling disability income insurance, it was most important to fully explain the potential problems as well as the solution. He made sure the prospect understood the grim reality of debt if he became unable to work because of sickness or accident. 'Tell the truth,' he would say, 'and all the glories and any limitations, make them clear.'"

Ray says, "Up front admission of any limitations — such as no benefits for intentionally self-inflicted injury — disarms the prospect. With a smile and in a good natured way, I would say to a prospect, 'Before I begin, let me say that my primary reason for being here today is to get your money out of your pocket and into my pocket. And that being the case, I insist that you have me prove beyond any doubt that what I tell you is the absolute truth and supported by impartial third-party testimony."

Lindop liked to tell about his friend Bill, who started an advertising agency after borrowing $29,000 from a bank. Bill worked like crazy; and three years later he suffered a massive coronary that sidelined him for four months. When he returned to work, his doctor told him to stay home for a few more months to avoid another heart attack. Bill refused to do so.

"Doctor," he said, "I've had four months now to think about living and dying. Financially, I'm prepared to die. I have more than $60,000 in life insurance. But I've got to go back to work because debt keeps piling up. I have no other choice."

Bill went back to work and ten days later he dropped dead. At this point in his narrative, Lindop would say, "But disability income insurance could have kept Bill alive. It would have paid his debts while he got better at home. But Bill decided that a 'dead death' was better than a 'living death' from debt piling up."

"The most important feature of the policy we sold was the ownership provision," says Ray. "The policy was non-cancelable and guaranteed-renewable each year at the same premium until age sixty-five. If the premium could be changed by the company or the policy cancelled, you didn't *own* the policy — you would only be renting it and you could be evicted at any time. Anything less than absolute ownership was a snare and a delusion. The company might wish you'd die or get well, but they'd have to pay and pay and you couldn't be cancelled. Most other disability policies were renewable annually at the option of the company."

Lindop drove home a point that no man who felt a responsibility to his family or himself could put out of mind: disability income insurance would take care of payments on the insured's home and car and buy groceries and the other essentials needed to keep the family together without going crazy with worry. And Lindop added, "Disability income and an adequate major medical insurance policy allowed a man to come out of a sick bed a well man. He can go back to work with a gleam in his eye and a jauntiness to his step — not as a hobbled, debt-ridden wretch."

Lindop religiously clipped newspaper and magazine articles about the necessity and the proven value of disability insurance, which he would take out and show to a prospect and say, "Look, *U. S. News and World Report* and *Reader's Digest* don't really care whether you live or die or face a future crammed with debt. And they couldn't care less if I ever make another sale. So let's read what these magazines and others have to say. They're impartial. They have no reason to lie to you." This would prove without any doubt that non-cancelable disability income insurance was truly essential and eliminated any logical objections why the prospect should not buy right then and there.

"If he didn't buy," Ray says, "I would hope to leave him miserable for the rest of his life. On some occasions I received calls later that evening or the next day asking me to come back and write the application for the policy. It was hard for someone not to buy from me. They couldn't deny me because they knew I was right — an exploding one hundred percent right."

But Lindop's winning sales method did not end there. The sale did not make a winner. The sale was merely the kickoff for more sales on the Wheel of Fortune.

STEP TWO WAS THE POLICY DELIVERY. Lindop emphasized the absolute necessity of personally delivering the policy. Ask for at least forty-five minutes and if possible have the spouse sit in on the delivery.

"I would call on a prospect to make an appointment for at least forty-five minutes," says Ray. "I'd ask that the spouse be in attendance and say, 'I've got some good news to share with you and Mrs. Jones when I see you.'

"Then before I delivered the policy, I would quietly sit down by myself and do what Lindop called 'pre-delivery thinking.' I would take out the policy and underscore in red ink the key provisions, especially any restrictions or limitations. A man is more interested in what a policy won't do than what it will do when buying something as complex as disability income insurance. I would highlight the non-cancelable features. With life insurance, it pays when you're cold and dead; but with disability there are many shades of gray. Absolute ownership was paramount. You can buy disability insurance out of the Sunday newspaper supplement or a TV ad for $5 a month, but if you take the time to read the fine print, you discover that you only receive the $1,000 a month if your arms and legs are blown off while flying first class on a Syrian airline from Iceland to Thailand on Friday afternoon in a year with an even number.

"In my quiet time I would then take a separate piece of paper and write down the categories of people the policy holder would probably know — church members, neighbors, relatives, business associates, friends, fishing or golfing buddies. Finally, I would make sure that I had a refund check for overpayment of premium at the time of purchase if there was one. When I wrote the application, I almost always overcharged in case the home office affixed a higher premium. It's difficult to go back to a buyer and say that he's got to pay another $50. But when I gave him a company refund check, I always saw a smile.

"During the delivery meeting I would briefly, but thoroughly, rehash the reasons he had bought the policy in the first place. I would go through the policy slowly and show him that I was delivering exactly what he'd bought earlier. I would go through the underscored policy, give him the check for the overcharge, and get a big smile. At this point I had done everything I had promised — and more.

"The new client understood what he had bought, why he had bought it and he felt much more assured about tomorrow — and so did his wife."

STEP THREE WAS PROSPECTING. "This was the moment of truth," says Ray, "my launch pad for marketing immortality. I would set the policy aside and look square in the man's eye and say, 'You now have financial peace of mind about getting sick or hurt but you have friends and associates who will never see this policy unless you tell me who they are. I don't knock on doors and the only way that they will ever see what you have done for yourself will be for you to tell me to show them.'

"At this point, the man and his wife trust me, believe me, and are confident that they have solved one of the major problems in their life. I would pull out my list of possible categories of people and say, 'Tell me the name of a neighbor who'd be in financial trouble if he got sick or hurt and couldn't work.' I would lead the man and his wife, who was usually more forthcoming with names than her husband. When the first name came out, it was like getting a kiss from a girl — the first one was difficult but the others came easier. Then the names would flow as freely as water down a mountain stream. On occasion I got as many as twenty names and I would average six. It was like a gusher going off. Because these people understood what they now had, they were excited to share me with their friends.

"When the names started flowing, I just jotted the name down and got the next name and the next name. I didn't ask any questions then about who a man was or what he did at that point. I just wrote down the next name. When I felt they were running out of names, I'd stop and go back to the first name and I'd say, 'Now, tell me about Billy Bob Jones. What does he do for a living? Is he married?' I'd get his age, all the particulars. And then I'd ask about his health history. And if they happened to say, 'He's always had problems with his lower back,' or otherwise indicated that a man had health problems, I would obviously scratch out his name and everything about him and say, 'Sorry, but I can't help him. He'll never qualify for this policy.' For the first time they realized that they were fortunate to have bought the policy while in good health and it had a profound impact on them.

"Now we are sharing the same heart. I would shove the pad back and say, 'Now Mr. and Mrs. Smith, there's a hard way and an easy way for these people on this list to see what this policy has done for you and what it can do for them. The hard way is for me to go knock on their door and ask for an appointment. The easier way is for you to call them, tell them that Ray Scott's coming and say, 'Listen to Scott. Buy or don't buy, but take the time to listen.' Sometimes they'd call. Most times they didn't, but I'd go see, face to face, every person on that list. I would *never* ever use the telephone. Lindop taught me that the telephone was a killer as people could easily say no, but it was much more difficult for them to say no when I was looking square in their eyes. Those names were too precious to burn with an impatient phone call.

"Lindop said that you could expect, on delivery, to walk away from each new client with an average of six names. Of the six, three would make an appointment to see you, and out of those three, at least one would buy. And the man who bought would give you six more names. Then the Cycle of Success, the Wheel of Fortune, the 1-6-3-1 Formula, would begin producing all over again."

STEP FOUR WAS "DEFINITIZING APPOINTMENT." At least that's what Lindop called it. In straightforward English that means making an appointment as soon as possible with a prospect — in person.

As Ray puts it, "A successful salesman never sits on the names of prospects while they're hot. He knows better. They're his ticket to tomorrow. So he promptly visits them asking for an appointment, totally confident that they'll buy and lead him to additional prospects. If he's a pro, if he does his job right, they will. And that's all he needs to be a success.

"Here's how I went about making an appointment with a prospect. I would never telephone for an appointment. I would appear on the front porch or in the office of a prospect and confidently announce, 'Your good friend, John Smith, told me to come and see you. Has he called to mention that?'

"If John Smith, the name giver, had not made the call, I would say, 'That's all right. I'm not here to talk with you today because I'm sure you're busy, and I'm already on my way to another appointment.' That immediately put the prospect at ease. I wasn't there unexpectedly to bother or harass him without warning and that made him feel better. He didn't have to make up any excuses to get rid of me. I was considerate enough to realize that he had a busy schedule and he appreciated that thoughtfulness. Yet, I regarded the prospect as someone so important to me that I dropped by in person, and he was flattered. That impressed him. He heard me say that I already had another appointment. And he was struck by the fact that I was a go-getter, a professional salesman on the move. I must be good. Why there were folks all over town just waiting to see me. Sometimes I did have another appointment, and sometimes I didn't. But I always made it a point to appear too busy to talk even if he invited me in.

"Next I would say, 'Please call John Smith before I come back. He wants you to know the kind of peace of mind he bought from me. He told me to tell you to buy or don't buy, just listen. He thinks it's important to you. Ask him if he did business with me, and if I deliver on every promise. If you buy, that's fine. If you don't, that's your decision. Will Tuesday be all right? Or is Thursday better for you?'

"In closing, I gave the prospect a choice of days when I could come back. I did not give him a chance to say no by asking, 'Can I come back?' Either answer he gave me was the one I wanted to hear. 'I'm off Thursday,' he might say, 'I won't be here.' 'Then how about Tuesday at two o'clock? Or would quitting time be better?' 'I close at five.' 'Does 5:05 sound all right?' 'That'll be fine.' 'Good, I'll be here. And please don't forget to call John Smith.'

"Over the years, very few prospects ever bothered to call their friends to check out Ray Scott. The very fact that I kept insisting they call made me acceptable in their mind. Personally, I wanted them to call. I tried to leave my buyers so satisfied that I sincerely believed they could have just about sold the policy for me before that Tuesday afternoon ever came around. I've seen that Wheel of Fortune turn losers into winners. It turned me into a winner. But you have to be dedicated to it. You can't take short cuts.

"Lindop convinced me that I could sell more life insurance by accident if I used disability income insurance as the entry. Before, I used to ride the streets of Montgomery wondering, 'Who can I sell life insurance to today?' It's a long way between getting into a man's house and getting into his pocket. If I said, 'I'm a life insurance man,' you'd throw me out the door, but if I said, 'I can give you peace of mind when you're sick or hurt and can't work,' chances are you'd want to listen.

"Prior to the Wheel of Fortune, my sales were spiked, my market was spiked. I might sell a dentist tomorrow, a truck driver the day after. I was up and down the economic scale. There was more money with professional people, and my objective was to fill up a void. With professionals, their life insurance man wasn't talking about disability insurance. But I was.

"I went to see Dr. Glenn Palmer, an orthopedic surgeon. Another client — a physician — Dr. Robert Lightfoot, had told me about him. Dr. Palmer told me that he had almost $1 million worth of life insurance, and I asked him, 'How much disability income insurance do you have?' And he said, 'What's that?' I said, "Doctor, you should know that the probability of your becoming totally disabled prior to age sixty-five is nearly ten times more likely than you die before sixty-five. Here it is in black and white in the *Journal of the American Medical Association*.' He said, 'I never saw those numbers before.'

"I shocked him into the reality that he had a complete void. His agent with Northwestern Mutual, a very fine company, had left him half-clothed against the winds of adversity. A man like the doctor has good money coming in, then disability crashes in. I'd draw a line that represents income sliding toward the pits, and then an expense line that starts soaring up with the cost of getting well. When those two lines cross, that's called debt, and a person has no control over it. It's economic reality and you can never feel it until you live it.

"I'd say, 'I guarantee your income line will never get down to that point where it crosses the expense line, and I would like you to take the time to get well.' I was selling more than a piece of paper and money. I was selling peace of mind. I sold Dr. Palmer everything in the book: $1,500 worth of tax-free income a month for personal disability and another $1,500 to help pay his office overhead expense. With that concept, doors around the city began to open for me. I had prospects. I was confident, I was cocky. I was selling peace of mind.

"With only one prospect, you go in nervous, scared to death, thinking if you use up that name you're out of business. Not with the Wheel. I had a pocketful of prospects to see, and I got so cocky that I'd open with the closer — buy or don't buy. I didn't have a prospect question my integrity. I'd have him challenge it. I knew what I knew, and I was one hundred percent committed to victory. You cannot discern the difference between a person who is ninety-eight percent committed to victory from a person ninety-nine percent committed, but you sure can tell a person who is one hundred percent committed to victory. There's a religious fervor."

WHEN OFFICIALS AT MONY in New York heard that another insurance company, Provident Life and Accident in Chattanooga, was courting Ray, they responded by bringing him to New York for a year as a training assistant to prepare him for moves up the corporate ladder to agency manager. Besides holding in-house tutorials on underwriting and policies, MONY would periodically dispatch Ray and the other trainees to the field. He spent a month in Raleigh, North Carolina, and two months in New Orleans. But most of all he loved the excitement and energy of New York City. He enjoyed seeing Lindop and his wife, who lived in Greenwich Village, and going out with them to the Coach House restaurant. And he relished calling on prospects in the big city where his Southern accent marked him as an interesting "exotic."

Thanks to the Wheel of Fortune, the name of one prospect on his list was a dentist named Dr. Bloomingstein. He went to his office and told the receptionist, "I am here to see Dr. Bloomingstein. His friend, Dr. Leo Smith, told me to come see him to discuss an appointment." She said, "Just a moment," and excused herself while she went to confer with the doctor. When she returned she said that Dr. Bloomingstein would see Mr. Scott at five o'clock. It was 4:30, and Ray decided to wait.

Promptly at five, the receptionist said, "Mr. Scott, Dr. Bloomingstein will see you now."

Ray walked into the doctor's office, introduced himself, and said that Dr. Smith had given him Dr. Bloomingstein's name. He asked for a sales appointment later in the week.

Dr. Bloomingstein, sitting back with arms folded across his chest, said, "I'm going to be busy. If you've got something to say, tell me now." Ray went into the benefits of disability income insurance. The doctor listened intently to Ray's every word for at least an hour without uttering one of his own.

Finally, Dr. Bloomingstein spoke after Ray asked him the application question, "When was the last time you saw a physician?" Ray noted the date in the application. Dr. Bloomingstein then answered all Ray's questions about his health, family background, and income, whereupon Ray said, "I need a check for $650 to cover your first annual premium."

Dr. Bloomingstein took out his checkbook, opened it, and put down his pen. He smiled at Ray for the first time and said, "You will never believe this. My receptionist came back and told me, 'Doctor, I know you are not remotely interested in talking to this character out front, but I just want you to hear his funny accent.' Mr. Scott, the only reason I let you in here was to listen to your accent and now you have sold me this policy."

Says Ray, "The moral of the story is to get in the door any way you can." Ray sold more insurance in two months in New York than he ever sold in two months anywhere else in his entire career.

MONY set a quota for every agency office and ranked them on their quota success. After Ray finished his training in New York, the company sent him to manage the Greensboro, North Carolina, agency which was close to the bottom of the pile. Two managers had died on the vine and had been fired, and the two salesmen left were dispirited sad sacks. The agency ranked a dismal 173rd out of 180 and was dropping fast. In the first five months with Ray in charge, the agency increased its performance quota by 390 percent, and only seven months later it had jumped from 173rd to second. "The salesmen were all the same," Ray says. "It was the Wheel of Fortune that made it happen."

In the late summer of 1964, Ray left MONY and Greensboro when Lindop asked him to move back to Montgomery and be the pioneer manager of the Alabama market for Underwriters National Assurance Company. Lindop had joined UNAC at its headquarters in Indianapolis. Ray stayed with UNAC in Montgomery until 1967 when he resigned after promoting his first bass tournament at Beaver Lake. Although he left the insurance field, he took the Wheel of Fortune with him and used it to build B.A.S.S.

6

Brainstorm in a Rainstorm

THE WHEEL OF FORTUNE gave Ray the confidence to create the world of big-time bass fishing that we now know. It gave boldness to his dreams. Just as more casts meant more chances to catch fish, more names to call on meant more chances to catch customers — in this case, fishermen.

Although Ray loved selling insurance, bass fishing often consumed his idle hours and his thoughts on the road. While driving from one prospect to another — or just sitting outside someone's office — he indulged in a fishing fantasy. In his fantasy he not only spent his working hours fishing but made a good living out of it as well.

Ray's fantasy began to assume reality in March of 1967. At that time his territory had been expanded to include Mississippi, Arkansas, and Louisiana; and he'd gone to Mississippi to call on insurance brokers. As he had done many times before, he arranged his travel schedule so that when the weekend came he'd end up in Jackson next to good bass waters. Once in Jackson, he dropped in on Don Norton at his Johnny Reb Lure Company. Norton told Ray with some pride that he had been invited to enter a fishing derby.

Ray was not impressed. "Yeah," he said, "I know all about those fishin' derbies. I've even been to a couple of those shindigs, and they're always won by the guy who has the most pounds of fish stored up in his freezer."

"Not this derby," Norton assured him.

Ray smiled and nodded. But to himself, he thought: these derbies are all alike, nothing more than little old Chamber of Commerce promotions where everybody pitches $2 into a hat, then finds out the winner is the one who can cheat without getting caught. And nobody ever gets caught. They give fishing — and honest fishermen — a bad name.

Ray learned years later there were a few well-run buddy tournaments — notably one circuit run by Waco *Herald Tribune* outdoor writer Earl Golding. In the early sixties he had already tapped into the burgeoning American subculture of bass fanatics and was well known in Texas.

On Saturday afternoon, as recounted in the introduction to this book, Ray went fishing with buddy Lloyd Lewis and got blown off White's Lake. Back at the Ramada Inn relaxing and watching TV, he had his revelation — his vision for a legitimate, honest, professional bass tournament that would attract the right kind of fishermen. Fishermen would compete, tournament-style. Fair and square. "It all just came to me," says Ray. "I knew it would work."

Forget those $2 derbies. High entry fees would attract high-caliber fishermen. And the tournament rules would be clear and concise — written in stone, like the tablets Moses brought down from the mountain — to guarantee a fair and equitable contest. No one would be able to cheat his way to victory with a sack load of frozen fish or any live ones caught against the rules.

Only the best fishermen would be accepted. Only the best would compete. In a Ray Scott tournament, anglers would compete for $5,000. In a Ray Scott tournament, anglers would compete for national recognition. That's what was going to make Ray Scott's All-American Invitational Bass Tournament different. It would be the PGA of fishing!

No longer would bass fishermen be looked upon as a bunch of redneck country boys whose idea of dressing up was buttoning the top button of a pair of bib overalls, who could plow the south forty, run a trotline, and wear out two chaws of tobacco before the corn mash got hot in the moonshine still. Bass fishermen had always been thought of as refugees from hard work, due neither honor nor respect. No more.

GREAT. RAY HAD sold himself. Now all he had to do was sell the rest of the country. It was time to use the Wheel of Fortune. Call the Wheel hokey, but it gave him the courage to give up his job in insurance and convert fantasy into reality. As Ray says, "You can afford to be daring when you're convinced your system can successfully take you into any market place — even if the market is brand new, untried and untested."

Few critics would have given him and his idea much chance of survival, but on that cold, blustery, rainy Saturday in Jackson, he was so fevered with excitement that he wasn't worried. Criticism would come later. So would the steady diet of bologna sandwiches. Critics first had to hear of Ray Scott before they could criticize him, and he didn't want to keep them waiting.

"I've often thought about that Saturday on White's Lake with Lloyd Lewis," Ray says. "If the sun had been shining and the fish had been biting, I just might have remained an insurance salesman all my life."

Ray couldn't sleep that night. The excitement was too much, like caffeine boiling in his brain. On Sunday he drove to Little Rock, Arkansas, and checked into a motel. He'd read a glowing article by Charlie Elliot in *Outdoor Life* about the bass fishing on Beaver Lake in northwestern Arkansas. That's where he wanted to put on his first tournament, and he needed help to do it. But no longer was he just one of tens of thousands of insurance salesmen, albeit a successful one. Now he was, in his own mind at least, the president and executive director of a brand new company, All-American Bass Tournaments, despite the fact that he had not even a business card to show for it.

In a hall of the state capitol building in Little Rock, a guard pointed out Bob Evans, the Arkansas director of tourism. Ray went right up to Evans and introduced himself. "Mr. Evans, I'm Ray Scott, the president and executive director of All-American Bass Tournaments. And I would like to talk to you."

Evans gave a broad smile and said, "I'm so delighted to meet you, Mr. Scott. I would be pleased if you and your staff would come right into my office."

Staff? Staff? "My staff isn't here at this time," said Ray, thinking

quickly as he followed Evans into his office. That was true. A staff was
about a year away, if he got lucky.

In his best salesman's manner, Ray pitched Bob Evans on the simple
fact that a national bass fishing tournament, repeat *national bass fishing
tournament*, with the best bass fishermen in the country competing for
$5,000, would generate tons, repeat tons, of favorable publicity for
Arkansas fishing and tourism. All the president and executive director of
All-American Bass Tournaments needed was a lake.

"Now, Mr. Scott, on what lake were you planning to hold your
tournament?" Evans asked.

"Beaver Lake," Ray said.

"A beautiful spot!" Evans exclaimed. "One of the best!"

Hmmm, Ray thought, sounds like he read the article in *Outdoor Life*.

"Mr. Evans, what *we* need to find out from you," Ray said, stressing
the *we* as if a staff of ten were with him, "is just which town on Beaver
Lake would serve best as our headquarters?"

"You've got two to choose from," Evans answered, "Rogers or
Springdale. Either town would be perfect. Both are beautiful little towns,
and both are conveniently located near the lake."

Ray smiled. Evans smiled. He was selling Ray as hard as Ray was
selling him and both were buying. Evans gave Ray the names of the
chamber of commerce directors in both Rogers and Springdale. Now he
had two names for the Wheel of Fortune. He walked away from the office
ready to click his heels. Round one was over and Evans hadn't seen
anything unusual or foolish in a big league bass fishing tournament. This
little venture was going to be easy after all.

Back at the motel Ray placed a long distance call to the Rogers
Chamber of Commerce and the chamber director answered. Ray took a
deep breath. "Good morning," he said, the excitement mounting in his
voice. "This is Ray Scott, president and executive director of All-
American Bass Tournaments. We are planning to hold our next invitational bass tournament at Beaver Lake, and I wondered if your fair city
might be interested in serving as a sponsor and host city for this
prestigious event."

Long pause. The long, fancy title was probably taking time to soak into the director's head. At last the director spoke up. "Look, Mr. Scott, I appreciate your calling, but I'm not interested one bit in your tournament. I'm quitting this job in three weeks and I don't want to get involved in anything new. I don't even want to sharpen a new pencil."

Round two. Can't win 'em all, but back to the Wheel of Fortune. Evans had given him two names. Time to spin the wheel for the last one.

As he placed the call to Springdale, he decided to be a little more positive, a little more forceful. The phone rang twice, and the chamber director, Lee Zachary, answered.

Ray said, "Mr. Zachary, this is Ray Scott, president and executive director of All-American Bass Tournaments. We want to congratulate you, Mr. Zachary, because we have selected Springdale as the site of our next invitational bass tournament. And your good friend, Bob Evans with the Arkansas tourism department, told us you would be the man most important to our success in Springdale."

"Yes, sir, Mr. Scott," Zachary said, "I've heard of your fine organization and we sure want you up here. Mr. Scott, I have been waiting for your call. We have needed something like this in our town for a long time."

Ray pinched himself. Only one morning in business and folks had already heard of his fine organization? Good news must travel a fast road in Arkansas. What Ray did not know was that Lee Zachary was a ball of fire who had only been on the job in Springdale for two months, and he had great confidence that he could wake up the town and put it on the map big time. He needed Ray as much as Ray needed him.

Ray's next step was to meet Zachary and the chamber board face to face. Back home in Montgomery, he called Zachary again to arrange a meeting with the chamber board in Springdale the next week. He could have written, but the president and executive director of All-American Bass Tournaments didn't have any All-American Bass Tournaments stationery.

Meanwhile, unknown to Ray, the board members had Zachary quietly checking with Ralph Murray, a Montgomery insurance man.

They learned three things: Ray Scott did live in Montgomery; there was no record anywhere of All-American Bass Tournaments; and that insurance salesmen in Montgomery seemed delighted with the prospects of Ray leaving the business.

At the meeting in Springdale, Ray came on strong with his sales pitch. He told about the value of publicity, how the eyes of the fishing world would be focused on the town, watching with a hypnotized fascination as the globe's finest bass fishermen challenged beautiful Beaver Lake for a record-breaking first prize of a whole $2,000. Why the tournament would pull in thousands of dollars in revenue as fishermen flocked to Springdale's motels, marinas, and restaurants. This was an invitational tournament so only the best would be on hand, only the top fishermen. In essence it was the World Series of bass fishing, and he wanted the chamber to put up $10,000 as the sponsor.

"How many fishermen you gonna have?" a board member asked.

"A hundred," Ray said.

"What will the entry fee be?"

"A hundred dollars." Men gasped, throats cleared, chairs scraped the floor. *A hundred dollars?*

"Yep, a hundred dollars," Ray said.

Ray did not know that Jim Cypert, a local attorney and Chamber member, had advised the board that some fishing derbies were having trouble getting a $2 entry fee, and that if Scott were lucky, very lucky, he might get $5.

The members looked at one another, and one of them said, "Mr. Scott, we'll discuss your proposition and get back to you at two this afternoon."

"By then, the veneer of my organization had gotten sort of thin," Ray recalls. "This business about 'we' that I had been giving them was nothing more than 'me and an idea.' Before I arrived, the Chamber of Commerce thought I had the $10,000 that I would need to pull off the tournament. I was hoping they had the $10,000. They probably did. But they sure weren't going to part with it unless they voted. Lee Zachary, perhaps out of hope, seemed convinced that I could do what I said I could. The board was being cautious."

Ray went to the Springdale Holiday Inn to wait them out. It was the start of a long wait. Meanwhile, the board put Ray under the close scrutiny of Joe Robinson, a veteran mountain man and coon hunter who was a real estate broker. He was also the owner of the War Eagle Boat Dock on Beaver Lake and a former member of the Arkansas Game and Fish Commission. Robinson and his son, Tub, met Ray for lunch. With a gleam in his eye, Robinson pushed his plate aside, pulled his chair close to the table, and, in a soft, quiet voice, asked, "Mr. Scott, what makes you think you can put on one of these tournaments?"

The inquisition was underway.

"Mr. Robinson," he answered, "I am absolutely certain that I can."

"How much experience have you had?"

"Not a dang bit. But I know I can do it."

Joe Robinson nodded. His assignment was at an end. If he learned one thing about Ray Scott, it was that he wouldn't lie to him. Actually, the truth did not upset Robinson at all. He and his son became Ray's allies.

THE CHAMBER BOARD met with Ray at two. They heard him again — this time he reduced the sponsorship money to $5,000 — and they sent Ray outside while they listened to Robinson's report. Then they deliberated.

It was a cold, gray day outside while Ray waited for their decision. Patches of snow covered the ground, and the wait seemed interminable. An hour and ten minutes later, Lee Zachary called Ray inside.

"The board has voted not to sponsor your tournament for $5,000," he said. "If, however, you want to produce the tournament on your own, we will permit you to use the back room at this chamber office. But I'm afraid you'll have to agree not to tie the chamber into your promotion in any way."

Zachary added that the board members hoped Ray would succeed.

Zachary and Robinson had even told them they believed Ray would succeed. But the board wasn't about to get in the same boat with Ray Scott, much less pay for it.

Looking back on that bleak time, Ray says, "I don't blame them. None of them wanted to jeopardize the good name of Springdale with some harebrained Alabama boy's fishing tournament. They couldn't afford the risk of a black eye. I learned later that Cypert, the local attorney, even suggested that they put me under a $5,000 bond if I stayed, just to prevent me from running off with any funds I might raise."

Robinson took the decision even harder than Ray. As competitive as an Ozark coon dog, he could see the tournament publicity bringing in a ton of people to buy gasoline and bait at his marina. A bass tournament would be a bonanza. In just a few days he could do a year's worth of business.

That thought also crossed the mind of Dr. Stanley Applegate. Dr. Applegate owned the Hickory Creek Boat Dock six miles down the lake from Robinson's marina. The doctor was such a strong believer in Springdale that he spent nearly as much of his time promoting civic activities as he did practicing medicine.

It was nearly dark when Ray and Joe Robinson wandered on back to Joe's real estate office where they would try to decide what the next step should be, if there should even be a next step. They no sooner sat down than the door swung open and Dr. Applegate burst into the room. He had been on the go all day and hadn't yet had time to catch either the latest news or his second wind.

"How'd the meeting go?" he asked.

"Turned us down," Robinson said. Dr. Applegate began slowly drumming a desk top with his fingers, his brow furrowed, his mind lost in thought.

Ray said, "I know it's risky, but I also know I can do it. The formula is simple. I'll get a hundred fishermen to pay a hundred bucks each. And that'll give us ten grand. I'll put $5,000 into prizes and $5,000 into promotion. Then if I have anything left over, I'll be ahead."

"Ray," said Dr. Applegate, "I know you wanted $10,000 and finally asked for $5,000. What's the least amount you could use and actually go ahead with your tournament?"

"Twenty-five hundred dollars. It'll be tough, but I think that's enough money to give me a working base."

Dr. Applegate pondered for a moment, then reached into his breast pocket and unfolded a checkbook. He wrote a check and handed it to Ray. It was to Ray Scott for $2,500, marked personal. "If the tournament works and you actually pull it off, you can give the $2,500 back to me," the doctor said. "If it doesn't work, all I ask is that you never tell my wife I gave you the money."

Without another word, the ever-hurrying Dr. Applegate glanced at his watch, jumped up, and headed for the door on his way to another civic meeting.

"Dr. Applegate!" Ray yelled. "Wouldn't you like a receipt?"

The doctor stopped, turned, shrugged and said, "Not necessary. If you were going to cheat us, you'd have already cheated us somehow." The door slammed, and he was gone.

With a big smile, Ray looked at Robinson. "Well, Joe, I do believe that you and me are in the fishing tournament business."

Robinson leaned back in his chair like a condemned man who'd just been given a last-minute stay by the governor. "We'll show, boy," he said. "We'll show."

7

The First Tournament

RAY PUT ALL his ingenuity — all his insight into the very soul of bass fishermen — into the First All-American Invitational Bass Tournament on Beaver Lake.

For starters, he decided to give cash prizes not to the top three finishers, but the top ten. The first place finisher would get $2,000 and the tenth place finisher $100. As a bass fisherman himself, he knew that most bass fishermen were conceited in a humble sort of way. Not one of the hundred fishermen invited to enter the tournament would think that he was a cinch to win the first place money of $2,000. On the other hand, no one thought he was bad enough to come in as low as eleventh place. As a result, every fisherman who sent in the $100 entry fee was dead certain in his own mind that he'd at least get his money back, if not more.

To sweeten the pot, Ray decided to give an all-expenses-paid fishing vacation in Acapulco to the first place winner, and Joe Robinson said he would give a lot on Beaver Lake valued at $3,500 to the fisherman who caught the biggest bass.

Ray's prizes were set. He had a beautiful lake for the tournament. Now all he needed was one hundred bass fishermen who would put up $100 each. And he needed them fast because the tournament loomed only fifty days away. But first he had to have a set of tournament rules. They had to be strict and assure each participant that he could win or lose in an atmosphere of total fairness. He locked himself in the Holiday Inn room for two days and carved out the rules, stopping only to eat.

Remarkably, Ray's rules remain basically intact to this day. Little has changed. He was obsessed with eliminating the possibility and the opportunities for cheating. He rejected buddies fishing together. No fishermen from the same state were paired. Anglers who resided in a county that touched Beaver Lake were ineligible. Partners changed every day. Fishermen could not leave the boat for any reason. Each angler had to stay within sight of his partner and his partner's fish at all times. Each fisherman verified his partner's creel by signing the official weigh-in slip. These were just some of the stipulations that have since been refined and refined again.

"I would come to find out," says Ray, "the tighter the rules and the more they were enforced, the better the fishermen liked it. When something went wrong, the rules did the talking, not me."

The tiny office that the Chamber let him use only had enough room for a couple of desks, a telephone, and a tall order of Alabama audacity.

To round the fishermen up, he took $1,330 of Dr. Applegate's loan and arranged for a WATS line to be installed. The Wheel of Fortune and the WATS line were key. The line put him in touch with any phone in the thirteen states nearest to Arkansas and he had the names of four prospects to start the Wheel. They were Charlie Bamburg and Marshal Tomblin of Montgomery; Tom Mann of Eufaula, Alabama; and Jack Wingate of Lake Seminole near Bainbridge, Georgia. If they had friends, and they surely did, he'd have entries.

"I am indebted to all of them," says Ray. "Jack Wingate and Tom Mann personify the character of the people who helped me." Indeed, Ray considers both Mann and Wingate true trail blazers of bass fishing.

Jack Wingate is the proprietor of the venerable Lunker Lodge on Lake Seminole outside of Bainbridge, Georgia, near the Florida border. A sign at the entrance to the Lodge greets visitors with the following inscription: "Cuz, They Bit Yesterday." The opposite side, the one you read as you drive away, says: "Cuz, They'll Tare It Up Tomorrow."

That quaint sign is one of the many icons at Lunker Lodge, a place where time stands still on the cypress-lined shoreline of Lake Seminole.

The dimly lit road to the Lodge is narrow and winding. Its canopy of Spanish moss-draped live oaks gives you the feeling you're headed down a peaceful path to the end of the world. There you'll find one of the last examples of what bass fishing was like long ago. And you'll more than likely be greeted by Jack and Joyce Wingate.

"You've definitely got to be coming here to get here," says Jack, a big bear of a man with a thick thatch of graying hair.

Ray had gotten a brochure about Wingate's Lunker Lodge and guide service from an insurance client. Ray had never even spoken to Wingate. When he desperately needed names for his All-American tournament, he called Jack one evening and gave him his spiel about the tournament. Did he have the names of a few crackerjack fishermen?

Ray will never forget his reply: "I've got a right many of them." Flipping through the pages of his client book, he reeled off some names that are now legendary in bass fishing.

"Here's two: Glin Wells and Stan Sloan from Tennessee," he said. Stan would win the tournament and Glin stayed with B.A.S.S. for years as a formidable competitor, winning a national tournament in South Carolina. After making follow-up calls to Wingate's prospects and after calling their buddies, Ray had twenty entries directly attributable to his phone call to Jack. And Jack, too, would be one of the 106 original contestants in the All-American.

"Jack Wingate is a true friend," says Ray. "Don't let the good ol' boy tone of his speech fool you. He's a very intelligent man who has left an indelible mark on our sport. Just one example is his Wingate's Fishing Camp for Boys which he established more than twenty-eight years ago."

Ray's next stop in Springdale was a print shop that just happened to be owned by a member of the chamber board. He was surprised to see Ray still around. Ray surprised him even more by saying, "I need letterhead stationery. I want the best paper that you have. It's gotta be high grade. It's gotta be like parchment. I want it to crackle and make noise when someone unfolds it."

"I don't have that kind of paper," the owner said. "I'll have to order it."

"Please do," Ray said with a smile.

When a prospect received that special invitation, Ray wanted quality to jump off the page and hit him right between the eyes. He wanted the invitation to put that old muddy fisherman up on a marble pedestal and make him feel important. To add to that feeling, he and the shop owner designed a letterhead inscribed with his new name and address: All-American Bass Invitational Tournament, Chamber of Commerce Building, Springdale, Arkansas 72764.

Ray told the manager of the Holiday Inn about the tournament, and the manager at once saw the possibility of filling up the motel for a few days. He told Ray, "Use the Holiday Inn for your headquarters, and we'll furnish you a room free of charge. We'll even give you your personal meals for half price." Ray accepted the offer. Then he allowed that he needed a secretary and the desk clerk recommended a young lady named Darlene Phillips. "Darlene would be perfect," he told Ray. "She has experience. She used to work, but now she is married and has a family. Since you just need temporary help, Darlene might be interested."

Ray insisted on meeting Darlene at once. He told her his plan, and she quickly shared his excitement. Ray could see that she was smart, charming, and efficient. In fact, she could recall telephone numbers off the top of her head. "I can only pay you $200 a month," Ray said.

"All right."

"And it might be three or four weeks before I can pay you at all."

"All right."

"Darlene didn't back off," Ray says. "I had told her the truth and I still had me a secretary. I had flat laid the negative on her, first thing, and we had no problem. I sincerely believed I could pay her quicker. But if I did, that would be my surprise. That would be that something extra, that something unexpected, that makes people appreciate you when you do deliver. Ralph K. Lindop was right. The Wheel was a philosophy of life, not just a cold formula for business."

With Darlene ensconced in the tiny office with the WATS line, a regular phone, and a rented IBM typewriter, Ray made a quick plane trip back home to Montgomery. His flight had an hour-and-a-half layover in

Memphis, and he used it to begin serious prospecting. "I got me a pocketful of nickels and ducked into a phone booth," he recalls. "I found marinas in the Yellow Pages and started dialing. I got the Lake View Marina. 'Good afternoon, this is Ray Scott, president and executive director of the All-American Bass Tournament, and we're lookin' for some top-quality bass fishermen.' The manager of the marina said, 'There's a young feller here named Billy Dance, and he's better than anyone.'

"Regardless of which marina I called, the first name they blurted out was Billy Dance. 'That Billy Dance must be somethin' special,' I would say. 'Tell me about him. Why do you think he's good enough to come to the All- American Invitational Tournament?' Just as in the insurance business, when someone gave me a name, I made him qualify that name. I wanted to know everything I could about the person behind that name. It makes talking to him later a lot easier.

"And the answer that I got was, 'Billy Dance is a young feller. Only about twenty-four or twenty-five. But he's good. If there are fish that can be caught, he'll sure catch 'em.'

"What does he do?"

"I do believe he works at a furniture store in town".

"Does he have a boat?"

"Yeah, a fourteen-foot johnboat."

"What kind of horsepower on his motor?"

"About eighteen."

"Thanks. You've been a great help. By the way, is he married?"

"Don't know. Never seen him with no woman."

As part of his spiel, Ray said, "'The tournament is not an event that everyone can compete in. Only the elite are being selected, then invited. I don't want anyone who's not a top-flight bass fisherman. We're looking, as well, for fine men who have outstanding character, who are honest and a credit to bass fishing. This is an enormous happening, perhaps the most important happening in the history of the sport. As a result, it's equally important to your friends that you tell me who they are.'

"They would think hard, and I would prompt them. 'Who fishes regularly out of your marina? Who has come back with the most fish? Who leaves their boats with you?'

"By the time my nickels ran out, I had about ten names. And, just as important, I had the names of the well-respected marina owners who had recommended them. That would make all the difference in the world."

THE FANCY PARCHMENT-like stationery with the ornate letterhead was waiting when Ray returned to Springdale. What counted now was what the letter said. Beg people to come and they'll ignore you. The text of the letter had to convince the recipient that it was a real honor just to be *asked* to enter the tournament. Ray wanted the prospect to believe that the fishing gods had smiled on him and that he had been chosen to participate only because men of sound judgment deemed him worthy of the invitation.

Ray put in a call on his WATS line to Tom Mann, one of the four prospects on his Wheel of Fortune. He knew Mann, a former Alabama game ranger who owned a small but growing tackle manufacturing company in Eufaula, Alabama, and had a high regard for his skill as a bass fisherman. Mann's wife, Nancy Ann, worked with him in the tackle business which was gaining fame with the Little George Tail Spinner, named after Governor George Wallace, and Mann's plastic stingray worms.

Mann immediately agreed to enter and mailed in the $100 entry fee. In fact, he thought the idea was so great that he urged Ray to contact several of his friends. Ray did, and as in all the letters on the fancy parchment stationery he sent to every prospect, he mentioned the name of the fisherman who had nominated them. This further impressed the prospect, and it pleased the nominator who was flattered to be recognized as an authority on bass fishing.

Here is what Ray wrote to each of Mann's nominees:

On June 6, 7, and 8, 1967, the most important event in sport fishing history will take place at Beaver Lake in Northwest Arkansas. It is the happening called the All-American Invitational Bass Tournament in which America's greatest anglers will come forth in a rod-to-rod combat of fishing skills. The awards are outlined on the enclosed brochure, as are the rules that will govern this event and ensure a fair competition. You have been recommended by your good friend Tom Mann. Tom says you are an honorable, decent gentleman who is also an excellent bass fisherman and devoted to the sport. For this reason, we extend our warmest invitation to you to participate.

Please read over the enclosed awards schedule and rules that will govern the tournament. After making your decision, please let me know within three or four days by calling me collect and indicating whether or not you intend participation.

Sincerely yours,

Ray Scott

Embedded in this beguiling blarney was the tantalizing message, *call collect!* That gave absolute legitimacy to the invitation and, by extension, to the tournament. Ray sat back waiting for the phone to ring. He certainly hoped that each caller would enter and get his $100 check in the mail. But even if he decided not to enter, Ray was going to milk him for another handful of names to work with.

But Ray's strategy went beyond this. Whenever a prospect called collect on the regular phone, Darlene would always say to the operator that Ray Scott was in conference or on the phone. And then with a warm welcoming voice that oozed smiles over the phone, she would add, "Please give me your number, and I'll have him return your call just as soon as he's free."

Once Ray got the name and number, he would look up background information on the prospect in his swelling card file. Then he would call the prospect on the WATS line. Collect calls can be expensive, but the full-time WATS line calls didn't cost Ray another cent. Ray could talk all day and usually did.

When Billy Dance called collect, Darlene gave him the standard razzmatazz and took his number. Five minutes later, Ray, his Billy Dance

Ray Wilson (Bud) Scott, Sr., was patriarch of the Scott family by the time this photo was taken in 1939 at the age of 31. He was the oldest of six brothers. Ray's mother, Mattie Laura (Matt), was the primary family disciplinarian but was also amused by her first born's never-ending antics. She would be his number one fan until her death in early 1991.

Eddie and Ray model matching Easter outfits made by their mother Matt in 1938 in front of the rented Cottage Hill duplex.

Ray and younger brothers Eddie and Danny grew up in this white frame house on Panama Street in Montgomery.

During the Depression, Ray's father supported the family with a small fleet of ice cream carts. He knew nobody had a dollar, but he figured everyone had a nickel.

Sixteen-year-old Ray and his fishing buddy and neighbor Dan Nolen would take off in the Scott family '39 Chevrolet to go fishing. Here they hold their catch at McIntosh, off the Tombigbee River in southwest Alabama.

PFC Ray Scott writes a letter home from Germany in 1955 where he was assigned to the 2nd Armored Division. He got his first chevron following a touchdown in a divisional football league game.

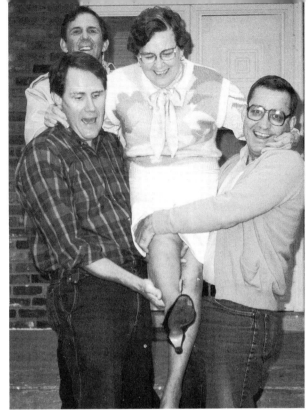

Ray and brothers Danny (L) and Eddie (R) tease their mother Matt in 1986 at Danny's house in Nashville, Tennessee.

Ray's father and his five Scott uncles all lived in Montgomery and formed a tight-knit family. (L to R) Leo, Lloyd, Sam, Paul, Ray Sr., and Marion.

Air Force Sargeant John Powell won the 1968 Eufaula National with 132 pounds of bass in a boat borrowed from Ray Scott. His partner for the day was 14-year-old Rhodney Honeycutt.

Ray with his right- and left-hand men in the early days: Bob Cobb, the first editor of *Bassmaster Magazine* and vice president of communications, and Harold Sharp, first tournament director.

OPPOSITE: Don Butler, a well-known lure designer and manufacturer (Okiebug), won the Beaver Lake Invitational in 1973 on the heels of his 1972 BASS Masters Classic win at Tennessee's Percy Priest Reservoir. His support and faith in Ray helped the young entrepreneur survive. Butler became the very first B.A.S.S. member and life member.

Don Miller of Brinson, Georgia, bought one of the first Classic Tournament Boats, a Rebel with a MerCruiser inboard/outboard and a MotorGuide trolling motor.

This superstar lineup was a common sight in the early tournaments: (L to R) Roland Martin, Tom Mann, Bill Dance, Johnny Morris, and Ricky Green.

Early bass legend Tom Mann (in 1975) would win several tournaments but also won fame for his lure inventions, including the Little George and Mann's Jelly Worms.

Father and son anglers, Rhodney and Blake Honeycutt. At age 14, Rhodney caught the big bass at Eufaula in 1968. Blake won the Eufaula National the following year with a 138 pound, 6 ounce catch.

Ray confidently arrives in Las Vegas for his very first "mystery" BASS Masters Classic. The charter flight destination was known to only a few individuals. On board were all the contestants and a contingent of invited press.

Young Billy Dance was one of bassing's first superstars. Dance remains one of bass fishing's most recognized personalities with his own cable TV fishing show and product endorsements. Always ready for a laugh, Dance won a hula contest at the 1974 Classic as emcee Scott egged him on.

Dave Newton helped Ray organize his Las Vegas fishing seminar and, with much secrecy, helped put together the first "mystery" BASS Masters Classic at nearby Lake Mead in 1971.

A fish fry marked the ground-breaking in 1972 of the new B.A.S.S. headquarters where an old farmhouse stood on Bell Road. (L to R) Helen Sevier, Bob Cobb, Barbara Spencer (Bazell), Martha Walton (Thornburgh), Ray, Kathy Holloway, and Lee Potzner.

Budding entrepreneur Johnny Morris was a formidable bass angler who qualified for numerous Classics on the B.A.S.S. Tournament Trail. Today he is founder and president of the highly successful Bass Pro Shops.

Current CEO of B.A.S.S., Inc., Helen Sevier was hired by Ray in 1970 and later made vice president of marketing. Her direct mail marketing genius would help spread the B.A.S.S. message to fishermen across the nation.

Still one of bass fishing's most visible personalities and competitors, TV fishing show host Jimmy Houston receives an award from Ray for placing in a 1968 tournament.

The seminar team gathers for the kickoff trip on November 1, 1970, as the tour bus representative looks on: (L to R) John Powell, Harold Sharp, Ray, and Roland Martin. It would be the first of 101 seminars.

ABOVE: As his wife looks on, Bobby Murray displays his winning third-day catch at the first BASS Masters Classic. He claimed $10,000, an amount unrivaled at bass tournaments in 1971.

BELOW: An early promotional photo brings Ray face-to-face with the formidable largemouth bass in a special holding tank developed during his highly successful efforts to promote catch-and-release.

With performances like this, Roland Martin would win 20 B.A.S.S. tournaments over a 30-year career, earn the B.A.S.S. Angler of the Year title nine times, and qualify for 21 Classics. In 1999, he is still fishing competitively and hosts his own cable TV fishing show.

Ray Murski, one of Ray's earliest and most avid supporters, was among numerous B.A.S.S. tournament competitors who would build successful careers on the business side of the booming industry.

Then Governor Bill Clinton looks on as Ray holds center stage at a news conference in Little Rock, Arkansas, announcing the 1984 Classic on the Arkansas River.

BELOW: Hank Parker retired from tournaments in 1989 with his second BASS Masters Classic win, on the James River in Virginia. He would parlay his bassing career into an equally successful business career with a cable TV fishing show and product endorsements.

NEXT PAGE: Rick Clunn and Harold Sharp get ready to weigh in Clunn's winning catch at the 1984 BASS Masters Classic. Rick's intuitive and cerebral fishing style ushered in a new era of bass angling. By 1998 his renowned consistency would win him four Classic titles (two back to back), berths at 25 consecutive Classics, and 12 tournament wins.

card in hand, called him on the WATS line.

Ray: "Mr. Dance, I'm looking forward to meeting you. Every top marina operator in Memphis thinks you're the greatest fisherman to ever wet a hook in Tennessee waters. Now I realize it's difficult for you to get away from the furniture store to come out here fishing, but we sure hope you can. I understand you have an eighteen-horsepower motor. That'd be just perfect for Beaver Lake."

That put Billy Dance in seventh heaven. Billy Dance was no stranger to Ray Scott. Ray Scott had checked him out and knew that Billy Dance was truly extra special. Ray Scott even knew that Billy Dance had an eighteen-horsepower motor. Billy Dance was overjoyed, Billy Dance was flabbergasted, Billy Dance was beside himself. Billy Dance's hand was shaking as he reached for his checkbook.

Billy Dance was treated no differently than any of the other fishermen that Ray called. He knew all about their achievements as bass fisherman. He knew that Lamar Gene Gumbody had caught three nine-pounders and that Joe Bob Bubba was the best man in all of Georgia with a crankbait.

"That's the way it should be when you make any sales call," Ray says, "regardless of the product. If you've taken time to find out about a prospect, then he's probably gonna believe you can solve his problem and fill his need. Impress him with your familiarity. Impress upon him that you care. Make him feel like a friend and he'll probably become one. It makes a difference.

"It did in Springdale. I hit that telephone early every morning, then followed the sun across the United States. At six o'clock I'd wake up Georgia and the Carolinas and the whole East Coast. Around noon I'd be working the heartland of the South. And as the day wore on, my calls would start easing further west with the sun and the clock. My letter had been just a short teaser, arousing his curiosity, nudging him into giving me an interview by phone. I figured a man had to be interested or he wouldn't have called me, especially if he had been recommended by a friend.

"It was when I got him on the telephone that I really went to work, romanced him, brought the tournament to life for him, then promptly 'closed' him. By talking to the prospect, I let him know that I existed and wasn't just some name on the bottom of a fancy letterhead. He found out in a hurry that I was a fisherman and could talk his lingo. And I asked him all about his fishing. Where he fished. How he fished. Did he use plastic worms? Or did he use other lures? I interrogated him. I made him worry about being good enough to qualify. And that made him want to come more than anything else in the world."

Ray left his little office only to sleep or eat. His work was certainly eased by the food at Herman's Rib House on Highway 71 between Springdale and Fayetteville. According to Ray, Herman's is not much to look at from the highway, but inside the food is fabulous. Herman "the German" Tuck, the owner, kept Ray alive on his great barbecue ribs.

"I felt sometimes as if I had sauce instead of blood running through my veins," Ray says. "And for some reason Herman wouldn't take any money for the barbecue. Instead, he'd just seat me over by the aquarium, the one where the piranhas were swimming, and pile ribs onto my plate until I would beg him to quit. Herman fed me when I was scratching. He wasn't much of a fisherman, but he was sure a blessing. Every once in a while, Herman would pass the wine bottle around his restaurant, announcing, 'If you can't pronounce it, it's gotta be good.' Herman was a great character and became my friend. He knew I was nearly broke but he never let on he knew."

The first fisherman to send in his $100 check was Leo Welch of Burlington, Iowa, who signed his letter, "Lunker Leo Welch, Burlington's Biggest Bomber Bass Boy." And his letterhead extolled his organization, "Bass Exterminators." The entire organization was comprised of Lunker Leo and his pal, Bill McManus.

Joe Robinson dropped by the office every day and Ray always greeted him with an air of confidence and aplomb even though his guts were beginning to knot with the race against time. As long as he had an unending supply of names he was in business, but he was inwardly afraid he might run out as the tournament drew closer and closer.

"How many fishermen have we got?" Robinson asked.

"Thirteen."

"We're gonna show, boy. We're gonna show." Robinson would give a smile, then slip right back out the door.

Those early visits from the postman were encouraging. Letters with checks came in little bundles. The Chamber of Commerce got even friendlier. Then, with less than a month to go, and only thirty-five entries banked, the mail started coming up empty. Ray knew that he could probably meet expenses with only sixty-five entries, but that meant he had to get at least one entry a day from then till tournament time. The knot in his guts was twisted so hard now that he had to tell Joe Robinson. He wandered on down to Robinson's office, feeling so low he'd have had to reach up to touch bottom. "Joe," he said, "we're stalled out on thirty-five. If you say the word, I'll go home, and we'll forget the whole thing."

"What do you mean go home?" Robinson sputtered. "My business isn't very large, but I've got enough funds to make up the difference in case we're a little short. We're gonna show, boy, regardless."

Two days later, the entries began to pour in again. The light at the end of the tunnel wasn't an oncoming train after all.

Clyde A. Harbin in Memphis was a great help. He had at that time the world's biggest collection of lures, and he got so excited about the tournament that he talked his entire Memphis bass fishing gang into entering.

Tennessee was strong, but Tulsa didn't care if Ray Scott and his tournament lived or died. Tulsa finally came through thanks to Bob Cobb, the farsighted outdoor editor of the *Tulsa Tribune*, who heard that a bass tournament promoter named Ray Scott was going to hold a press conference over in Springdale. Instead of driving the hundred miles, he picked up the phone and called Ray. Ray wouldn't tell him a thing. He just said, with as much humility as he could muster, that he was going to talk about the greatest happening in freshwater fishing since the invention of the hook.

"I need the story, now," Cobb insisted. "I'm sittin' on top of a deadline."

"I'll make a deal," Ray said. "I'll give you the information for your paper now if you promise to attend the Springdale press conference anyway.".

Cobb paused a moment and then agreed. That was a break for Ray because he needed any help he could get from the Tulsa press.

At the press conference, Ray's talk hit most of the writers with about the same impact you'd expect from an announcement that another nut was going to challenge Niagara Falls in a newly designed barrel. They listened courteously, ate the cold cuts, belched, and then disappeared with nothing to show for it in their newspapers.

Bob Cobb was the exception. Cobb sat with Ray for two hours and picked Ray for more of his plans. That started a friendship that would last for more than thirty years. In Cobb's Sunday column in the *Tulsa Tribune*, he wrote, "Ray Scott is like the fellow building mousetraps. He has an idea for a better fishing tournament." His readers got the word, but Oklahoma bass fishermen were very slow to react. Ray decided to stoke the fire. He put Clyde Harbin in Memphis in touch with Cobb, and Harbin laid down a challenge to the Tulsa area crowd. Great stuff for Cobb, who led off one column stating, "Help Wanted: Ten to fifteen of the roughest, toughest, two-fisted black bass fishermen in Tulsa County for three days of hard fishing on Beaver Lake to put down a gang of Memphis, Tenn., bass dabblers who claim to be the 'world's best.'" Cobb went on to write that he believed Tulsa "spawns the wildest and most enthusiastic bunch of bass fishermen in captivity."

Two and a half years later Cobb would become the editor of *Bassmaster Magazine*.

Clyde Harbin kept up the Tennessee challenge: "All I've heard around Beaver Lake is how that Tulsa bunch keeps the road hot coming over to Beaver and about all the bass they catch. We don't think another group can outfish Memphis, even on their home grounds." And in his column Cobb quoted young Billy Dance as saying, "There will be some Tulsa bass fishermen with good reputations who won't enter because they are scared they will get their 'reps' damaged if they blank."

With Ray throwing more and more gasoline on the fire from behind the scenes, the Tulsa fishermen finally realized they were being burned to a crisp by Cobb in the *Tulsa Tribune*.

Don Butler, the owner of a lumber company and later of the Okiebug Lure Company, put a group together, and they sent in their checks. Ever the man to put his money where his Okiebug was, seven months later Butler became the first member — and life member — of the Bass Anglers Sportsman Society. His framed $100 receipt occupies the place of honor on Ray Scott's office wall at his home in Pintlala, Alabama.

The rules for the private Tulsa-Memphis grudge match were simple. The total score of the top ten Tulsa bass boys would be compared against the total catch of the Memphis top ten. And the winners got the privilege of plucking a lure of their choice from the losers' tackle boxes. "This doesn't sound like much to the average person," Harbin said, "but to me, to get to pick out any bait I want from a man's fishing box is a rare privilege."

Ray's prospecting had yielded just over five hundred names; and every day he had new prospects. Thus far the Wheel of Fortune had not failed, but he wondered if he had given himself enough time for the wheel to work.

Joe Robinson stuck his head the door and asked, "How many?"

"Sixty-three. It's tough."

"We're gonna show, boy."

Jack Powers of the Heddon Lure Company in nearby Rogers, Arkansas, believed that the tournament would be good for fishing, and he provided All-American Bass Tournament patches for each participant.

When Ray mentioned the idea of a bass fishing organization to Jack, he said it was a good idea, but cautioned him not to limit it to one species. It was advice Ray would get many times. Advice he refused to follow.

Fishermen were entering at such a rate that on Friday, a week before the cutoff date for tournament applications, Ray had ninety names and ninety checks in the bank. He closed the office that afternoon so he and Lee Zachary could fish Beaver Lake. It may have been Lee's first fishing experience. Later Lee said Ray spent the whole time hugging and kissing and sweet-talking his fishing rod as the bass kept biting. "Maybe I did," says Ray. "All I know is I kept that trusty WATS in place for one last weekend. That phone burned hot. When the phone company finally unplugged the WATS on Monday morning, the All-American Bass Tournament had 106 entries."

"We showed, boy, we showed," Joe Robinson exulted. Ray wallowed in one last meal at Herman's, and this time he let the sauce drip down his arms and off his elbows.

THE 106 BASS FISHERMEN came from thirteen states; and Ray couldn't wait to put faces with voices, and rods in their hands. A last-minute entry was Bob Hamilton from Fairfield, Alabama. A thirty-year-old steel company employee, he had caught the world-record spotted bass, an eight-pounder, using a Whopper Stopper Hellbender lure made in Sherman, Texas. Hamilton wanted to try his luck at Beaver Lake, but was having trouble putting the entry fee together. Ray called Jodie Grigg, the president of Whopper Stopper, and explained Hamilton's plight. "Tell Bob not to worry," Grigg said. "We'll take care of his fishing tournament." Thus Bob Hamilton became the first honest-to-goodness independent professional bass fisherman with a paying sponsor.

Lunker Leo Welch hit town with a Bass Exterminator patch that proclaimed, "Catch every bass that swims. Never be caught using live bait. Keep only the ones four pounds or better. Win every fishing contest in the area and denounce any fisherman who catches bigger bass than me." His pal, Bill McManus, a cop back home in Iowa, couldn't come, but he made dadgummed sure that Lunker Leo had a local police escort with flashing lights and sirens when he came roaring through Fort Madison to Springdale.

Entrant Bud Buchanan had lost the lower part of his leg in an accident. Complications set in and ten days before the tournament started, he was rushed to the hospital. He wanted to enter so badly that he put himself on a rugged daily exercise schedule, and he made it to Beaver Lake.

Twenty-two teachers in Bowling Green, Kentucky, looked around and realized they had a couple of the country's most competitive anglers in their ranks. So like a betting syndicate at Hialeah, they put up $5 to $10 each and bought shares in the entry fees for Alderson Clark and Douglas Hovious. Another windfall came Ray's way from Bowling Green when Ben Corbin, president of Pedigo lure company, agreed to buy the trophies in exchange for having his company's name on the trophy plaque.

Mark McDonald of Joplin, Missouri, had the distinction of being the youngest pro. He was fourteen, but he figured that the experience he had after seven years of serious fishing was worth $100. Unfortunately, he raised more eyebrows than fish. But Mark represented the future of bass fishing.

With 106 entries, the fishermen had to start from five different marinas precisely at six a.m. The D-Day landing had less confusion. Some fishermen brought boats. Others didn't, so Ray had to double them up. They could either agree on where to fish, or argue. That was entirely up to them. But nobody argued. They seemed to be in awe of each other. "It was an amazing sight," Don Butler recalls. "There were all kinds of boats in that tournament. I had a Kinzie Craft with a thirty-three horsepower motor and a backend trolling motor, and I thought it was pretty fancy equipment."

And Bob Cobb remembers, "Most had those uncomfortable flat-bottom boats that looked like coffins with a seat. Ray Murski had gone to the trouble of putting a tractor seat on the back of his boat, sticking it on top of the motor. It was, in reality, the first advance copy of the pro throne that everybody uses today."

Just before the six o'clock send off, Ray took a megaphone and prayed that everybody would get back to the marinas safely. The shotguns fired and engines growled as the boats leapt into action. "The motors were so doggone small," says Scott "that it took the boats thirty minutes to get out of sight."

Billy Dance and partner Troy Anderson of Little Rock tore out of the marina. Dance went a few yards, spun his little boat around and cast toward shore with a seven-and-one-half inch blue Fliptail Worm with a one-quarter ounce slipsinker. His bait had barely touched the water when a two-pounder inhaled it. It was the first fish caught in a Ray Scott tournament and it was caught less than one minute from the opening shotgun blast.

The crowd on shore screamed and whistled, and that catch scared the living heck out of the fishermen who saw Dance land it. "I had borrowed a sixty-horsepower motor so I could go a lot faster than most of the other boats," Dance says. "I caught that first bass and looked around, and I could see that most of the boats weren't even half as far as I was."

Was Dance some kind of a magician? The other fishermen immediately realized that they were already two pounds behind in the first two minutes. It was the start of the Bill Dance legend.

"I watched them all fan out into the lake, and I felt on top of the world," Ray says. "I had promised, and I had delivered. No one could have been happier than I was. I didn't know it at the time, but no one could have been more unhappy than my wife, Eunice, back in Montgomery. Later I heard that the whole Eastern Hills Baptist Church back home had been praying earnestly and diligently that Ray Scott would give up his foolish new calling and come on home to the insurance business where he belonged. But I knew I was now standing where I belonged."

Joe Robinson had rented the official scales from a grocery supply house in Fort Smith, and as a former member of the Arkansas Game and Fish Commission, he had gotten a dozen uniformed game wardens to weigh in the catch each day. On the second and third day, the top twenty in the standings were paired. Robinson arranged for Bryan Works, an old friend and tombstone salesman, to round up ten impartial observers to ride in the boats with the leaders. Three men in a small boat was a load, but it assured that no one even felt tempted to cheat. And nobody did.

Each afternoon, the weigh-in took place in an open lot on the corner of Tyson's turkey farm. A crowd jammed Highway 71, gawking, talking, and wondering who had caught what. Stan Sloan, a Nashville policeman, had the heaviest stringer of bass that first day. He declared he was wearing his lucky britches and wouldn't change 'em for anything.

Carl Dyess of Memphis gained immediate notoriety. He was fishing with Don Miller, a writer from Elyria, Ohio, when he made a cast using a beat up old Lucky 12 lure. It *was* lucky. Two bass promptly jumped on the hooks and Dyess landed them both. He cast the Lucky 12 again. And again two more bass jumped on.

At the second day weigh-in, Jimmy Holt, the outdoor writer for the *Nashville Tennessean*, came in with a stringer of ten bass that weighed a total of one pound, thirteen ounces. He had them strung on a shoe string. "I know they aren't nothing but minnows," Holt said. "But someone told me to keep them, they may count. So I did. Heck, I was afraid to throw 'em back." Holt still holds the record for the smallest total weight on a limit of bass in a Ray Scott tournament. That has never really bothered him. "Heck," he says, "It's the only record of any kind that I've ever held."

All the bass went to an orphanage called Boys Land. Joe Robinson told Ray, "You ought to see Lee Zachary now. He's rounded up a bunch of his chamber of commerce buddies, and they're all out there cleanin' those fish." Jim Cypert, the attorney who had advised the chamber that Ray Scott should be placed under a $5,000 bond to keep him from running off with the money, was wearing an apron and pitching in with an electric knife.

Stan Sloan and his lucky britches won it all with a grand total of thirty-seven pounds, eight ounces on his "bomber spin stick lure." He pocketed $2,000 and later headed off to Acapulco. Sloan was the first of only a few men ever to win a tournament with a top-water bait.

Billy Dance placed second and helped Memphis whip Tulsa after all. Alderson Clark, the teacher from Bowling Green, took third place and $500. All of those sponsoring teachers doubled their money, and he and Doug Hovious split the remaining hundred bucks.

Ray Murski finished fourth, fishing mainly a Texas-rigged Creme worm and a frog-colored Zara Spook. A former footballer under Bear Bryant at Texas A&M, Murski went on to become, as an owner and a rep, a giant in quality hunting and fishing paraphernalia. He owns Strike

King Lure Company, named after the celebrated spinner bait, and has a cadre of pros headed by Denny Brauer and Kevin VanDam who fish his baits. Murski deals with Bass Pro Shops ("Johnny Morris is a good friend of mine"), Wal-Mart ("our biggest customer") and "Anybody that's got change for a $20 bill. I'll sell anybody anything."

From this first tournament on, Murski was all out for Ray Scott and B.A.S.S. "I had started a weekly hunting and fishing newspaper in 1965," he says, "and when Ray Scott came around, we started talking to each other on a kind of a weekly basis. I had about ten thousand subscribers who were getting the paper, and a lot of them were fishermen. Later on, when B.A.S.S. got started, I invited him to come with me to visit some of the bass clubs in Texas and see if we could sell some memberships. Anyway he stayed at my house for about a week after Beaver Lake. I felt like he had something that was a pretty good little ol' deal for fishermen. We thought we were going to be fishing tournaments like the golfers were doing, and they were making a few thousand dollars. Ray Scott had a vision, and I believed in him, and I just did everything I could to support him. We kinda have a big time together."

Ray Scott didn't make a penny at Beaver Lake. In fact he lost $600. He felt like the longtime gambler who left the racetrack and said, "I broke even today, and Lord knows I needed it." But he had a long metal box crammed with five hundred names on three-by-five cards, and they were more important to him than dollars. Those names were his future. With them, he could prospect forever. Using them, he would, within ten years, get 1.5 million names and build the Bass Anglers Sportsman Society into an organization with more than half a million members, making it by far the largest fishing organization in the world.

In his "Sports Afield" column in the local *Rogers Daily News*, Homer Circle wrote, "Well, I tip me hat to an Alabamian named Ray Scott . . . Ray Scott has now proved that he is a man who came into the project cold turkey, and walked out with warm congratulations from participants and partners . . . By his initial performance, Ray Scott has earned his place in the sun." And Charles Elliott, outdoor columnist for the *Atlanta Constitution*, hailed Ray's tournament as "a tremendous success" and that anyone who had "dreams of becoming a world champion fisherman" should contact Ray Scott.

And the Wheel of Fortune made it all possible.

8

The Birth of B.A.S.S.

RAY LOST $600 promoting his first tournament at Beaver Lake. Some might have considered that a failure, but not Ray. He felt in his very bones that Beaver Lake was the first step to success. The two loves of his life — selling and bass fishing — had long been on parallel courses. Now, at last, they were on a collision course.

When he returned to Montgomery in July of 1967 he had two more tournaments in mind — one at Smith Lake in Alabama and one at Lake Seminole in south Georgia. He requested a three-month leave of absence from his insurance job. "I did that for two reasons," he says. "I knew they would suspect my sanity if I told them my plans. And I wanted to be able to borrow two desks, two chairs, and two file cabinets. I dragged them across the hall to a ten-by-twelve office that cost me $30 a month to rent."

The idea of a bass fishing organization was already percolating in his brain. He was convinced that bass fishermen could make up the largest group of active sportsmen in the world. He firmly believed they represented the heart and soul of America — good, hard-working, red-blooded boys who liked to keep in touch with the outdoor world around them. More than anything, he felt, they longed for information and a forum.

He looked forward to upgrading their image from that of the tobacco spittin' good ol' boy. Ray knew that a lot of black-tie gentlemen traded their cummerbunds for tackleboxes every time they could get away to a creek bank without someone watching. Why not? Bass were as unpredictable and challenging as Wall Street.

"It's amazing," says Ray. "I learned from my very first tournament that bass fishing is a great equalizer. When those windburned fishermen weigh in at my tournament in their bill caps and grungy blue jeans, you can't tell the doctors from the pipe fitters. And it makes no difference to the bass if he's caught from a shiny new $30,000 rig or an old johnboat."

Ray was convinced his organization could and would cut through every social, cultural, and economic strata. He would charge a $10 membership fee. Ray was determined to give every member information and services worth a whole lot more than ten bucks.

Little did Ray Scott dream that some thirty years later, there would be an estimated twenty-five million bass anglers in the United States and that bass fishing would represent the largest and fastest-growing segment of the more than $100 billion sportfishing and boating industry.

The ideas were coming fast and furious. But first, he had two more tournaments to plan and he needed help — bad. Who could help him? He mentally ran through his acquaintances. He thought about his high school sweetheart, Sara Boyd, now Sara Smedley. She was smart, capable and calm. He had always admired her. He called her immediately and told her about his dreams of bass tournaments and a bass fishing organization. Would she run the office while he did the leg work?

"After Ray called" says Sara, "I asked him to come over to the house and talk to my husband, Doug, and me. He did that very night, and his enthusiasm was contagious. By the end of the evening I had committed myself to help turn his dream into a reality and, hopefully, a very profitable venture. I did know that if anyone could do it, Ray could."

Ray and Sara worked in the minuscule office at 513 Madison Avenue in Montgomery. Like the office in Springdale, it was about the size of a large closet and barely had room for the two desks facing one another. Ray had his telephone and Sara had her typewriter, and in the next three months they burned up wires and ribbons.

"We were working with a very tight budget," Sara recalls. "We referred to our company as BASS, though we had not officially named it at that time. But we did need a name. About October or November, Ray and I sat in the office for some time throwing names around, and he kept coming back to BASS. We were having a difficult time coming up with the long version of BASS.

"In frustration Ray called his friend, Homer Circle, the outdoor writer, and asked for help. Homer referred Ray to the outdoor editor of the *Nashville Tennessean*, Bob Steber. Ray called Steber and Steber said he would call back. Fifteen minutes later the phone rang and Steber said, 'How about Bass Anglers Sportsman Society?' Ray said 'That's kind of long, isn't it?' and Steber said, 'Yeah, but that's another reason they'll call it B.A.S.S. for short,' Ray said, 'Fine, thanks Bob.' He put the phone down and said, 'We've got a name.'"

Sara continues, "Ray gave me the checkbook, and for several months that was our entire 'accounting system.' My accounts ran from general office expenses to Mrs. Scott's household money. I paid the house payment and household utilities along with car payments for Ray and Mrs. Scott.

"One of our biggest early expenses was a WATS line, but we could only afford the line for a month. I know Ray got more mileage out of that line than has ever been gotten out of any WATS line. He contacted every lead, working into the night. He was always at his desk early in the morning when I got to work. I recall the day that the man came to remove the WATS line. Ray had the man wait so he could make 'just one more call.' The man was kind and laughed, and he waited until Ray called 'just one more fisherman.'

"We ran close most of the time as far as money was concerned. I tried to keep all our bills current to keep our credit in good standing and his family cared for. But occasionally we would run very, very low on funds."

A major crisis came one day when Ray saw Neva Brown, who had a typing service, get out of her car and come toward the office. He owed her $240. He said to Sara, "Here comes Neva Brown. I promised I'd pay her, and I've put her off for two months now."

Sara said, "We can't, Ray."

Ray: "What do you mean we can't?"

Sara: "We don't have but $30 in the bank."

Ray: "Write her a check anyway."

Looking back now, Ray says, "My mind was thinking that it takes three days, sometimes four days, for a check to clear. I was broke as heck. The next day when I went to the post office, I had four $150 entry fee checks for the Lake Seminole tournament. I immediately deposited them in the bank. Fortunately, the invitations for Seminole, which was a February tournament, were mailed early. I needed the revenue from Seminole to carry the earlier Smith Lake tournament. I was piggy-backing, as they say."

Sara says, "Ray was relentless in his efforts to gather enough fishermen for the Smith Lake tournament in Cullman, Alabama, in October of 1967. We both worked many hours putting that tournament together. Our money was so tight that I did not draw a salary for several months. I even recall Ray asking me to get money from our account to get hot dogs from Chris's Hot Dog Stand for a quick lunch. He loved those hot dogs and still does. Many times, I simply took the car and bought lunch myself. We needed every cent we could get to keep going.

"One day as we were discussing how we could afford to go on, Ray stated that he would risk everything but his home. He would not jeopardize his family's security.

"I might add that though we were close to failure financially, Ray never lost hope and was always confident that we would make it. One way Ray provided for needed cash was to sell his personal effects. I remember he sold his camper, his half interest in a Boston Whaler he shared with Roy Hines, several guns, and an old five-horsepower outboard."

Ray and Sara drove up to Fairfield, a suburb of Birmingham, where his old college pal, taxidermist Archie Phillips, let them copy the names and addresses of hundreds of customers for whom he had mounted bass.

"It seemed logical to me that they were bass fishermen," Ray says, "and I sent each one a letter inviting them to enter the Smith Lake tournament. Later on, I invited them to join B.A.S.S. and a sizeable number did."

"B.A.S.S. finally came about because many things simply fell into place for Ray Scott," Sara says. "It was like a miracle at times. It took terrific determination on his part but there also were many people who really believed in Ray, his integrity, and his ability to do the impossible.

"Dr. Robert Lightfoot, a prominent Montgomery physician, was one of those men. Dr. Lightfoot had told Ray two years earlier that if he ever needed an investor in something that he might do, to let him know and he would be interested in investing in the project. Well, the time came when our money was very low and we had exhausted most of our sources and extended our credit to the limit. Ray went to Dr. Lightfoot and told him about his fishing tournament idea. Dr. Lightfoot asked how he might become involved and Ray told Dr. Lightfoot that he would allow him to put up $8,000. He could either have stock or provide a high-interest loan. If he had stock and we failed, he would lose his money; but if he lent Ray the money and we failed, Ray would personally guarantee the doctor that he would be paid off. Dr. Lightfoot said that he would lend Ray the money."

Although money was still tight, the very day before the Smith Lake tournament began, Ray had enough to pay off all the expenses with enough left over for a kickoff banquet, featuring entertainment by the Skunk Hollow Gang from Springdale, Arkansas, the band that had played at the Beaver Lake tournament.

From there it was on to the Seminole Lunker Bass Tournament in Bainbridge, Georgia. Jack Wingate, who still runs Lunker Lodge on Lake Seminole, had fished Ray's previous two tournaments and was the man responsible for the Seminole tournament.

Wingate recalls, "When I got to Beaver Lake and walked into that Holiday Inn, there were prime bass fishermen everywhere I looked — in the dining room, coffee shop, sitting room. I just was flabbergasted. Stunned. When I got back to Bainbridge I called ex-Governor Marvin Griffin, publisher of *The Post-Searchlight*, and told him about it. He said,

'Yeah, we need some of that down here,' and we put it together in my lodge dining room."

Wingate lined up the support of Pop Alcorn, manager of the Army Corps of Engineers operation, which controlled Lake Seminole, and Governor Griffin went to the local bank to get the $2,500 that the Chamber of Commerce needed to sponsor the tournament. On Thursday, October 19, 1967, Griffin put out a "Special Fishing Edition" of his newspaper with the banner headline, "NEXT: SEMINOLE LUNKER BASS TOURNEY, SAYS SCOTT."

SARA SMEDLEY went on maternity leave and when she returned to work, she found Ray had a new project. He was starting a magazine called *Bassmaster*. He had no editors, no writers, no advertisers, no subscribers, and a sorely depleted bank account. But he knew he needed the magazine if members were going to pay ten bucks a year.

Ray says, "My whole aim with *Bassmaster* was to give inside information on bass fishing that the angler could get nowhere else. I would tell them such things as how to use the single-spin spinner in brush-clogged shallows, or how to rig the plastic worm for productive down-deep fishing. I knew fishermen were hungry for hard-core information, so I wasn't about to weigh my magazine down with long, dull paragraphs about azure sunrises and reflections of the moon on a silver spinner."

The first issue wasn't much given that it was written by a man who had flunked high school and college English. "But it was more than they expected," says Ray. "It gave them down-to-earth information on how to catch bass. Besides, I was to find out that even Ph.D.s didn't mind misspelled words and misplaced commas and dangling participles as long as the stories were crammed full of know-how, straight from the minds of experts."

Most of the early articles were written by honest-to-goodness fishermen, not writers at all. They were just good ol' boys who knew how to catch fish and who didn't mind sharing their ideas, techniques, and secrets. Ray asked Harold Sharp, a railroad man from Chattanooga,

Tennessee, to contribute an article on his favorite topwater bait, one he had made himself and fished with for fifteen years.

"I'm no writer," Sharp said.

"Well, just write me letter," Ray told him, "and put down everything you know about the bait and about topwater fishing."

And that's just what he did. The letter came in with sentences running two feet long.

A secretary came to Ray's desk and announced, "We can't use the article by Harold Sharp."

"Why not?"

"It has two thousand words."

"So?"

"It only has two paragraphs in the whole thing."

"Honey," Ray said softly, "you just get yourself a pair of scissors and cut him in some more paragraphs, but don't change a word."

A few top writers, like Bob Cobb, also began sending articles to *Bassmaster Magazine.* In one, Cobb wrote, "I've come to the conclusion that a tournament bass fisherman is just as much an athlete in his field as a professional tackle for the Green Bay Packers. Bass fishing takes stamina, imagination, and, sometimes, a little guts."

Scott agreed. He promptly offered Cobb the job as editor of a magazine that would ultimately become a national leader in the outdoor publishing field.

Bob accepted Ray's job offer and moved his wife, Barbara, two children and two bird dogs to Montgomery. On December 7, 1969, Cobb walked into the office for his first day at work. Ray pointed to a cardboard box crammed with the *Bassmaster* files and proclaimed him the new editor. He sat down, swiveled around in his chair, an adjustable "Pro-Throne" bass boat seat, and began digging through the files. Ray knew *Bassmaster Magazine* was on the launch pad, ready to lift off.

Every click of Bob's rickety 1960-model Royal typewriter worked editorial magic in the pages of *Bassmaster.* A gifted outdoor communicator, he was also the catch-man for many of the ideas that laid the foundation for B.A.S.S. in the early years. For example, he brainstormed the concept of the BASS Masters Classic while on a road trip with Ray.

"Ray came in one day and told me that we needed a mass mailing telling fishermen why they should join B.A.S.S.," Sara says, "He had a friend, Morris Dees, who would sell us three automated devices that only had to be fed the names, addresses and a few personal words into the typewriter. Ray had arranged to pay $500 for the machines when he could manage it. This sounded ideal — the answer to our prayers — but we knew of no one who could operate the machines. So I had someone instruct me on how to use them.

"You really needed to be there to appreciate the humor in the situation, but Ray and I squared the machines off with my chair in the middle; and I literally turned around in circles with each machine as it came to a name or a town that had to be injected. Every hour or so, I would simply leave the building and walk around trying to get my mind back to normal. But it was a success and I'm not much dingy-er for the experience."

After all the letters were prepared, they needed to be folded and put into envelopes which had to be stamped. Ray called in reinforcements from his family and Sara's. He put three ironing boards end to end to serve as a table for the assembly line and everyone went to work. Their only compensation was a meal of Chris's hot dogs. Ray's cousin, Helen, later swore that her mouth was permanently glued together from licking so many stamps.

But first Ray had to get the stamps. He tried to get a loan from a bank, but didn't have enough collateral for the several thousand dollars needed for postage. He went to the post office and tried to persuade them to lend him the stamps. That story is probably still a good one at the post office. Then his friend, Don Butler happened to call and asked Ray how things were going with his hundred-dollar investment. Ray told him about the bank and the post office.

The next morning there was a call to the tiny office from Western Union saying a money wire was waiting. Ray assumed it was a fisherman's entry fee. When he picked it up, he found himself holding a Western Union money order for $10,000 and the only clue about the sender was that it was from Tulsa, Don Butler's hometown. Indeed Butler had sent the money and Ray was able to pay it back in three weeks. The bond between Don Butler and Ray Scott has never been broken. "The world will never know all the things Don's done for other people," says Ray. "He's one of my heroes."

Ray had many "angels" in the early days. John "Soup" Campbell, a local printer, printed the first issue of *Bassmaster Magazine* (typeset on an old Linotype) on ninety-day credit. The bill was paid on the eighty-ninth day. A few issues later they would go to offset printing with a young go-getter named Irvin Wells of Wells Printing Company. He provided continuing printing education for Ray and B.A.S.S. and got them through many a deadline on all types of projects. Irvin also led Ray to Margaret Carpenter, an attractive widow and civic leader who ran a successful typesetting business called Compos-It.

"These were just some of the people who made everything click in the early days," says Ray. "I almost hated to see the day we got so big we needed to go to web presses and bring our graphics work in house."

"In those early months and years at B.A.S.S. we worked at a frantic pace," says Sara. "A few fragile secretaries ran screaming from the office never to return, but Ray was always a good boss. He never really gave any of us totally impossible tasks, but I'll bet that even our dear Lord would have had to move fast to keep up with Ray. He was busy burning the candle at both ends — trying to reach each and every fisherman in the United States and trying to get a buck to make a buck."

BY DECEMBER OF 1969, B.A.S.S. was doing well enough for Ray to hire Bob Cobb full time. The following July, he hired a bright young woman named Helen Sevier. Both came on board accepting less money than in their previous jobs.

These two individuals would form the nucleus of his organization, becoming, respectively, vice president of communications and vice president of marketing, and Ray sold both stock in the up-and-coming company.

Helen Sevier was working for Fuller and Dees Marketing when Ray met her through the now well-known civil rights attorney Morris Dees. Ray and Bob Cobb had gone to see Dees about reprinting Henshall's *Book of the Black Bass*. Dees, who at the time was reprinting antique cookbooks, saw no copyright problem with the Henshall book. He told Ray, who wanted to sell a reprint of the Henshall book and offer it as a premium to new members of B.A.S.S., that he was free to do so. Ray then asked Dees, who is a direct mail marketing genius, "How do you mathematically calculate how to break even with direct mail?"

"I don't have any idea," said Dees, "but there's a gal down the hall who's good at it." It was late in the afternoon, and Dees added, "Sometime when you have time, I'll introduce her to you."

"I don't have time to wait," Ray said. "Let's do it now."

With that they walked down the hall and Dees introduced Ray and Bob to Helen Sevier, a slim brunette with a big smile. She'd been working for Fuller and Dees for four years. They started talking and Ray was impressed with her marketing savvy. Helen had gotten her bachelor's degree from Southern Mississippi where she majored in business administration and marketing, and then she went into retailing for several years.

"I was working for Rich's in Atlanta when it hit me like a ton of bricks," Sevier recalls. "I didn't like it, and I decided that I didn't want to do this the rest of my life. So I decided to go back to school and get my master's at the University of Alabama, where I got a scholarship. For whatever reasons, the professors took me under their wing and kept telling me, 'You need to speak to a guy named Morris Dees.' Finally, Morris called me at school and asked if I would come and see him. He was brilliant. He was about to start a new business and wanted to know if I would be interested.

"The company was Fuller and Dees. They marketed everything from toothbrushes to cookbooks. We put *Southern Living* and *Progressive Farmer* in the cookbook business. Our cookbooks featured home-tested recipes. We would mail to subscribers and ask for their favorite recipes, and these homemakers would send in their recipes. In three and a half years, we had 700,000 or 800,000 members involved in cookbook clubs.

I was the consumer marketing director — really a glorified direct mail person."

At B.A.S.S., Ray made Helen marketing director with the primary goal of increasing the membership. "I used everything," she says. "*Field & Stream, Outdoor Life, Fishing World*, anything related to fishing. I can remember *Sports Afield* was having an article on bass; and I thought, gosh, a good time to run an ad. We never ran an ad before. So we ran one in February 1971 concurrently with the article. The ad ran as follows: 'Will this patch make you a better fisherman? We think so. Bill Dance improved his fishing by 500 percent.' It worked marvelously. So we said, let's do it again. The next ad read: 'Not every fisherman wears this patch, can you?' It worked equally well."

"I will not take the slightest credit for direct mail," Ray says. "Helen did it." Within a year after she went to work at B.A.S.S., membership jumped from fifteen thousand to twenty-five thousand, and then to sixty-five thousand the following year.

Not long after Helen joined the small staff, Ray added another young woman to his team. Martha Walton (now Thornburgh) was an attractive divorced mother of two young boys, who could swing from accounting to customer service to tournaments without ruffling a hair. She would remain with B.A.S.S. for twenty-eight years until her retirement. "She's another of those nuggets I found," says Ray. "She could wear any hat I gave her."

Another "nugget" that rolled Ray's way was Harold Sharp, who came on board in November 1970. A diehard bass fisherman, Harold was a crew dispatcher for the Southern Railroad in Chattanooga. Because he could get the right crews on the right train at the right time, Ray figured he'd be a natural to organize a countrywide seminar tour he was about to launch.

Harold would later gain fame as the iron-fisted B.A.S.S. Tournament Director. Some would call him pig-headed. But the tournaments ran smoothly, honestly, and safely. He shared Ray's abhorrence of cheating. Those unfortunate souls who tried to bend the rules — even slightly — found Harold didn't give even a millimeter. He was Ray's kind of man.

Harold had fished Ray's second tournament at Smith Lake in 1967 and caught the biggest bass — six pounds, one ounce. He was impressed with Ray's organization and showmanship. On the way home with a friend, Glynn West, he started talking about organizing a Chattanooga bass club. He knew that Bob Cobb and Don Butler and others had formed the Tulsa Bass Club after the Beaver Lake Tournament, so he asked Bob if they had any rules and regulations to organize a club.

Ray heard about Harold's idea and it wasn't long until he contacted Harold and told him about his own Society concept. The two anglers were on the same wavelength.

Shortly after their conversation, Ray traveled to Chattanooga where he and Harold talked some more. That same evening the Chattanooga Bass Club was formed and became the first to be officially affiliated with the new Bass Anglers Sportsman Society. Nineteen members joined the Chattanooga Bass Club and B.A.S.S. at the same time and Harold was elected president. Since Don Butler had just given Ray a hundred dollars to be the very first member, Harold claims to be the second member of B.A.S.S.

Harold retired from B.A.S.S. in 1987 and now lives in Hixson, Tennessee, where he heads up Fishin' Talents, Inc., which helps professional anglers with endorsements and personal appearances. He is also an environmental activist and a leader in the fight against aquatic herbicides. In that fight, he would join forces with Ray Scott once again.

Another pioneer in the baby B.A.S.S. organization was James "Pooley" Dawson, a young black man Ray had met through a friend at the National Guard Armory where Pooley had worked for some ten years. "Pooley was recommended primarily as a cook," says Ray "and I needed someone who could throw together a first-class casual buffet for a bunch of hungry fishermen and wives. Short notice. No paper. No plastic."

Pooley more than proved his abilities on a part-time basis for two years and then joined the staff full-time in 1972. Like everyone else, his job would defy description. "Pooley was the kind of guy you give a job and he'd move the earth to get it done," says Ray.

Pooley rescued Ray more than once. In one early tournament, Ray had a small disaster at the kickoff dinner. The designated "caterer" had set up one little "catfish cooker" to feed a fried fish dinner to 175 people. Ray recalls, "There were hungry people lined up everywhere. Everyone was being really nice, but it was such a disaster. I was so embarrassed. I fired the caterer and immediately called Pooley and told him I wanted a steak dinner for 175 people three days later at the Friday night awards banquet. He did it, and it was first rate."

Pooley is still with the organization in the Tournament Department and is a welcome and familiar sight to many fishermen, especially those at the BASS Masters Classic who are greeted by him as they drive up to the weigh-in stand.

"If I have a single outstanding business talent," says Ray, "it is hiring good people. I'm pretty darn accurate in spotting good people. And I know how to turn them loose and let them do their job. It's the only way a business can grow. B.A.S.S. would still be in my brain without those early people like Helen and Bob and Harold."

Shortly after Ray conducted his first tournament, he realized that his fledging group, as well as the entire bass industry, had a bleak future, considering the polluted state of so many of America's waterways at the time. This inspired Ray to lead a two-pronged attack against water pollution. In 1970 and 1971, he filed more than two hundred lawsuits against polluters large and small in Alabama, Texas, and Tennessee under the little-used 1899 Refuse Act.

At the same time, he launched a publicity campaign designed to awaken the public to the threat and create a groundswell of support that would encourage the courts to do the right thing. He appeared on NBC's Today Show and ABC's Dick Cavett Show, and later on ABC's 20/20. In between, he was preaching the clean-water gospel in literally hundreds of smaller forums — local radio and TV shows and local newspapers across the nation.

9

Spreading the B.A.S.S. Gospel

RAY KNEW ONE day he would have to defend his tournament trail. That day came in late April of 1970. While B.A.S.S. was preparing for a major tournament at Ross Barnett Reservoir near Jackson, Mississippi, Ray uncovered a wave of uneasiness in the community. People were afraid that those busloads of professional fishermen were going to swoop down out of the night and fish the lake dry. It was an absurd thought, but those sentiments could become a real problem, not only for Jackson but future tournaments as well.

Ray was determined to allay the unrest in Jackson quickly. He figured he could ease local worries by explaining his tournaments and his mission to the people themselves. He and Cobb decided to hold a free bass fishing seminar at the old War Memorial Building in downtown Jackson on the eve of the tournament. They would have pros like Bill Dance, Tom Mann, Ed Todtenbier, John Powell, Pete Henson, and Grits Gresham, an outdoor writer from Louisiana, on hand to impart their wisdom. Ray himself would tell them all about B.A.S.S. The *Clarion Ledger* announced the seminar in Herb Sandusky's popular outdoor column.

The seminar was to start at 7 p.m. in the four-hundred-seat auditorium. Ray and Cobb wondered if anyone would actually show up. They arrived at the auditorium an hour early and found, to their amazement, people already standing on the steps waiting to get in and get good seats.

It was a sweltering day and made all the hotter by the crowd that began jamming inside. By 6:45 the auditorium was packed with people standing, sitting in the aisles, and in the windows, where they blocked any airflow. Ray recalls, "It was so crowded, a lizard couldn't get in." When Grits Gresham got up from his folding chair on the stage, he returned to find someone had stolen his seat. Local TV crews were among those who couldn't squeeze in, which made for an even better news story about the incredible popularity of bass fishing.

When Ray entered the auditorium, he spotted a piano against the front wall. He had no idea what the mood of the crowd would be like. So, like the saloon owner in Western movies who always has the piano player ready to play in case a fight breaks out, Ray got a volunteer pianist to play "God Bless America." He asked the crowd to stand and join in, and almost five hundred good ol' boys, many presumably hostile to the tournament, made the walls shake with their vocalizing. The air was filled with a wonderful, revival spirit.

Each pro stood and talked on one particular phase of bass fishing. One extolled the glories of the "jelly" worm. Another explained the art of top-water fishing. A third told how to select the right equipment. And the last removed all doubts on deep-water angling.

The crowd response to the seminar was so favorable that it not only put out any fire about the tournament but it made Ray wonder if he might be on to something bigger. Hmmmm . . . suppose folks had the "opportunity" to pay to get in? And suppose he could get them to join B.A.S.S. at the same time? It was an idea worth trying.

Ray gave it a try in Tulsa. He brought along Bill Dance, Ed Todtenbier, Roland Martin, and his Tulsa buddy Don Butler, as well as a copy of Elgin Ciampi's prize-winning underwater film documentary on bass, *Still Waters*. He expected maybe a couple of hundred fishermen to show up at a dollar-a-head. Instead eighteen hundred came piling through the door, and each was handed membership applications for B.A.S.S.

As Ray was leaving after the seminar, he looked across at the ballpark where the league-leading Tulsa Oilers were playing a night game. He noted the number of fans in the stands; and to his great satisfaction he found that, probably for the first time in history, a crowd of bass fishermen outnumbered the crowd at a baseball game — and at a buck a head. On top of that, Ray got almost a ten percent return on the membership applications dispensed in Tulsa, 170 to be precise. Following his standard practice, he sent every new member a personal letter offering congratulations and asked them to recommend friends. He got more names to add to the Wheel of Fortune, and that meant more members. All seminar attendees signed up for door prizes and that provided another great source of names for later mail invitations.

With the Lake Sam Rayburn Tournament in Texas scheduled for late September, Ray announced a seminar for Houston. Thanks to the drumbeating of a local radio D.J. who was a devoted bassman, Houston would set a record. The three-thousand-seat auditorium was packed at two bucks a head. Ray's head was spinning. The more you charge, the more they come. And again, nearly ten percent joined B.A.S.S.

His first seminar experiences confirmed many of Ray's hunches about this amazing American subculture. First, the fishermen were indeed out there. Second, they had an insatiable thirst for knowledge. Third, they enjoyed the fellowship of other anglers. There were lone, contemplative anglers, but by and large these men and women enjoyed belonging to and being part of a group that shared their passion. Finally, they wanted to share their knowledge.

Ray's tournaments were already creating names and heroes. *Bassmaster Magazine* was tantalizing anglers with more information than they had ever had before. But as a salesman, Ray knew nothing was better than face-to-face communication and live demonstration.

He decided to build on his seminar success and take to the road to "spread the gospel of bass fishing." Ray is very comfortable with including the Almighty in his plans. "After all," he says, "Jesus Christ was the greatest salesman of all time. He had the greatest product and the greatest message. And I'm happy to say that at least four of his disciples were fishermen. He knew fishermen were good men."

Indeed Scott is very comfortable as a prophet, apostle, and supreme evangelist for bass fishing. And in fact, many a tournament winner has given thanks to his "Lord and Savior" well before acknowledging his sponsors.

With an unabashed evangelistic spirit, Ray planned his official seminar tour. He hired and put railroad man Harold Sharp in charge. Then he bought a secondhand Bluebird travel coach complete with sleeping berths for four, bathroom, kitchenette, and lounge for meetings.

Ray and Harold mapped out a seminar route that would take them from Bangor, Maine, to Los Angeles, California. In ten months, they put on 101 seminars, with Ray often flying back and forth from Montgomery to join the road show. Every few days the team would check into a motel to shower, do laundry, and sleep in a real bed.

John Powell and Roland Martin were also hired as part of the seminar team. On occasion, Bill Dance, Don Butler, Stan Sloan, Pete Nosser, Tom Mann, and other stars on the B.A.S.S. circuit would take part. At each location, they would show Elgin Ciampi's *Still Waters*. The crowds were awed. It was their first underwater glimpse into the life of the storied Florida largemouth bass.

On the road, Roland, Harold, and John would occasionally treat themselves to a nice restaurant and drag Ray away from his beloved Krystal hamburgers. Ever the practical joker, Ray would carry a life-size red toy telephone that would ring realistically at the push of a button. Once seated in the restaurant, he would set the phone down on the table and sneak a peek at the nametag of a nearby waiter. The phone would ring. In the days before cellular phones, every head turned at the sound. Ray would pick up the phone and begin a very convincing one-sided conversation.

"Just a moment," he would say and look around him. Then he'd call out, "Is there a John Smith here?" using the name of the server he had spotted. The dumbfounded server would come forward and Ray would thrust the toy phone at him. "It's for you." Inevitably, the server would take the phone and cautiously put it to his ear and say, "Hello?" At that point, the table of men, who had gone along with the joke, would burst into laughter, usually joined by the good-natured waiter. Anything that would break the monotony and stir things up was fair game.

Ray credits the tour with ten thousand new memberships, jumping B.A.S.S. membership up to twenty-five thousand. But just as important, he made his way home with bundles of prospects that in time would form the nucleus of his more than half-million members.

For the first several months on tour, Ray made it a point to have an organ and organist on hand to get the crowd pumped up by singing "God Bless America." "We had done that with a piano for the first seminar and it put the crowd in a good mood," Ray says, "so I thought, well, that must be the secret."

This didn't work when Ray ordered an organ for the basketball arena at Southwest Missouri State University in Springfield. When he walked in at 6:30 p.m., an hour before the seminar was to start, two girls' basketball teams were scrimmaging, and their coach refused to get off the court until the practice was over.

"We couldn't even set up our stage, screen, and projectors," says Ray. "This was terribly embarrassing, unprofessional, and my temper was rising. Then I looked over and saw that the organ we had hired looked as though it belonged in some great theater. This thing was seven feet high, about seven feet wide, and three feet thick, with a little wimpy fellow named Percy preparing to play. I asked this skinny-fingered boy, 'Why in the name of heaven did you have such a big organ brought in here, and what did it cost?' He said, 'Well, you wanted an organ and this was the only one available. It will cost you $150 for the organ and me." Only three hundred people had shown up; and, to add to Ray's ire, the organist was going to take a quarter of the gate home for himself.

Ray's anger kept rising while he stood around waiting for the girls to get off the court. He noticed that the organist was talking to a friend at the organ keyboard, so he walked over and peeked at the back of the organ. He saw a little square door on hinges. He quietly opened it, and found two four-inch long fuses. Looking around to make sure no one was watching, he pulled out the fuses, put them in his pocket, and closed the door.

Ray sidled over to Harold and asked, "What happens if this guy doesn't play the organ?"

Harold said, "If he doesn't play, then we don't pay. But what are you getting at? He's ready — he's gonna play."

Ray said, "Look here in my hand," as he took the fuses out of his pocket.

"Where did those come from?" Harold asked.

"From the organ," Ray said with a confident smile. Harold laughed, and a few minutes later the girls left the court. The seminar team set up the stage and Ray called out to the organist, "Percy, fire up the organ! We're ready to start!"

Percy sat down, flipped some stops, and flexed his fingers. Ray chuckled to himself while he waited for the organist to hit the keys for "God Bless America." Ray says, "When he did, the most awesome, powerful sound of music came out. I thought, what in heavens name! I checked my pocket to see if I still had the fuses. I did. Of course, I had to pay him $150; but till this day I don't know what in the dickens those two fuses controlled."

AS FATE WOULD have it, at the Springfield seminar and organ fiasco was a sharp young student at Southwest Missouri who was working part-time as a fishing guide and part-time in Gibson's Discount Store in Springfield. He was very excited about the prospects offered by B.A.S.S. after he fished the tournament at nearby Table Rock Lake in November of 1970. He was, in fact, so excited that his enthusiasm and brains were to give rise to a merchandising empire.

His name was Johnny Morris, and the empire-to-be was Bass Pro Shops Outdoor World. Its headquarters in Springfield now attracts four million visitors a year, easily making the 320,000-square foot store, with its own museum and waterfalls and pools of fish, the number one tourist attraction in the entire state, outdrawing nearby country-music Branson, by about a million folks.

"Ray was then giving birth to the whole sport of tournament fishing and development of bass gear," Morris says. "Everything from reels and lures to the development of electronics and boats — everything. It was like a fire and he was fueling the incredible growth of the sport and the entire fishing and boating industries. His tournaments and magazine worked together to inform and inspire anglers, manufacturers, and retailers alike.

"At Ray's tournament I met people like Tom Mann, who had these 'Jelly Worms' he was making in his kitchen and garage and who went on to become a famous lure designer. And Stan Sloan who had his own bait company, Zorro. I fished with an electrical contractor, Blake Honeycutt from North Carolina [who had won the 1969 Eufaula National with 138 pounds, six ounces, still the all-time tournament record as of 1999], and he was deep jigging with a Hopkins spoon, which was never heard of around here. There also were Bill Norman, Jim Rodgers, Jim Bagley, Forrest Wood, and Don Butler — all fishermen and entrepreneurs. Now, there is still room for upstart guys with baits, but it's harder to go national compared to those early days.

"So I made a list of all this stuff," Morris continues, "and I took it in to the department manager in Gibson's Discount Store which had the largest selection of fishing tackle in the Springfield area. I told him, 'We've got to get all this stuff. This gear would really sell.' I kept going back checking and checking with him, and finally he said, 'Sorry, but I just can't get permission from the home office to carry all this bass gear you're telling me about. We can't stock it.'

"I went to my dad, and asked him if he'd back me. He said yes, and gave me a budget of $10,000 to invest in inventory that I could stock in one of his liquor stores on the way to the lake [Table Rock]. He gave me eight feet of display. Then I called Don Butler in Tulsa. I just barely knew him from some fishing trips and being around Ray's tournaments. Don had a great tackle store in Tulsa called Okiebug, and it was probably the finest in the country as far as bass gear was concerned. And he wholesaled. I hired a fishing buddy, Steve Reed, who worked in a convenience store, and we took a U-Haul trailer and went over to Tulsa and backed it into Okiebug. I spent the whole $10,000 right there with Butler and loaded the U-Haul with Bombers, deluxe stringers, Tom Mann Jelly Worms, and a nickel's worth of everything — just like a smorgasbord.

"Then my buddy and I went to a get-and-go, got a seventy-nine cent padlock, put it on the trailer, parked it in the hotel parking lot, and went out on the town for a while before we went to bed. When we got up the next morning, the trailer was still there. I always thought that was a close call. If somebody had made off with that trailer, it would have been the end of Bass Pro Shops. That's really how I got started in the fishing tackle business — by going to Ray's tournament in 1970.

"We used the name Bass Pro Shops because it was real descriptive of what we wanted to do. I was in the local bass club, and at first customers were primarily local fishermen. When Ray's magazine, *Bassmaster*, came out, it would have the tournament reports and interviews with the winners. Man, these guys were like heroes — half the time they were Bill Dance or Roland Martin — and they'd talk about the lures and equipment they used. Bass club guys who were just getting started would read about this stuff.

"Part of what made it so magic for us was that guys couldn't find these baits at most of the big mass-market merchants because they weren't tuned into what was going on. Because I was competing as a regular on the early B.A.S.S. tournament circuit, I had a good insight into which products were really hot. Everybody who read Ray's magazine would want this or that. Ray was creating a frenzy for tackle, and he was also creating heroes in the sport. There was a tremendous demand, and fishermen simply couldn't find the stuff elsewhere. That's what gave birth to my business. When our catalog came out, we created more demand and more awareness because we'd have little editorials or advertorials describing the merchandise."

Morris published his first catalog in 1974 — 180 pages with some 1,500 items. It was an immediate success. He fulfilled the needs that B.A.S.S. had created. Today, 500 customer service operators handle thousands of daily telephone orders 365 days a year.

His Outdoor World Bass Pro Shops are a combination of a sporting goods store, natural history museum, art gallery, restaurants and aquariums loaded with gamefish. A refrigerated, flowing, stream is stocked with rainbow trout.

Like Ray, Morris's love of fishing brought him success beyond his wildest imaginings. Like Ray, he saw a need and filled it. And like Ray he knows the future of sport fishing and his business depends more on good conservation and environmental practices than anything else. He, too, has received conservation awards for his efforts in national and state projects.

The kinship between Ray and Morris is strong. "He's never let me down," says Ray. "He was the prime mover in getting support for the Eagles of Angling Tournament on my lake that raised over a million dollars for a new church sanctuary. He gets it done."

FEW PEOPLE REALIZE that the dream of a Bass Pro Shop and its dreamer nearly died in a 1974 B.A.S.S. tournament. Morris continued to fish tournaments as his business grew, but in the first week of April 1974 at the Arkansas Invitational at Beaver Lake, he almost lost his life when his boat capsized. He had a pretty good boat, but this was before Ray demanded that all boats have upright and level flotation for safety. Fortunately, Morris and his partner, Bob Craddock from Kentucky, were wearing Ray's required life jackets. Even so, it was a close call for both fishermen because the water temperature was forty-seven degrees, enough to cause death by hypothermia in a very short time.

"We were fishing way down the lake from the tournament site, down by the dam," Morris says. "The fish were biting real good, but a storm was building up and we headed back toward the weigh-in site. The rain was light, but the wind was very strong, and the waves built up. This was a freak deal because you're usually protected from the wind by the high bluffs in the Ozarks. Then my bilge pump stopped working. I wasn't real good mechanically with my gear — I'm still the same way — and as I started to cross the open water, my battery shorted out because I'd taken on so much water. Two waves later the boat filled with water and we capsized.

"I'd seen this ad to grab anything that floats, so I swam and got a gas can that was floating and swam back to the boat. I started to rest on the boat but at that very moment it sank to the bottom. I had a life vest on — that was a Ray Scott requirement — and so did Bob. After the boat went down, I was trying to conserve energy and drift with the waves which were four, five, six feet high. There was an island maybe one hundred yards away. Bob started to swim for it, and I almost got into a fight with him because he was working against the current and the waves. Then he came back and we were both drifting holding on to the gas can. We were deteriorating fast. My hands were so weak that they felt like I'd gone to sleep on them. Then they began to burn so much I couldn't tell if they were in a furnace or the deep freeze.

"I remember I managed to get a coin out of my pocket. I was going to write a note to my parents because I knew I was history, and I tried to scratch on that Mercury gas can, 'Mom and Dad, I love you.' I got so mad because that paint finish was too good. I knew that this was my last chance to tell my mom and dad that I loved them. I'm trying to scratch that paint and I couldn't do it.

"We were getting in bad shape. It was real rough and we were coughing and spitting. I could smell the fumes in the gas can, and I'd just about given up hope. Craddock told me about his children and grand-children, and we both said our prayers out loud. All of a sudden, he started laughing. I thought he's either seen somebody coming to save us or he's gone nuts. Then I saw this big hand reaching down, and it's Billy Westmorland. His was one of the few boats that had been down there, and he had seen the red gas can. It was our last chance, a miracle, answered prayers. He almost capsized his own boat to drag us in and take us to the Lost Bridge Marina. When we got there, the fellows at the dock pulled our clothes off. This old guy put us in front of the heater and said, 'Boys, I've got a little whiskey here,' and Craddock says, 'Sir, I don't mind if I do.' I was shook up. I called my parents and told my dad that I was happy to hear his voice."

Billy Westmorland also remembers the day well. He recalls that a freak storm had passed over the lake and many boats had been capsized that day. He and his partner were skirting the rough waters about one-half mile from shore, when Billy saw a gas can bobbing up and down in the middle of the lake. From the way it was submerged, he thought there might be someone hanging onto it. He approached more closely, to the dismay of his partner who did not relish heading into the violent swells, which were reaching seven to eight feet.

"I got close enough to see Johnny's head," says Billy. "I slowly made my way toward him. I had to reposition the boat constantly to get through the swells. I didn't even see Bob Craddock. He was hanging on to Johnny from the back with his arms around his neck. By that time we had a boat full of water too. Can you believe, by sheer coincidence my boat had been rigged with two strong bilge pumps? If it hadn't been for that, we'd have been in big trouble too.

"Anyway, we got over to Johnny. First we had to pry Bob's arms loose from his neck and then we had to pry Johnny's hands loose from the gas can. His fingers were frozen. My partner got Johnny by the arm and I got him by the neck and we flipped him into the boat on top of rods, reels, treble hooks, everything. We took on a lot of water, too. I have to tell you I was scared to death after I got them in the boat. The water was up to my knees and I started shaking. The doctor said they had twenty more minutes maximum and they would have died of hypothermia."

10

The Making of Heroes

RAY SCOTT'S tournament concept succeeded beyond his wildest dreams. It allowed wholesome competition for competitive Americans. It provided fellowship. It spread down-to-earth bass fishing information. It educated everyone about the world of bass fishing. It created heroes and a whole new class of sports celebrities.

In five years, by the end of the 1972 tournament season, legends were already born. Bill Dance, Roland Martin, Tom Mann, John Powell, and Bobby Murray had won multiple tournaments. Early B.A.S.S. believer and lure maker Don Butler would win the second Classic at Percy Priest Reservoir in Tennessee. Roland Martin would still be competing and winning thirty years later although the Classic title would elude him.

In the next few years more future legends joined the tournament trail and won: Rick Clunn, Tommy Martin, Jimmy Houston, Al Lindner, Billy Westmorland, Ricky Green, Woo Daves, Gary Klein, Paul Elias, Jack Hains, Guido Hibdon, Basil Bacon, Bo Dowden, Larry Nixon, and Charlie Campbell. In 1979 a young Hank Parker won his first Classic at Lake Texoma and repeated his Classic win ten years later on the James River. He then retired from tournament competition to concentrate on his popular TV fishing show and product endorsements.

Even Ray could never have predicted the effect tournaments would have on fishing technology and products — including an entire marine and fishing tackle industry. The bass fishing industry evolved from the humblest glass-eyed wooden lures to sleek, state-of-the-art bass boats. Manufacturers sought endorsements by the pros. B.A.S.S. sought tournament sponsorship from the industry (and outside the industry) which led to bigger purses. It wasn't long before fishermen could actually *fish for a living*. The tournament not only made millionaires out of some fishermen; it made many, many millionaires and multi-millionaires in the fishing retail industry. New products and new technologies were born. Sleeping companies revived and grew. New companies were born.

Fishing fans can smile at Pulitzer Prize-winning sports writer Red Smith's account of B.A.S.S. tournament fishermen in a 1973 *Sports Afield* article:

> They are a strange new breed, somewhat like the professional golfer or rodeo hand in that they put up entry fees and compete for cash prizes, but while the rodeo cowboy may tow a roping horse in a trailer, the bass pro pulls a carpeted fiberglass boat rigged with a 150-horsepower outboard, electric stalking motor, sonic depth finder, bow steering stick, electric fuel gauge and meter, tachometer, speedometer, bilge pump, water temperature thermometer, light penetration meter, upholstered swivel seats, electric winches, running lights, and enough lures, lines, rods, reels and 'lunker lotion' to supply the state of Maine.
>
> Such a rig runs about $4,000 and the fact that there are more than 125 thousand in operation reflects the soaring popularity of the black bass. He deserves his high repute, for among freshwater game fish the bass is Joe Frazier without Joe's cheerful disposition.

"Red Smith came to the tournament to do a hatchet job," Ray says. "Who are these rednecks turning a contemplative sport into crass tournaments? Well, he saw our operation and wrote a classic of an article. It is still one of the most objective and insightful pieces ever done on B.A.S.S. and bass fishing. That man could write."

In 1967 Ray conducted two tournaments and in 1968 he conducted five. By 1997 B.A.S.S. was putting on an average of sixteen tournaments a year, not including the Classic and the federation divisional competitions and championship.

For several years, Ray ran the tournaments virtually single-handedly. Eunice helped out with pairings, scorekeeping, and other duties at some of the earlier tournaments but it was difficult with three small children at home. Most of Ray's help was in the form of volunteers arranged by the local chambers of commerce.

Ray never missed a tournament for the first twenty years. He figures he has weighed in well over fifteen million pounds of bass.

TODAY, AFTER MORE than thirty years, B.A.S.S. tournaments are a masterpiece of planning and logistics. There is no tournament trail today that has not borrowed directly from the B.A.S.S. formula — from rules to procedures. After Harold Sharp retired in 1987, tournament director Dewey Kendrick was the restless commanding general, constantly checking to make sure everything was proceeding correctly. His unflappable assistant, Glenda Cobb, had grown up on the trail, coming to B.A.S.S. in January 1982.

Registration, pairings, check-outs, launchings, check-ins, weigh-ins . . . there were thousands of details, always with the overriding concerns about safety, cheating, keeping the fish alive. Usually everything ran like clockwork, with a few exceptions, naturally, depending on the whims of mother nature and human nature and faulty alarm clocks. The veteran fishermen easily led newcomers into the rhythm of the event.

They formed a brotherhood, these road warriors, towing their rigs with vehicles loaded with tackle and provisions. Early mornings. Early dinners. Early bed hopefully. Some would travel with wives and even small children. The wives had learned to "camp out" in aging motel rooms. Some would bring their own sheets and towels, devising ingenious homemaking systems of hot plates, little microwaves, and even small refrigerators.

The contestants fished in all kinds of weather. They broiled under the Georgia sun. Their fish froze to weigh-in baskets in Oklahoma. They battled six-foot swells on the St. Lawrence River in New York. If there were nerves, few would betray it. Faces were impassive, stoic at the early morning launches. Brains doing a mental countdown on strategies, equipment, weather, and a new fishing partner.

"Many people do not understand how physically strenuous tournaments are. If anyone thinks these guys are going out having fun 'just fishing,' they're dead wrong," says Ray. "It's not only physically demanding, it can be dangerous, too, as Johnny Morris found out."

Earl Bentz, the competitive president of Triton Boats, found his first bass fishing tournament somewhat humbling and it left him with a great respect for the pros.

In 1976, while working at Hydra-Sports Boats in Nashville, Earl shared a house with Bobby Murray, the winner of the first Classic. "Of course, he was a pro on the B.A.S.S. circuit, and I was a pro on the boat racing circuit," Earl says. "Neither of us was home very much. I was gone about six months of the year racing, and he was gone about an equal amount fishing and giving seminars. We were having lunch one day, and he bet me a hundred dollars that I couldn't even finish in the top fifty in a B.A.S.S. tournament on Kentucky Lake."

Earl soon found out that fishing a B.A.S.S. tournament was different from racing and difficult in its own way. "In racing I was one of the elite three drivers for Mercury World Wide and had the best equipment. And even though racing was competitive, I found that bass fishing was a very humbling experience for me. I did not finish in the top fifty.

"In racing I had an entire contingent of engineers, mechanics, boat riggers, and other people with me, and all I was responsible for was getting my helmet and life jacket there. They even made my plane and rental car reservations. The crew took care of everything.

"In the B.A.S.S. tournament, it was three days of practice, three days of tournament. I had to put my own fuel in my boat and my own oil, charge the batteries, and put new line on my reels every night. In fact, Bobby and I shared a room during this particular tournament, and he had me stripping my reels of line and putting new line on every night. To make a long story short, I was getting to bed at 11:00 at night and getting up at 3:30 and 4:00 in the morning, and by the end of the fifth day I was dead. I was a young man in good shape, but the physical demands of this sport were far greater than I expected.

"The phone rang early on the fifth day. It was Ray Scott on the other end of the line and he said, 'Boy, what are you doin'?' I looked at my watch and I leapt out of bed and said, 'My goodness, I've overslept.' He said 'Look, these ain't boat races that start at noon. These are bass fishin' tournaments that start at 6:30 in the morning and your partner's down here as mad as a wet hen.' So I immediately ran out and had to spend the day in a boat with a guy who wasn't very happy with me because I had overslept. But I was just worn out."

"Unfortunately my partner did not do very well. I caught a limit of fish that day and had about twelve pounds. He was not in the running, fortunately for me, and actually he took it much better than I would have. At that point, I gained even more admiration and respect for bass fishermen who were doing this for a living."

Beyond the retail world, there were collateral benefits of the B.A.S.S. tournaments that no one could have anticipated even with the most astute foresight and painstaking planning. The tournaments fostered safety. Ray insisted on functional ignition kill switches which would shut the big engine off if the driver left his seat. In 1968 Ray required that personal flotation devices (PFDs) be worn and fastened every time the big engine was in use. This PFD requirement preceded the U.S. Coast Guard's regulation by eight years. Tournament boats had to have adequate positive upright flotation. Engines could not exceed a certain horsepower. The list went on.

And when Ray instituted the rule of catch-and-release at his tournaments (with mandatory livewells) little did he know how his tournament example would become unwritten law among the rank-and-file fishermen. Livewells appeared on the most modest of fishing boats. "If you ever told me a fisherman would shed a tear over a dead fish, I would have said you were crazy," says Ray. "But I've seen it happen. It is genuine remorse. Of course, some cry over the two-ounce penalty for a dead fish."

One of the most gratifying aspects of Ray's thirty-plus year career is being able to see his boys — some of them grandfathers now — become celebrities in their own right. Indeed he is now on a second generation of successful professional fishermen. There's Chad and Denny Brauer; Bo Dowden, Sr., and sons Bo. Jr., and Eason; Woo and Chris Daves; Roland and Scott Martin; and Guy Eaker and son Guy, Jr. And of course there's Guido and Dion Hibdon of Missouri, both Classic champions.

Ray is not above giving his fishermen spontaneous advice on the weigh-in stand.

"Lose the gum, son."

"Take off your sunglasses for the camera."

"Hold the fish out, it looks bigger."

"Smile for the camera, come on, let's see a smile."

"Is that your sweetheart out there? Come on up front, Sugar, and get a *good* picture."

"Are you his mother? Come on up here."

Ray has stood on the weigh-in stand for hours upon end, rain and shine, weighing his boys in. Talking to the crowd. Weighing small children in the Rubbermaid laundry/weigh-in basket. Making $1 bets on weight (the crowd roars with delight when Ray loses). Hawking hot dogs and drinks for the local chamber of commerce snack wagon. But always he has a handshake for the fisherman, an arm around the shoulder. A little reminiscing with the old timers. Trading lighthearted insults with the superstars.

A tournament is show time for Ray. From the beginning, he was determined to make it just that — a show. Today thousands can come to a weigh-in at an out-of-the-way lake near an even more out-of-the-way town. Some bring folding chairs but most stand for hours. Sometimes there are a few bleacher seats. If it rains, the umbrellas come out. But almost all remain to the end. The people in the crowd know these fishermen and can recite their stats just like they would for baseball and football players.

RAY IS RICH IN friendships from his early tournaments. Bill Dance was an early friend who would gain great fame and fortune on the B.A.S.S. tournament trail. Indeed, Bill won eight of the first twenty

B.A.S.S. tournaments. Although he has not fished tournaments in a long time, he is still arguably one of the most recognized bass fishermen in the world from his product endorsements and popular TV fishing show.

According to Ray, "Bill was just born ahead of everyone else. Even in the early days, he had an instinctive relationship with fish. He was just incredible at finding them. I swear he can communicate with bass. He's great with them, just like he is with people. He reads people, too. Time after time I would watch him sit down in a bull session with other fishermen after a day of tournament fishing. There were tall tales told, believe me. By the time everyone left, Bill knew exactly what he needed to know. He had a Sherlock Holmes way of deducing facts and a Bill Dance way of weeding out the lies."

Bill and Ray together spelled double trouble, especially on the B.A.S.S. Seminar Tour which Bill would join on a regular basis. Bill could pick up immediately on Ray's pranks and Ray on his. Even today they can carry on mischievous double talk conversations that totally baffle people. "No doubt waitresses all across the country are still talking about those two crazy fishermen," says Ray. "I had a little furry fake mouse. I took it into the restaurants and hid it up my cuff. It was soooo realistic."

One of Ray's favorite recollections was of a tournament practice on Santee-Cooper Reservoir in the early days. Bill made a long, high cast and caught a fish-eating cormorant in mid air. He pulled the large flapping bird in and managed to put it his livewell.

Bill was sharing a small cabin with Billy Primos of Jackson, Mississippi. Billy was a notoriously fastidious and organized individual. When he returned from practice each day, he would carefully put his neatly organized tackle down and head to the tiny bathroom in the cabin he shared with Dance.

That day Dance hurried to get to the cabin first and stuffed the bird in the toilet and shut the lid. Ray dropped by to visit and decided to wait for Primos to come home. As usual, Primos put his tackle down and headed right to the bathroom. He closed the door to the small enclosure. Bill and Ray waited. "It was like a tornado," Ray recalls. "Billy was squalling, the bird was flapping its wings violently and Billy couldn't get the door open. When he finally came out, he was soaked with toilet water and went straight for Dance, who fled from the cabin."

Roland Martin was another rising young star on the early tournament trail who is still making history today. Strikingly handsome with his tanned face and sun-bleached platinum hair, Roland was a well-known guide at Santee-Cooper in South Carolina. Although he had a biology degree from the University of Maryland, he chose to make a living fishing. He joined B.A.S.S. as soon as he heard about it and came to his first B.A.S.S. tournament as a spectator in July of 1969 at Lake Eufaula, Alabama.

When the first boat came in, Roland ran down to the water's edge. Gerald Blanchard of Memphis had eighty-eight pounds of bass and his partner Californian Rip Nunnery had ninety pounds, fifteen ounces — the largest fifteen-bass creel in B.A.S.S. history. They had so many fish they had tied their stringers to a boat paddle to carry them in but the paddle broke from the weight.

A wide-eyed Roland told Ray, "I've got no business here." But Ray encouraged him to stay. He did and went on to win frequently. He placed second in his very first B.A.S.S. tournament in January 1970, and won his second tournament at Lake Seminole. He has earned the Angler of the Year title on nine different occasions, which is the highest honor on the B.A.S.S. Tournament Trail next to the Classic Championship.

"Roland was one of the earliest to grasp deep water structure fishing," says Ray. "Before depth finders, he mastered the triangulation technique to locate structure and later became an early advocate of sonar technology. He was one of the first 'scientific' anglers on the B.A.S.S. trail."

Ray's good Tulsa friend and benefactor, Don Butler, would also help another famous fisherman in the early days. Jimmy Houston was a twenty-three-year-old insurance salesman from Oklahoma when he fished his very first B.A.S.S. tournament. In June of 1968 he came into the Okiebug tackle store in Tulsa where owner Don Butler encouraged him to enter the Lake Eufaula B.A.S.S. tournament. Jimmy had the desire and the skill, but he didn't have the money. Don not only paid his entry fee but gave him a ride to the tournament as well. Jimmy placed in the money and the rest is history. The blond mop-topped angler has qualified and fished fifteen Classics and is a popular host of his own TV fishing show. His appearance on the scene brings near rock star adulation. Wife Chris is an outstanding professional angler as well.

Bass fans have a wide choice of heroes. Every top fisherman has not only his own style of fishing but a very distinct personality. One of the most unusual is Rick Clunn who began fishing the B.A.S.S. trail in 1973. Always neat, polite, and somewhat reserved, he did not fit the good ol' boy image of a fisherman at all. But he had that same burning desire to commit to bass fishing. Giving up a good computer-programming job with Exxon in Texas, he went full-time on the B.A.S.S. trail and to date has fished a record-breaking twenty-six consecutive Classics. He has won four of them — two back to back in 1976 and 1977 and again in 1984 and in 1990.

He brought in the all-time best Classic weight of seventy-five pounds, nine ounces (twenty-one bass) from the Arkansas River in Pine Bluff in 1984. Standing alongside then-Governor Bill Clinton and Vice President George Bush, he said, "Only in America can a boy grow up to make a living chasing little green fish."

"Rick's greatest strength," according to Ray "is his ability to concentrate and focus to the exclusion of everything else. He can focus in an unparalleled way. He becomes the fish. He becomes part of the environment. And his concentration doesn't just stop with the tournament day. It is part of him twenty-four hours a day during competition and practice."

Asked what particular trait is common to all the greatest names of fishing, Ray does not hesitate to answer: "Versatility. It is the universal ability to be versatile, to adjust to changing conditions. I have often said you can drop our boys on any water in the world and they'll catch fish. Luck plays an absolutely negligible part in their success. All successful fisherman who have hung in there over the long haul have to have that quality.

"Young Kevin VanDam has that talent in spades. He can compute all the variables — and they're staggering — and come up with a winning strategy. He is highly versatile and like so many of these pros, Kevin is not only a super fisherman, he's a super human being. He's living proof that you can be a winner and a gentleman."

RAY MADE A VERY special friend at his second tournament on Smith Lake. It was there he made the acquaintance of a tall, impossibly slim, slow-talking fisherman from Flippin, Arkansas. His name was Forrest L. Wood. With wife Nina he operated a successful guide and outfitting service on Bull Shoals Lake and the White River in Arkansas's scenic Ozark region.

When Ray first met Forrest, Forrest was wearing a straw cowboy hat. "That's a good lookin' hat you've got on there, Forrest," said Ray. "Much obliged," said the laconic Forrest. A week later, the postman brought Ray a box. He opened it and found a new cowboy hat in his size. It was by far the best hat Ray had ever owned up to that time. From then on, he was never without his signature cowboy hat. The white cowboy hat became his trademark as well as Forrest's. Today when Ray sees that look of recognition on someone's face, he loves to extend his hand and say, "Hello, I'm Forrest Wood."

More than the hat, Ray came to appreciate the quality of this man. At the time he was fishing Ray's tournaments, Forrest was using a fishing boat he had developed himself. He had named it "Ranger" after the law enforcement Texas Rangers whom he admired. Ranger Boats was a sideline business but when Forrest saw this young fireball from Alabama, he knew they were traveling different trails, but they were heading to the same place.

Forrest was impressed with the caliber and the friendliness of the B.A.S.S. fishermen. He was struck especially by their eagerness to share their thoughts on fishing boats and what real fishermen wanted in a bass boat. He wisely turned this unique pool of anglers into his own research and development team. Orders began coming in for his boat and more and more Rangers showed up at B.A.S.S. tournaments.

The first Ranger boat bore little resemblance to today's sleek models.

The early boats, by Forrest's admission, were little more than glorified johnboats with a flat hull and a center keel. He moved on to a tri-hull design with a keel and side sponsons. The fishing world embraced this design and as the tournament concept became more refined, so did Ranger boats. Forrest placed full-page ads in *Bassmaster Magazine* and his business snowballed.

Despite the success, Ranger Boats came close to extinction.

In the early evening on May 4, 1971, Forrest was sitting at his kitchen table in Flippin with Roland Martin. They looked out the window and saw a red glow across the hill and heard fire engine sirens. The Ranger Boat Company was on fire. Roland and Forrest raced to the site and managed to drag an army surplus desk and a file cabinet out a window before the roof fell in. Everything else was lost — molds, boats, materials, everything. All that was left was the slab and Forrest was not insured.

The next morning, Forrest and Nina calmly hung a telephone box from a hickory tree near the slab and continued to do business on the phone, vowing to fulfill orders. Ray sent a telegram to say he knew Forrest would come back — better than ever — and that in the meantime, his ads would continue to run in *Bassmaster Magazine* free of charge.

As B.A.S.S. grew, so did Ranger. Ray bought Ranger Boats for his second BASS Masters Classic at Percy Priest Reservoir. Together, he and Forrest put together a special Classic edition, a TR-3, fully loaded with all equipment pre-rigged and factory installed. It was a revolutionary concept — the first fully rigged bass boat ever put together at the factory and marketed nationally. After the Classic, the boats were sold to eager B.A.S.S. members. And the fully rigged bass boat eventually became an industry standard.

Ranger boats became part of the B.A.S.S. tournament family and many a pro will tell you right away he would never have made it without Forrest and Nina Wood. Ray and Forrest's friendship flourished. For the next twenty-six years, Ray and Forrest and Nina would ride to the first-day Classic launch together in the pre-dawn hours, Forrest with his ever-present thermos of coffee.

Then the two tall men in white cowboy hats and boots would climb into a waiting Ranger Classic rig, don their life vests and launch into the sea of idling, identical boats. Once in the middle, as the boats gently bobbed about with all engines off, Ray would address the Almighty through a bull horn, praying for a good day, the safe return of the fishermen, and a good catch.

11

The Cheater

I N ALL HIS YEARS AT B.A.S.S., Ray was fanatical about the
prevention of cheating. With the sordid history of bass derbies and
the dangers of buddy tournaments, he knew his tournaments had to
be above reproach. His rules were ultra strict and with different partners
paired every day of the tournament, the possibility of cheating was
greatly diminished. But he knew that people intent on cheating could be
very cunning. Several known cheaters were warned not to even think
about entering a B.A.S.S. tournament.

Ray's vigilance was tested in 1974 at the All-American B.A.S.S.
Tournament at Clark Hill Reservoir in South Carolina. Out of deference
to his family, Ray has chosen not to use "the cheater's" full name here. He
was not, after all, the first nor probably the last to try to breach the
B.A.S.S. rules.

Ray was alerted to the case shortly after the tournament when he
received a call from a Georgia B.A.S.S. club president who said that two
members of his club who fished in the tournament had been paired the
first and second days with Wade S., a used car salesman in his fifties from
Virginia.

Driving home together after the tournament, the two club members
began comparing notes. They were surprised to learn from each other
that at the start of the first day and the start of the second day, Wade had

asked, "Have you got any fish located?" And then he would add, "If you don't have any fish, I have an ace in the hole."

Ray called the two club members to ask if they had anything else to add. They did not, but Wade's comment to both men on successive days, "I've got an ace in the hole," echoed in Ray's mind, and he asked Harold Sharp to get the name of Wade's partner on the third and final day of the tournament. That partner was twenty-five-year-old Bob Martin of Springfield, Missouri.

Ray called Martin and asked, "Bob, did you have a good tournament?"

Martin said that he had.

"And you qualified for the Classic?"

Martin said that he had.

Then in a move that Ray says was just intuition on his part, he asked Martin who his partner had been on the first day.

Martin said that he had been paired with So-and-so.

"And what kind of a day did you have?"

Martin said that he had had a good day.

"And who were you paired with on the second day?" Ray asked.

Martin said that he had been paired with So-and-so.

"And what kind of a day did you have?"

Again, Martin said that he had a good day.

Whereupon Ray said to Martin, "Now I'm going to ask you one more question, but I don't want you to answer it right away. I want you to think about it for five or ten minutes and then call me back. I want you to think about *everything that was said and done that third and final day*. It's very important that you remember *everything*. Here's my number." And with that Ray hung up the phone.

Ray says, "Harold Sharp was sitting there with me, and he said, 'What are you doin'?' And I said, 'If this guy Wade pulled any bull, Bob Martin's going to be honest about it. He's a good kid."

MARTIN DIDN'T TAKE ten minutes — not even five minutes — to call back. He called back in three and a half minutes, and he was sobbing as he told Ray about the final day. Martin said he figured he needed to catch four pounds of bass that day to clinch a spot in the BASS Masters Classic. He was paired with Wade in Wade's boat, and they immediately went to a place that Wade picked. Right off the bat, Martin caught a three-and-a-half- or four-pound bass, then a keeper, and then another keeper. With that, he was certain to qualify for the Classic. In contrast, Wade did not catch a single fish.

"Wade didn't announce he was going to an ace in the hole, he simply went," Martin said. "He headed up a creek where two of his buddies were camped. Then he got hold of a rope and pulled a basket up. I would say there were a dozen bass, most of them dead, three or four alive. He said to me, 'this is my ace in the hole.'

"I said to him, 'What are you doing?' Three or four times I said to him, 'Wade, get rid of these fish.' He said, 'No, I need some of these to get my money back.' He said, 'You want a fish? Here's a fish for you.'

"I took the fish and put it in my side of the livewell. All the time I'm thinking I'm going to take this fish as evidence and say that this fish came out of a basket and that this guy had a basketful of fish. Wade dropped the basket in the water, and I said to him, 'Let's get out of here.'

"I just wanted to fish," Martin continued. "As we headed back, he said, 'You're not gonna say anything about this.' I wouldn't talk to him. I'm running the boat, other boats are coming in, and I'm thinking about what to do. My brain's going a hundred miles an hour. Finally, I stopped off a point and said, 'Wade, get rid of those fish.' I took my fish out and threw it up on the bank, thinking it would be there if I needed to come back and prove what had happened. I said again, 'Wade, get rid of them.'

"And he said, 'No, I need them.'

"At the weigh in, I got out with my fish to see if I qualified for the Classic. I did. I never looked back at Wade. I wanted to go up there and say that Wade, who finished twenty-fifth, got someone else's money. But I didn't. I know I'm guilty, I know it's my fault. I went right on through the weigh-in line."

Ray told Martin, "Bob, that's not the only thing you did wrong. You signed the slip that said in so many words, 'I hereby certify that the fish caught by myself and my partner were caught under the rules and regulations of this tournament.'

"Now Bob, what I'm going to do is call Wade and I'm going to ask him to think about the tournament. And I'm going to tell him to call me back in ten minutes. I guarantee you'll get a call from him because he'll want to know what you told Ray Scott. When he calls, you say, 'Wade, I'm not going to talk with you about this subject,' and hang the phone up. If he calls back, tell him the same thing. He'll be pumping you, trying to find out what you told me. I appreciate your being honest with me, Bob, and I understand how this could have happened. He's an older man and you're a young kid — it was a bullying kind of thing.'"

Ray called Wade and asked, "How you doing, Wade?"

"Fine."

"Did you have a good tournament?"

"Oh, yeah, I had a good tournament."

"Who was your partner the first day?"

"Some kid from Georgia, Ray."

"Did you get along with him okay?"

"Yeah."

"Anything happen that day at all, anything that was a little out of the ordinary?"

"No."

"Who was your partner the second day?"

"Another young guy from Georgia."

"Anything unusual happen that second day?"

"No."

"Now, Wade, I'm going to ask you another question, and it's very, very important. I want you to be very careful when you think about this, and don't answer right away. I want you to hang the phone up, wait ten minutes and then call me back. Now the question is this: During the third day of the tournament, who were you paired with? Don't answer now. Just think about the third day. Everything that happened that day.

If anything out of the ordinary happened, it's real important that you tell me every detail. Anything that was even a little bit off course. Call me back in ten minutes."

Ray hung up.

Harold looked at Ray and asked, "What do you think is going to happen?"

"I know exactly what's going to happen," Ray replied. "He's on the phone right now with Bob Martin."

Ray told his secretary that if Wade called back, she was to tell him Ray was tied up on the phone and that he'd call back in a minute. Ray called Martin's number. The line was busy.

After a couple of minutes passed, Ray called Martin again. This time the phone rang, and Ray asked, "Did you get that call from Wade?"

"Yes, sir, I did."

"What did he say?"

"He wanted to know if I had told you anything."

"And what did you tell him?" asked Ray.

"I told him that I couldn't talk with him about it."

"Thank you, Bob, I'll get back to you later," Ray said and he called Wade.

Wade began crying when he answered.

"'Why did you do it, Wade?' Ray asked. 'I want to know the whole story. I know the truth, but I want you to tell me in your own words.' And he told me the whole story, the whole bloody conspiracy of how he did it. Before the tournament, he'd gone in with his buddies, caught fish and put them in the basket. Then they tied a string to the basket and hung it to a willow so it was suspended in the water. He was just torn apart."

Ray banned Wade from B.A.S.S. tournaments for life, and he suspended Bob Martin from the Classic and competition for a year.

But the story wasn't finished. Several months after Wade was banned, he called Harold Sharp and asked if he could take a polygraph test about the tournament incident. Harold recalls, "I said, 'Yes, you can. I don't know why, but if that's what you want to do, yes.'"

"And Wade said, 'Well, would you arrange it for tomorrow?'

"I said, 'Well, it depends on the polygraph man.' I checked and he was available, so Wade said he'd be there the next day. I couldn't figure out what he was trying to do. He came down and I met him and took him to the polygraph test man. Wade went in and took the test, and when it as all over, I asked the polygraph man, 'What happened?' He said, 'Well, to start off with, Wade told me what I was supposed to ask him, and I told him, 'That's not the way it works. I ask the questions, and you supply the answers. But what is it you want me to ask? He said that he had been disqualified for weighing in an illegal fish at your tournament, and he wanted me to ask him if he caught those fish. But that's *all* he wanted me to ask him.' To make a long story short, Wade totally flunked the polygraph test."

Harold adds, "I had an idea of what was going on. I confronted Wade and he confirmed my suspicions. George Oates was a guy who had been fishing our tournaments and had started a tournament organization down in Florida. When we disqualified Wade, he entered a tournament that Oates was conducting. Oates told him that he couldn't fish it because he had been disqualified by B.A.S.S. Wade told him he hadn't done what B.A.S.S. said he did. Oates told him if he passed a polygraph test he could fish the tournament.

"So Wade concocted this single question to have the polygraph man ask him, 'Did you catch these fish?' He would answer, 'Yes,' which was the truth, and then he'd get in the tournament down in Florida. The only problem was he caught the fish two days before the tournament started and put them in a basket."

"It was a bad experience," says Ray, "but it showed the world that we did not put up with any monkey business. A news release was generated and sent to every outdoor writer on our list. And after his suspension ended, Bob Martin fished in our Bull Shoals Tournament and placed nineteenth."

Today, Martin owns a very successful restaurant, The Repair Shop, in Springfield, close to the Bass Pro Shop. He says that single incident changed the course of his life. "I qualified for the Classic. Who knows what would have happened if I had done well in the Classic?" He wants the story to be told. "It holds lessons for everyone, especially young tournament fishermen and anyone who even considers cheating."

12

The Classic

RAY KNEW TOURNAMENTS were critical to the success of B.A.S.S. and vice versa. But to be really effective, B.A.S.S. and the tournaments had to get the attention of the press.

The press was not really that interested. For too many years, outdoor writers had been besieged by promoters of $2 fishing derbies, all craving front-page coverage. Ray had to prove he was different. He had to prove that B.A.S.S. tournaments were a legitimate sport, on a par with golf and tennis.

He and Bob Cobb discussed the lack of publicity as they drove to Atlanta in August 1970 to attend a regional fishing tackle show. They batted ideas around during the three-hour drive and came up with the rough concept for the Classic, a "test of the best." Ray proposed to take the top twenty-four fishermen of the 1971 season, along with twenty-four writers, to attend a three-day championship tournament he would call the BASS Masters Classic.

It would be the fishing equivalent of the World Series, the Super Bowl, the Masters. Only the best, the ones who had scored the most points throughout the year, would qualify. Everything would be first class. First prize would be $10,000 — a sum unheard of in fishing circles in those days.

Ray and Bob were excited now. Ideas were flowing. They both agreed they needed a "hook," something that would really get people talking and keep them talking. Ray hit on the idea of a "mystery lake." The pros and the press would have no idea where the Classic would be held. Talk about suspense. Talk about novelty. So, even though a site had not been selected, Ray publicized the upcoming Mystery Lake BASS Masters Classic.

Someone else liked the idea — a fellow by the name of Dave Newton, a writer for the Las Vegas News Bureau. Dave was an outdoorsman born and raised in Moultrie, Georgia, and a 1962 graduate of the University of Missouri Journalism School.

The idea of a mystery tournament was welcome news to Dave Newton in more ways than one. First of all, he says, "It was our job to get publicity for Las Vegas as a family destination, so I called Ray Scott in Montgomery about getting this mystery tournament. After thirty seconds on the phone, Ray realized that Las Vegas would be a super destination. He said, 'You got a lake out there?' I said, 'Yeah, Lake Mead.' And he said, 'Are there any bass in it?' And I said, 'Oh, yeah.' Actually Mead was a pretty good clear-water bass fishery.

"Then Ray said, 'I'll have to call you back. Give me your phone number.' He went out to a pay phone, called me back and said, 'I can't talk in the office because this thing has to stay a secret. If word gets out, it will blow the whole deal. I'll tell you what. We're taking our seminar tour west to Los Angeles, and we can come back through Las Vegas. Why don't you set up a seminar site for us?' So we set one up at the Dunes."

Newton was also excited because, he adds, "B.A.S.S. sounded like a great organization and a great place to work. Ray's dynamism, of course, came across over the phone. I was looking forward to meeting him because my wife, Gayle, and I wanted to move back to the South, and maybe this was the opportunity. Before attending the University of Missouri, I went west with the Air Force and became a survival instructor at Stead Air Force Base outside Reno. As a survival instructor I lived in the woods for four years. I also wrote outdoor columns. Ray's coming to Las Vegas was a tailor-made situation for Gayle and me because as a former survival instructor I wanted to get into the outdoor industry in some way.

"I saw that phone call from Ray Scott as a possible ticket back to the South and into the outdoor industry, but I never let on to him that I was interested in anything like that. Yet Gayle and I pinned a lot of hopes on how things would develop."

"Ray, Harold Sharp, John Powell, and Roland Martin drove in from Los Angeles in the Bluebird," Newton continues, "and our bureau photographer, John Cook, and I met them when they arrived. John was a B.A.S.S. member, and had told me about the 'Mystery Lake.' We're standing there watching them unload, and they just stood out as different. I think John Powell was wearing one of those polyester B.A.S.S. jumpsuits, and then here comes Ray Scott, cowboy boots, a big cowboy hat, the whole works. By that time I'd been in Nevada for sixteen years, and I knew what a real cowboy looked like, and I knew where real cowboys came from, and they sure didn't come from Alabama.

"So I looked at Cook, a West Coast hippie type who had no exposure to the South, and he looked at me, and he said, 'Snake oil?' All at once there was great suspicion just from this first appearance. We were really set back on our heels. I went back home and told my wife, 'Gayle, honey, don't pack. You're not going to believe this, but this may not be the deal I thought it was. I think this guy is a con man of some kind.'

"But anyway, the die was cast. We had the room set in the Dunes. We had done a lot of local promotion, and we just had to see what would happen that night with the seminar. That afternoon Ray had to ditch John Powell and Roland Martin while he and Harold went out to Lake Mead with me to look at the marina, and, I guess, verify that there was a big lake out there. They loved the whole set up. They spent the day questioning whether we could pony up the amenities that they needed — rooms, meals, airline tickets.

"That night, we had a great turnout for the seminar. Three hundred to four hundred people filled the room. None of the people had ever seen Ray before or heard this kind of Southern evangelism, and it really just lit up the crowd. It really lit it up. The seminar was kind of a combination of an old-time revival meeting, a tent show of some kind, and a little bit of snake oil. Ray had that audience, a sophisticated Las Vegas audience, in the palm of his hand. I mean these were sophisticated people who wouldn't cross the street to see Frank Sinatra or Dean Martin. They were jaded. They'd been there and done that, but they were just putty in Ray's hands.

"It was really exciting and entertaining. Halfway through his routine, the house was absolutely rocking. I knew then that any fears I had were unfounded, and we quickly got everything in place for the first mystery BASS Masters Classic tournament — the hotels, airfare, the meals — largely through the efforts of my boss, Don Payne, news bureau manager. Vegas put up about $25,000, and B.A.S.S. paid the $10,000 prize money.

"The next day Roland wanted to go out and fish Lake Mead; he had no idea it was to be the secret destination lake for the Classic. He just wanted to fish it. but Harold Sharp took care of that. He said, 'Roland, you get your butt back on the bus. We're leaving here in five minutes.'"

From Las Vegas, Ray flew to Chicago where he was to attend a tackle show with Bob Cobb. While there, he decided it would be a good time to talk *Playboy Magazine* into sending a writer down to do a story on the BASS Masters Classic at Lake Mead.

Ray recounts: "I marched into the magazine's offices and the first thing I saw was a secretary in a little getup that couldn't have taken very long to get into. She looked up and stared at me as though I had gotten off on the wrong floor. 'Hello,' I said. 'I'm Ray Scott with B.A.S.S.' She hesitated a moment, gave me another curious look, and invited me into the advertising manager's office. He later laughed and told me, 'You'd have never gotten in, but the secretary thought you might be with the Bass Shoe Company and wanted to place an ad. She was afraid to take the chance of turning you away.'"

Not long after his visit to *Playboy*, Ray felt a pain in the right side of his abdomen. It was like the one he felt in Las Vegas before the seminar. Only this time it didn't go away.

It was so excruciating that he had Cobb take him to a hospital. The cause of the pain was a kidney stone, and after a day and a half of major misery, he underwent surgery. He felt so good that evening that — in defiance of hospital rules — he checked himself out and went to his hotel. Not long after, he felt as if his stomach was about to explode. The pain was unbearable. Cobb took him right back to the hospital where doctors discovered that the surgeon had punctured the right ureter, the duct leading from the right kidney to the bladder. He spent five days in the hospital recuperating and this time he did not check himself out.

The Classic plans continued and were made in extraordinary secrecy. No one would know the Classic destination except for Ray, Bob Cobb, and tournament director Harold Sharp — not even their wives. As Ray had hoped, rumors spread, some started by Ray. Whispers were repeated. Outdoor writers got into a guessing game in their columns.

But no one was to make the mistake that Ray was not serious about the secrecy. As a matter of fact, his concern bordered on obsession.

Employees of B.A.S.S. headquarters had no idea where the mystery lake would be and they took great delight in "sleuthing" and making guesses. One day Barbara Spencer (now Bazzell), an early employee who stayed for eighteen years, bounded into Ray's office and announced she had "guessed" the tournament site. Unknown to her, she had guessed correctly. Ray was not amused. Barbara would recount in later years how Ray rose up and out of his chair, murder in his eyes. She quickly exited the office, not hanging around for any further reaction. And she kept her guesses to herself.

In October, Newton and John Cook flew east to Atlanta to join Ray on the Delta charter flight carrying the Classic contestants and outdoor writers to Las Vegas. The charter had been reserved in the name of the Golden Age Garden Club. No one had known what clothes to pack because Ray had helpfully told them to bring hot *and* cold weather clothing. When Newton boarded the plane, Roland Martin stared at him as if he knew him from somewhere but Vegas didn't click in Roland's mind, and none of the contestants or writers was able to guess where they were going.

"Ray had the heavy hitters of the east and southwestern press, plus Homer Circle on board," Newton says. "I thought, I'm in good company. Those fishermen and writers gave us more press in a year for our family-related outdoor activities than we could ever have possibly gotten by calling writers individually and saying, 'C'mon and fish with us.' The BASS Masters Classic really put Lake Mead on the map as a bass fishery."

The three-day Classic ended on October 22, 1971, with Bobby Murray of Hot Springs, Arkansas, the winner with a total catch that weighed forty-three pounds, eleven ounces.

The Classic weigh-in was conducted on the marina roof with the press, wives, and a few spectators in attendance. As Harold measured and weighed the fish, Ray announced the proceedings through a bullhorn to the sparse crowd. "A peanut salesman would have starved to death," says Ray.

The next day the fishing world almost lost both Ray Scott and Bobby Murray. On the lake filming "fill-in" shots for the Classic movie, a sudden windstorm almost sent the three Rebel boats to the bottom. They were saved by sheltering in the lee of John Cook's big Slickcraft.

Not everyone shared Ray's enthusiasm for the Classic. One fisherman who qualified for the event, Johnny Adams from Florida, said that he couldn't be bothered fishing the Classic because he didn't want to take the time off from work.

STARTING IN 1977 at Lake Tohopekaliga in Florida, the Classic went "public." Ray no longer needed a mystery lake to intrigue the media. He announced where the Classic would take place, and the crowds came.

Ray threw himself into the Classic with even more joyous abandon. For a number of years he retained a gourmet chef, Frank Martinelli, just to cook for the event, and he gave Martinelli a blank check to come up with culinary wonders. "We can't make the fish bite," Ray exulted, "we can't make the weather bright, but we sure can send them home with great memories and their tummies full of exotic food they'd never tasted before." The only time Martinelli did not preside over the fare was on those nights when Pooley would prepare soul food, and Martinelli cheerfully served as sous chef.

The Classic became more and more creative. For the 1979 Classic at Lake Texoma on the Texas-Oklahoma line, Ray dispatched a King Air

A-100 prop jet to Chicago to pick up a belly dancer named Santana, her dresser, and a three-piece Middle Eastern band to perform for one night. Ray had hired her on the recommendation of half a dozen Greek restaurant owners in Chicago. The night that Santana entranced the Classic banquet crowd, Ray, dressed like a sheikh, came on stage, borne aloft on a canvas stretcher shouldered by six heavy-set, shirtless, turbaned outdoor writers with their pants rolled up to their knees. He tossed plastic worms to the crowd. After Santana and her ensemble performed, Ray had them flown back to Chicago, where the plane picked up Franz Bentler and his all-violin orchestra, the Royal Strings, who performed the next night.

Without question, the Classic became the greatest fishing tournament in the world. A combination of the Masters Golf Tournament, NASCAR, and the Grand Ol' Opry, the five-day spectacle attracts up to 125 thousand people from all over the country and various parts of the world, as well as three hundred media representatives, both domestic and foreign. Vice President George Bush and Governor Bill Clinton attended the 1984 Classic in Pine Bluff, Arkansas, and Chuck Yeager and former President Jimmy Carter showed up at the 1986 Classic.

There are those who plan their annual vacation around the Classic week, which begins with Monday registration, Tuesday official practice day, Wednesday media day (just like the buildup before the Superbowl), followed by competition on Thursday, Friday and Saturday. The day of the final weigh-in is complete with an award-winning show directed and produced by Dave Ellison, who also edits the B.A.S.S. publication, *Fishing Tackle Retailer.* Accompanying the Classic is a big outdoor show featuring boats, trucks, tackle, and a cornucopia of bass-related goodies for the fishing frenzied. All in all, it is a monument to Ray's determination to make weighing a fish a *spectator sport.*

Classic first-prize money is now $100,000, but a win can be worth $1 million to the victor. An estimate of how much the winner makes from sponsors can be made by counting the advertising patches on his post-tournament shirt. Some years ago, Rick Clunn, who has won the Classic an unmatched four times, calculated that each patch was worth $50,000, "which is one reason he wears long-sleeved shirts," says Ray.

In 1997, the last year that Ray emceed the Classic, so many bass fanatics — more than twenty thousand to be exact — tried to pack into the Coliseum in Birmingham, Alabama, for the final weigh-in that a live video of the proceedings had to be fed into a theater next door for the overflow.

It had been a long, exciting journey from the rooftop of a Las Vegas marina to Ray's final appearance in Birmingham. The Classic had evolved into a spectacle of laser lights, fog machines, indoor fireworks, huge TV screens, and booming music — mostly gospel, country, and patriotic. B.A.S.S. member Lee Greenwood has performed at the Classic extravaganza on numerous occasions, always bringing the house down with his signature song, "God Bless the U.S.A.," the Country Music Song of the Year in 1985. The song's lyrical but unabashed patriotism would remain the unofficial theme song of the Classic event.

The Classic weigh-in is a phenomenon in itself. Some consider it a carnival atmosphere. Some complain it is too close to a religious revival. Some protest it is a maudlin display of patriotism. But it is All-American and it is a heckuva show. Ray is the masterful impresario who keeps all the elements together and moving in the same direction.

His fans are not at all surprised to see him dramatically appear in the darkened arena amidst a spotlight and swirling fog to the dramatic strains of *Also Sprach Zarathustra*, the theme from *2001: A Space Odyssey*. Arms outstretched, microphone in hand, he welcomes the audience to the world of B.A.S.S. They roar in approval.

While Ray stands in the center of the arena in his flamboyant fringed leather jacket, boots, and white cowboy hat, the fishermen make their own grand entrance. Seated in identical boats and pulled by coordinated trucks, each contestant makes a triumphal three-quarter lap around the darkened arena, dramatically highlighted by a moving spotlight.

In front of the weigh-in stand, each fisherman yanks his catch out of a livewell for the cheering fans. All the while, Ray, cordless microphone in hand, is working the audience, feeding them pertinent bits of information. His love for the crowd is palpable. He feeds off their energy and they feed off his. By the end of the show, they have a virtual conversation going. They'll do anything he tells them — stand up, sit down, scream or yell on command, execute a football "wave" around the entire coliseum. Ray makes them feel they're not *at* the weight-in, they're *part of* the weigh-in.

His manner with the contenders is downright affectionate. He knows these men. Most of the superstars got their start on his trail more than twenty years ago. He has followed the careers of the younger ones on the B.A.S.S. tournament trail and he knows the long, arduous journey each has traveled to make that walk to the microphone in front of tens of thousands of fans.

He makes sure each has his day in the sun. He cajoles the audience and builds suspense as the weigh-in progresses. Sometimes only a couple of ounces — even one ounce — determines the crown of bass fishing. The crowd is in a frenzy.

And when the triumphant angler — the Classic Champ — joins Ray on the weigh-in stand, there are tears in many eyes, even those of big, strong, sunburned fishermen and cynical journalists.

13

Saving Fish . . . and Fishermen

WHEN RAY TOOK bullhorn in hand and prayed for a good catch at the beginning of each tournament, he also silently prayed for a good release. That is, the release of the tournament bass back into the water alive and well.

Ray Scott first pitched catch-and-release to B.A.S.S. tournament competitors at the start of the 1972 season. It was a request . . . a plea. He asked every fisherman to make every effort to bring every fish in alive — and keep them alive — to be released back into the water.

As there were few livewells at the time, fishermen had to use rope and chain stringers and ice coolers and whatever they could concoct. But they honored his request. In the second tournament of 1972, he sweetened the incentive by giving a one-ounce bonus for each fish brought in alive.

As a fisherman, Ray knew that fishing resources were finite even though biologists had assured him that the tournament pressure would not harm the fish population. As a businessman running a company to make money, he realized that what was good for the sport of fishing was good for the bottom line.

As the tournaments grew in size and popularity, he also knew the sight of stringers of dead fish could be deadly to public perception. It was a win-win situation to practice catch-and-release at B.A.S.S. tournaments.

Little did he know that his policy would end up saving more fish than any regulatory step since governments first began putting legal limits on catches in the last century.

Ray points out that the tournament rules allow the fishermen the option of mounting lunker bass. "So far, in the history of B.A.S.S., not a single competitor has exercised that option," he says with great satisfaction.

B.A.S.S. publicized the catch-and-release philosophy every way it could and even made decals and patches that read "Don't Kill Your Catch." The concept swept the fishing world. Today virtually all fishermen practice catch-and-release, at least part of the time. A generation of young fishermen knows nothing else. The practice has also spread into saltwater angling.

Ray described his catch-and-release policy in the January/February 1972 issue of *Bassmaster Magazine* in his Scott on the Line column:

> Beginning with our 1972 tournament schedule, all contestants will be asked to keep all bass alive. Tournament bass will be promptly weighed in and immediately placed in a large five hundred-gallon aerated livetank. Our study indicates that we can save up to ninety-five percent of all bass caught. After the weigh-in is completed, the bass will be released to swim away and be caught again. The few bass that don't survive will be cleaned and presented to a deserving charity.
>
> It is a fine feeling to catch a good sized bass and show the trophy off to your buddies. But, it is an even greater feeling to catch a good fish, admire it, weigh it and then lean over the boat and gently release the fish. When you see a big bass slowly swim off out of sight beneath the boat, then, and only then, will you know the complete thrill of bass fishing.

Ray's projection of the live-release rate was too pessimistic. Today more than ninety-eight percent of fish caught alive at B.A.S.S. tournaments survive, even when delayed mortality is factored in.

For all the accolades that have come his way for catch-and-release, Ray has never taken credit for the concept. He gives that credit to the trout fishermen.

In the summer of 1971, Ray was invited to speak in Pensacola, Florida, to a regional meeting of the Outdoor Writers Association of America. After he returned home to Montgomery, he got a phone call from Al Ellis, who had heard Ray speak in Pensacola. A maker of custom fly rods, Ellis asked Ray if he would be the master of ceremonies at the annual conclave of the Federation of Fly Fishermen in Aspen, Colorado, that September.

"We'd love to have you," Ellis said, "but we have no money. There's no fee and no travel expenses. However, we can give you room and food."

"What a deal!" said Ray. "Can I bring my wife?" Ellis said yes, and that September Ray and Eunice went on vacation to Aspen.

Ray had a wonderful time at the conclave. "Conclave," he says, "is a trout fisherman's name for a convention" — and there, like a Don Rickles of bass fishing, he teased the fly fishermen about the elegant way they dressed right down to their "funny lookin' britches."

Ray was fascinated with their fishing paraphernalia, especially their vests. "You could do minor surgery or major plumbing with all the gizmos and gadgets on their vests," he says. "They had ten pockets fore and aft and rings for all kinds of implements like fly disgougers, line snippers, scissors, cubes of beeswax, line dressing, you name it. And of course there was the patch of lamb's wool to park flies, as well as the hat. And they wore rubber britches up to their armpits."

At the conclave he met Nathaniel Reed, the Assistant Secretary of the Interior for Fish and Wildlife and National Parks, Lefty Kreh, Jack Hemingway, Gardner Grant, Leon Chandler of Cortland Line, and other leaders in the field.

The day before Ray left Aspen, his hosts invited him to go fly fishing with them. He was not a complete stranger to this side of angling, at least not when it came to using a cane pole with handmade wire guides and a Cortland fly line on a $2.50 Pflueger fly reel to cast a popping bug for largemouths and bluegill.

"We got out to this river — a stream really — that was so small and narrow you could cast across it," Rays recalls. "All the fishermen were dressed up in their fancy suits and were casting about twenty yards apart.

Suddenly, downstream, a guy stuck a fish. All the other fly fishermen dropped their rods and moved back up the hill to watch this guy fighting his fish and to comment on what he was doing.

"Somehow the guy reached behind for a net and brought the fish up with it. The trout was not more than eleven or twelve inches long. Lord have mercy, I thought — *bass bait.* The guy brought out some little tool that he had stored somewhere on his vest, wet his hands and used the tool to unhook the trout. Then he released it, very, very gently. All the other fishermen began cheering and high-fiving each other. I couldn't believe it.

"The next day on the way home, I replayed this scene in my mind. I thought, if they had so much fun releasing this piddlin' little trout, what would it be like if a big, hairy-legged bass fisherman released a five-pound bass?

"The biologists told us that tournaments had no impact on the fishery. And we always gave all the bass we caught to an orphan home or some charity, but there was always the grouchy old timer in the bib overalls standing by the weigh-in saying, 'Thass why ah ain't catchin' no fish.'"

THE FIRST CATCH-AND-RELEASE tournament, the Florida National, was held March 9-11, 1972, on the Kissimmee chain of lakes. Tom Mann won with forty-seven pounds, fifteen ounces. For the weigh-in, Ray and Dave Newton had designed and built a twelve-foot long, five-foot wide, five-foot deep livewell with an efficient aeration and water cooling system. It had inch-thick, bulletproof glass windows, and was mounted on a tandem axle horse trailer chassis. When they first filled it up with water, the livewell, which then weighed almost five thousand pounds, sank down into the soft Florida sand to the chassis frame. Unable to jack it up, they had to drain the water. On their second attempt, they succeeded in keeping the livewell up by slipping railroad ties beneath the chassis. The huge live-tank, filled with big, healthy Florida largemouths, was a smash hit with the crowd. Hundreds had their picture made beside one of the viewing windows, where a big bass would obligingly pose. The likes had never been seen before.

Everything went fine at the next three tournaments in South Carolina, Arkansas, and Tennessee. "The fishermen were following the leader," Ray says. "They were being led on the straight-and-narrow path of righteousness." Attitudes were changing. The tournament anglers were beginning to have a new regard for the well-being of their quarry.

But there was a big bump in the road when Ray arrived in Jackson, Mississippi, for the Rebel Invitational on Ross Barnett Reservoir in August. Tournament Director Harold Sharp told him, "Hey, we got a bad problem. One of the fisheries people said that we can't release these fish." Ray asked, "Why?" "I don't know," Harold replied. "All I know is that we can't release them. If we bring 'em in, we gotta keep 'em."

Mississippi B.A.S.S. Federation President Les Johnson supported Ray's catch-and-release program one hundred percent. However, a local group, the Mississippi Association of Bass Clubs, was not releasing fish and did not want any adverse publicity. So they sent a lawyer-member to speak to Governor William Waller. The Governor, in turn, sent word to his appointed Fish and Game Commissioner, Avery Wood, that the fish were to be kept — not released, but kept.

Ray and Harold went to see Wood. He was sitting in his office, arms crossed, feet up on the desk, a cigar butt in his mouth. A nervous biologist named Jack Herring sat to one side, Ray says, "trembling like a dog who had swallowed a pocketful of peach seeds."

Ray asked Wood why the fish could not be released. "I'll tell you why," Wood said. "Because we don't want you to turn those fish loose that have been stressed or diseased and go out and spread disease all over the lake."

Ray said, "Mr. Wood, I'm not a biologist, but I think your man sitting here by you will tell you that there's no scientific evidence that will happen."

"Well, you're not gonna do it," Wood said. "You catch 'em, you keep 'em and that's that!"

Ray said, "Mr. Wood, we're trying to teach people that you don't have to kill every bass you catch. We're trying to set an example."

"Well, I don't give a dang!" Wood shouted. "I don't care!"

Amid the crescendo of hot words, Ray fired back, "Well, Mr. Wood, I hate to tell you this, but what we're gonna do is catch our bass within the legal rights and rules of our license. And we're gonna bring the fish in, and we're gonna weigh 'em! Those that are alive and can swim, we're gonna put 'em back in your lake unless you have someone there with a baseball bat to kill 'em!"

Wood shot out of his chair and started stalking back and forth across the room, cussing Ray out. "He called me everything," Ray said. "He just went into a rage." Ray and Harold walked out, and Harold said, "You got his hockey hot. He ain't our friend." "Well, I'm sorry," Ray said, "but we'll find out what happens tomorrow."

Right after the blast-off to start the tournament, Harold came over to Ray and said, "Good news. They changed their mind. They're going to let us bring the fish in."

"That's good," Ray said, "that's fine, that's wonderful."

It did not turn out to be so wonderful.

When the fish came in and were weighed, state biologists put the fish in an aerated tank truck and deposited them a mile down the causeway in a shallow area netted off from the rest of the lake. The average depth was only two feet.

"This was a tragic time of the year," Ray says. "It was hot under that August sun, and we learned then that we would never again hold a tournament like that in August. Probably thirty percent of the fish were dead on arrival. Then every day a fishery man would wade in the shallow area and collect the ones that had died after release. When all was said and done, twenty-five percent of the total catch survived. The fish that died couldn't stand the combination of the livewells, the handling, and the hot shallow water where the temperature was almost ninety degrees.

"In my experience, most fish and game people are brutal in handling fish. They need to take a lesson from people who are motivated to keep them alive. If it costs me two ounces to bring in a dead fish in a tournament, I'd give the fish mouth-to-mouth resuscitation. *I've seen men do that.* Bureaucrats and fishery biologists don't do that. Seems like they go for 'the big picture' and lose sight of the individual fish."

"Let me tell you something," says Ray emphatically. "If we had rolled over and let them kill those fish, it would have broken the catch-and-release movement. In 1997 when we returned to Jackson for a tournament, Wood was almost afraid to meet me. He said, 'I never thought you'd speak to me.' And I said, 'Man, do you know what you did? You know what you did? You made me more determined than ever. It made us more fervent. Ross Barnett was the turning point. It was gut check time!'" Ray and Avery Wood are friends today.

Catch-and-release had a major impact on both conservation and technology. "In the course of the catch-and-release evolution, guys like Forrest Wood and Don Butler were coming up with new things," Ray says. "Don Butler, the first member and life member of B.A.S.S., designed and patented a practical aerating system for a bass boat. He needs to be credited for being the first man to do that. You can imagine the jackleg schemes the bubbas came up with. They weren't using anything until I gave them an incentive and a one-ounce bonus for every live fish. It didn't take long for the industry to react. Boom! Soon we had livewells in every bass boat — every boat. Boat manufacturers quickly learned they could not give away a boat that had no livewell."

AS PARTICIPATION IN B.A.S.S. tournaments increased, Ray grew more and more concerned about the safety factor of the more than one hundred boats plying the competition waters. Even in their infancy, the tournaments were fertile ground for safety innovations.

Two long-standing B.A.S.S. tournament rules have had a tremendously positive impact on boating safety on and off the tournament trail. One such rule evolved in 1968 when Ray began requiring that every contestant wear a fastened life preserver while his outboard was running. And Ray was proud that B.A.S.S. leadership played a role in the U.S. Coast Guard's later requirement that a Personal Flotation Device (PFD) be on hand for each person aboard a motorboat.

Ray recalls, too, when an enterprising B.A.S.S. angler, Dave Hilton of Dyersburg, Tennessee, rigged what eventually became the first ignition kill switch, at the 1968 tournament held on Alabama's Smith Lake. His ingenious invention was adopted by his peers who wanted a way to turn off their engines should they be thrown from behind the wheel. They knew that a circling, driverless boat was a deadly weapon.

Tournament director Harold Sharp and Ray were so impressed with Hilton's invention that they shared the idea with the marine industry. They were met with stiff resistance, except from Mercury Marine. But they eventually prevailed and today kill switches are standard equipment on most bass boats. Ray and Harold followed up by mandating that a functioning kill switch lanyard be attached to the driver every time the boat was under power at B.A.S.S. tournaments. Each driver demonstrated his kill switch for Harold at boat check-out each tournament morning.

Ray's record as a staunch advocate of boating safety was rewarded with an appointment to the U.S. Coast Guard Boating Safety Advisory Council. From 1976 through 1978, he used that post to lobby for safety reforms such as positive upright and level flotation in boats.

At the time, most boats lacked adequate flotation and some could sink to the bottom in seconds after being swamped. But with upright and level flotation, even a boat that is filled with water can serve as a life raft and perhaps prevent the loss of valuables. The Coast Guard adopted the recommendations and passed them into Federal law and on to the manufacturers.

Concerned about unsafe boating in Alabama, B.A.S.S. worked hard for passage of the 1994 Boating Safety Reform Act. Alabama was the first state to pass such legislation, thanks in large part to the efforts of one man — Charles Grimsley, then Commissioner of Alabama's Department of Conservation and Natural Resources.

"At the time," says Ray, "a six-year-old child could legally operate a two hundred-horsepower boat. People were being slaughtered on the water by disabled, unqualified, incompetent and drunk boat drivers. Charlie Grimsley sent a videotape, that he personally paid to have made, to every member of the legislature in a package as a Christmas gift. 'Open it on Christmas Eve,' he wrote. The videotape was called 'Dead in the

Water,' and in a typical scene a mother holds a doll with blood stains on it and says that is all she has left of her daughter after a boating accident. The bill sailed through the legislature."

Today boat operator certification and testing is required by law and boating safety is being taught in driver's education courses. The concept is spreading to other states. And as far as Ray is concerned, it shows once again what courage and determination on the part of just one individual can accomplish.

As Ray celebrated the thirtieth anniversary of B.A.S.S., he embarked upon yet another safety crusade: getting all boaters to *wear* PFD's *whenever* they're on the water. According to Coast Guard statistics, more than eight hundred people die in recreational boating accidents each year and almost all of those who die aren't wearing life jackets.

Ray says while laws require that a Coast Guard-approved PFD be on board for everyone in a boat, nobody says you have to wear them, or even have one handy, unless you are a contestant in a B.A.S.S. tournament.

"Accidents happen when you least expect them" says Ray, "and when you are least prepared for something to go wrong. In cold water, a person begins to become disoriented in a matter of seconds, and hypothermia very likely will prevent even a strong swimmer from even getting back into the boat. As a matter of fact, hypothermia can kill within twenty minutes when water temperatures are in the fifties.

"I'm convinced that hundreds of lives would be saved each year if people would only wear some sort of Coast Guard-approved life jacket *whenever* they're on the water, whether the big engine is running or not. People fall out of idle boats all the time. Remember, and it may sound obvious, but a life jacket is absolutely worthless unless it is worn. It's too late to grab the vest from under the seat when you're flying out of the boat. Unfortunately most popular foam-type vests are bulky and hot. The truth is, when vests aren't comfortable, people simply won't wear them."

Knowing that, and with the memory of friends who had died in boating accidents while a life vest was securely stowed in the boat, Ray was very interested when a young man from Fruitland, Idaho, approached him with a novel idea: a truly comfortable and truly life-saving PFD.

The innovator was Scott Swanby and over the next ten years Ray would come to have a deep respect for his perseverance and sheer tenacity.

"Thanks in large part to Swanby's efforts over the last decade, the U.S. Coast Guard has finally approved a comfortable life jacket people will actually wear even when they aren't forced to do so."

Swanby's quest began about fourteen years ago, when a close friend drowned while duck hunting. The friend's life jacket was stowed in his boat.

"I had to relay the terrible news to his wife and children," Swanby recalls. "As a result, we went on a mission to find a life jacket that was comfortable for active sportsmen and sportswomen to wear."

He found that product in SOSpenders, a lightweight, compact vest that indeed resembles suspenders and inflates instantly when a tab is pulled activating a built-in CO_2 cartridge. With investors, he founded Sporting Lives, Inc., and bought the company that manufactured SOSpenders. Then he set out to gain Coast Guard approval for inflatable personal flotation devices. The Coast Guard had never approved an inflatable, even though the "Mae West" saved thousands in World War II.

Swanby joined the Personal Flotation Device Manufacturers Association and chaired its Inflatable Committee. It took ten years as he, along with other manufacturers and boating organizations, worked to obtain the Coast Guard's approval which most states require for PFDs. But he didn't sit idly by while waiting for the bureaucratic wheels to begin turning. He traveled to Europe and gained approval for SOSpenders in nineteen countries.

Swanby also traveled to Ray's home in Pintlala and demonstrated his vests for Ray and several B.A.S.S. staffers. Ray slipped into a SOSpenders and jumped into his swimming pool. "I was immediately popped to the surface and my head and face were held very securely out of the water."

Ray was especially impressed because many USCG approved vests, especially foam versions, will not hold a person's head out of the water if he or she is unconscious. And they say so on the label. The SOSpenders unit not only kept Ray's head out of water, it provided nearly three times the buoyancy of the popular conventional foam-type vests.

Immediately Ray knew this could be the single most important development in boating safety since the kill switch and upright flotation in boats. He knew that most people who die in recreational boating accidents are not wearing life jackets and the reason most people don't wear life jackets is because they're hot, bulky and uncomfortable. And they greatly hamper an angler's use of rod and reel.

"I knew it was hard to get people to wear life jackets," says Ray. "That was why ever since the earliest days of conducting B.A.S.S. tournaments, every competitor is required to wear a PFD, zipped up, and with the kill switch fastened to the operator while the outboard's running. Very few boating accidents have occurred during our tournaments over the years, but I know that some would have died had we not strictly enforced those rules."

Ray believes that inflatable PFD's are so compact and comfortable that many people will wear them even when they don't have to and hundreds of lives will be saved every year. The Coast Guard agreed and changed its rules to include these comfortable life preservers as approved PFDs in 1996. They are so unobtrusive that Ray has worn them under his sport coat in public meetings without detection. "I've given them to many of the pro fishermen," he says, "and they've told me they wore them all day. They forgot they even had them on."

Ray admits the SOSpenders are a bit more expensive than the standard, bulky PFD, but adds, "It amazes me that people will spend $20,000 or more on a bass rig and then settle for a $49 life vest. It just doesn't make sense."

Ray marvels at Swanby's tenacity.

"He's like the Energizer Bunny," he says. "And he's an absolute stickler for quality. One day while he was in the middle of water testing some technical aspect of the inflatable, his secretary came to tell him he had a call from a Mr. Spielberg. He told the secretary that he was too busy, he'd call back. His secretary said, 'Mr. Swanby, I think you'd better take this call.'"

It was movie producer Steven Spielberg personally calling to place an order for vests to use while filming. The Hollywood mogul is notorious for his fanatical attention to detail and quality. "That was quite a compliment to Swanby," says Ray.

14

Federations on the Frontline

AS THE SEMINAR team rolled across the country in those early days, they left in their wake a trail of newly formed — and B.A.S.S.-affiliated — bass clubs.

Harold Sharp was the first to recognize a link between B.A.S.S. and bass clubs. For months in 1967 he had been thinking about organizing a Chattanooga bass club like the one Don Butler headed in Tulsa. When he competed in Ray's second tournament at Smith Lake in Alabama and heard Ray's idea about a national bass fishing organization, the spark of an idea became a flame.

In January of 1968, when Ray and Harold emerged from a Chattanooga motel room where they had taken refuge from an ice storm, the two men had hammered out the by-laws for the first B.A.S.S.-affiliated club. Before he left Chattanooga to come to work for B.A.S.S. on November 1, 1970, Harold had started fifteen clubs in the area.

"It's hard to describe the enthusiasm of these early anglers," says Ray. "They were so thrilled to be able to get together with like-minded fishermen. I was always struck by the way a group of guys could sit in a coffee shop for hours at a tournament site and talk about lures and techniques and how to find bass at different times of the day and year.

"There was so much information out there just looking for a forum. *Bassmaster Magazine* really helped fill the void. But these guys went way beyond. It would be like reading a great golf magazine on how to improve your game and then go and play by yourself. It is just human nature to want to interact with others. Nothing replaces that human contact, the face-to-face communication, the sharing — the fellowship. And of course there is the natural urge to compete. I've always believed the whole fishing industry should say a little prayer of thanks every day for bass clubs."

Ray saw that bass clubs were a logical outgrowth of everything he'd done to this point, and that it was time to actively pursue the development of B.A.S.S.-affiliated clubs. B.A.S.S. could provide support in a lot of areas. It just made sense.

He got together with Harold Sharp, Dave Newton, and Barbara Spencer, the savvy, can-do young woman who had made the mistake of guessing the mystery Classic site.

Barbara was appointed "Mama Bass" and given the responsibility of nursemaiding new chapters as they formed and affiliated with B.A.S.S. She had a huge national map in her office and every time a new club affiliated, a loud cheer would go up from her office and a pin was placed, signifying the location of the club. Chapters sent in their club patches which were handsewn to a big green velvet banner. They bore names such as Scales of Justice, Bad Boy Bass Busters, Empty Bucket Bassmasters, and, of course, Happy Hookers.

True to Ray's insights, these chapters first and foremost wanted information from B.A.S.S. They wanted speakers like Roland Martin, Tom Mann, and other angler-heroes. They wanted films, especially of the "how-to" variety. They were starved for knowledge and, not surprisingly, these cravings reached a fever pitch in the dead of winter. Ray quickly learned that this was the time of year when his B.A.S.S. membership soared. Denial intensified the hunger.

"In the beginning the club concept was simply a melting pot for ideas and techniques on fishing," says Ray. "But as more clubs joined, I got more involved personally. I started getting phone calls at night with members telling me about their ideas and what they were thinking, which was great. But then, they started telling me about going fishing and finding some pukey green stuff running into a lake and asking,

'What are you going to do about it, Ray?' I knew I couldn't do it all on my own, so I decided these boys needed to organize into state federations where they could attack state or local problems on their own. Then, when we faced a national issue like the passage of Wallop-Breaux [which provides funds for state fisheries] we could organize the federations behind one B.A.S.S. cannon and fire a shot across the bow of those who were threatening our sport."

"We saw each federation as an intermediary between the local chapters and B.A.S.S. headquarters," says Dave Newton. "We envisioned a state convention every year, with all the federations sending their officers to the national convention, maybe in conjunction with the Classic."

There was the great temptation to put B.A.S.S. chapters under the direct control of B.A.S.S. headquarters. However, Ray was adamant that each federation be autonomous. "I warned Ray that I could see the potential for rebellion because he can be didactic, overbearing at times," Dave says. "Ray could say, 'Here's the plan,' and the assemblage could stand up to him and say, 'No, Ray, we're going to do this instead.' My question to Ray was, 'Aren't you afraid you're setting the stage for the federations to take control away from you?' And Ray said, 'I don't want people to stay in my organization because they *have* to. I want them to follow me because they *want* to. If we lead right, they'll follow.' So it was full speed ahead and damn the threat of rebellion."

THE CHAPTER-FEDERATION-NATIONAL headquarters structure was designed to strengthen the ties in both directions: out to the members, and back to national headquarters. The concept took wing under the enthusiastic leadership of the first Federation director, a personable young Georgia native named Bill McGehee.

The guiding purposes of the new structure were simply a modification of Ray's original set of "The Purposes of B.A.S.S.," which he set forth in the very first issue of *Bassmaster Magazine* under the heading "B.A.S.S. will make you a better fisherman," but also included was the pledge to "find and stop water pollution wherever it exists." Ray instinctively knew that water pollution could put him out of business faster than any other threat. He also pledged to help bring along the next generation of bass anglers. "Take a kid fishing" was a subtext to much of the other activities at B.A.S.S. Kids were the future of B.A.S.S.

These three principal ideas — dissemination of bass fishing knowledge, environmental action, and youth fishing activities — guided the federation concept.

Meanwhile, National Headquarters was being overwhelmed with reports of environmental problems. It was clear to B.A.S.S. that each federation needed to appoint and support an energetic conservation director who would evaluate complaints in his state. In most cases, the problem could be handled on a state basis. A few required a national approach, and when that happened, B.A.S.S. headquarters took the lead.

It wasn't long before the federation system was tested. In 1973 the U.S. Army Corps of Engineers attempted to institute user fees at all its facilities. They planned to charge so much to enter, so much to launch, and even so much to use the toilets.

B.A.S.S. became involved when member Richard Long of Fort Worth called Ray with the details, which he had gleaned from the February 1, 1973, *Federal Register,* the official publication in which government agencies publish proposed rules and regulations. Like Long, Ray was outraged. The taxpayers had paid for the lakes, the launch ramps, the toilets, the picnic tables, and the parking lots. Why should they be forced to continue paying and paying and paying for something they already owned?

Besides, before the Corps came along, there was plentiful public access, free of charge, to the fishing waters later dammed by the Corps. Generations of Americans had accessed the nation's rivers long before the Corps of Engineers began pouring concrete. Now the Corps was proposing to deny free access to a national resource that had always been open.

"I blew the bugle," says Ray, "and Dave Newton and the B.A.S.S. staff took up battle stations against the Corps." Word was passed to each of the twenty-one state federations and in turn, each federation mobilized its clubs — more than six hundred of them by this time — asking members to write their Congressman and Senators protesting the Corps' money-grab.

The Corps was caught off-guard and off-base. In response to a question from the Associated Press, a Corps spokesman said, "Maybe we're trying to discourage so many people from using these facilities. I understand some areas are overcrowded." Ray remembers thinking, "So much for the riff-raff. Price 'em out."

Dave Newton's specialty at B.A.S.S. was writing, although he was nominally in charge of film productions (he wrote and directed the film of the first Classic at Lake Mead, and the first B.A.S.S. how-to film, *Spinnerbait*). Ray instructed him to go after the Corps with bare knuckles. "We characterized the Corps as the 'New Water Barons,'" Newton said, "denying access to public waters to all those citizens who could not pay. We pointed out that often, these were the people who needed access the most, because fishing provided them with much of their diet."

To add insult to injury, Newton revealed in *Bassmaster Magazine*, the Corps decided that "to allow more than fifteen days for public comment would be contrary to the public interest." That fifteen-day period was to expire three days after Mr. Long's call. Congressman Jim Jones of Oklahoma, with help from a few others, got the deadline extended.

"Man, did the public respond!" Ray says. Thousands and thousands of telegrams and letters poured into Corps headquarters, the Congress and the Senate. After a few days, Corps secretaries stopped opening the mail. They knew what was inside. After a few more days, they stopped counting the envelopes. "Thousands" is all they would say when asked for a count.

"Those generals up there in Washington had to feel a close kinship with General Custer," Ray says, "except they're wondering 'where the heck did all these fishermen come from?'" The Senate convened an emergency hearing, and Ray testified as chief spokesman for the fishermen. He suggested that if the senators approved the fees, they should send out news releases stating their support of the fees, and then run on that platform in the next election. He said this to senators who were still digging out from under piles of mail. Not one senator supported the Corps' position.

After one especially bad day in the Senate for the Corps, General John Morris, project manager and the officer most directly on the spot, introduced himself to Ray. He gave Ray his office *and* his home phone numbers, and said, "Please, *please* call me whenever you have a problem and I promise you I will personally handle it."

A year later, Dr. Wayne Shell, dean of the fisheries department at Auburn University, came to ask for Ray's help. He had been frustrated in getting funding for an important $750,000, ten-year baseline study of a new Corps lake under construction on the Chattahoochee River at West Point, on the Georgia-Alabama line. At his last stop at a Corps office, he had been told, "You're wasting your time asking for money."

Dr. Shell came to Ray, hoping the fledgling Bass Research Foundation might be able to help, but to Ray's regret the foundation simply did not have that kind of money. Soon after, Ray was invited to the dedication ceremony of the West Point Dam. Also there, lo and behold, was Ray's former adversary, General John Morris. They met cordially and Ray congratulated the general on the design and plan of the lake.

Ray then reminded Morris that one vital ingredient, important to B.A.S.S. and the public, was missing: $750,000 for Dr. Shell's study. "General, the Corps has turned Dr. Shell down cold," Ray told him. Without the slightest hesitation, General Morris replied, "He's been talking to the wrong man," and the Corps not only ponied up the money, but later increased the amount to $1 million.

Ray fully appreciated the power of properly placed clout from the Federation. And it would serve bass fishermen again and again. Most important it showed any doubters that organized bass fishermen were to be taken seriously. Today the Federation represents more than twenty-seven hundred clubs in forty-six states and eight foreign countries and has more than fifty thousand members. There are federations in Canada, Japan, Zimbabwe, South Africa and Italy. These are the hardest of the hardcore — the diamonds in the crown of the B.A.S.S. membership.

Through many and varied activities, federation members form the backbone of B.A.S.S. environmental efforts. Affiliated chapters within each state and region provide a united voice on issues that affect the quality of natural resources. Pressure from state federations and local clubs was instrumental in the passage of the Sport Fish Restoration Act — also known as Wallop-Breaux. Signed by President Ronald Reagan in 1984, the act established a federal excise tax on fishing and boating equipment with the proceeds channeled to state fisheries agencies to be used in fisheries restoration and access programs.

Each state and international federation has a conservation/natural resource director who is involved with habitat improvement, boating and fishing regulations, and water quality. Conservation directors also serve as watchdogs for legislation that will impact the water resources of their own states. These directors meet annually for seminars and workshops conducted by state and federal fisheries biologists.

Don Corkran, Federation director since 1991, is a retired Army sergeant-major. Under his leadership, the federation has grown by sixty percent, although he credits Bryan Kerchal's Classic victory (the first Classic win by a federation angler) and the federation CASTINGKIDS program for boosting membership.

Hard work and dedication on the part of B.A.S.S. chapters coast to coast are responsible for the success of the CASTINGKIDS competition, which has involved almost a million boys and girls since its inception in 1991. "This is a program we had wanted to get started for years," Corkran explains. "But we simply didn't have the money. Now, thanks to the Federation sponsors, it's possible." (National sponsors are Zebco and Kmart.)

The stated goals of the program are to teach youths better fishing skills, family values, and environmental awareness. But it's the competition that draws the kids. Contestants flip, pitch, and cast a hookless lure at a stationary forty-two-inch target from distances of ten, twenty, and thirty feet. The winners advance to state, regional, and national competition, with the finals taking place during the BASS Masters Classic.

"It's a sight to see," says Ray. "Some of these kids are half the height of their fishing rods. It's fantastic to see them — and their parents — get so involved."

AT THE STATE LEVEL, federations take on service projects of their own.

For example, the Indiana Federation, in cooperation with the U.S. Forest Service, recently built a five-acre pond, complete with handicapped-accessible docks, restrooms, and parking lot, in Bean Blossom. "We needed a place we could take youths as well as physically and mentally challenged people from around the area to fish," says Indiana Federation President Dan Pardue. "Since we couldn't find such a body of water, we built our own." Through its Adopt-an-Angler program, the Indiana Federation also loans fishing tackle and lures to more than twelve hundred children who can't buy their own. The Indiana Federation is also known for its support of the Children's Miracle Network and many other youth-oriented service organizations.

Federation members in Maryland donated a pontoon boat to be used by fisheries biologists to conduct research and to release bass into the Potomac River. They also installed navigational markers on the upper Potomac, making it safer for boaters. And in a highly publicized case, the federation helped uncover an illegal netting operation in which more than forty thousand pounds of largemouth bass were taken from the Potomac River.

In Washington State, the five hundred-member federation campaigns for recognition for warm-water fishing in a state where trout and salmon rule. "Our federation won the National Conservation award three years, mostly for our work with the Department of Fish and Wildlife and the state legislature," says Washington Federation President Jim Owens. "This state is very salmonid-oriented, and for years the warm-water program was only getting table scraps when it came to government funds. We got a warm-water enhancement bill signed by the governor and obtained an extra $1.25 million through a special warm-water stamp."

"When people join a federated bass club, we try to make them understand that they have an inherent responsibility to help protect the resources and preserve the sport of bass fishing," Corkran says. "Those who come in solely to fish tournaments usually don't last long. There are other circuits that allow them to just fish."

However, Ray would never forget the love of sport that created the B.A.S.S. chapters. He knew that a major reason fishermen joined B.A.S.S. clubs was to have the opportunity to fish competitively in their home waters. Ray made an important decision — to allow one Federation member to qualify for the BASS Masters Classic. So in 1974, the winner of the National Federation Championship tournament was invited to the Classic. It was a stroke of genius. Now, these dedicated after-work anglers could aspire to the pinnacle of tournaments — the Classic. It was a long, hard journey but one that many Federation anglers would enthusiastically undertake. Charlie Campbell of Branson, Missouri, was the first Federation contender. Today there are five from the Federation ranks.

To reach the Classic, Federation anglers must qualify for the state tournament via club events. The top twelve anglers from each state compete in one of five divisional tournaments — north, south, east, west, and central — and the angler with the highest total weight from each state in the divisionals qualifies for the Wrangler/B.A.S.S. National Championship. Finally, the top angler from each of the five divisions goes on to compete in the Classic as a Wrangler/Angler, named for their sponsor — Wrangler Rugged Wear. (As a bonus, Wrangler also sponsors each of the five in one of the Bassmaster Invitational tournament circuits the following year.)

Federation fishermen follow this rigorous tournament trail knowing they have a real hope of winning the world's most prestigious bass contest. After all, there is always the Cinderella story of Bryan Kerchal, a young short-order cook from Connecticut who won the 1994 Classic on High Rock Lake, North Carolina [his story follows in the next chapter]. He was the first Federation member to win the Classic and represented the hopes and aspirations of amateurs everywhere. Although Bryan was killed in a plane crash a few months after his win, he still personifies "The Dream."

Others have come oh, so close! In 1986, Danny Correia of Massachusetts finished thirteen ounces behind veteran Charlie Reed of Broken Bow, Oklahoma, and Alabama's Dalton Bobo finished one ounce shy of tying Dion Hibdon after taking a four-ounce penalty for a dead fish in 1997. Gerry Jooste of Zimbabwe is another outstanding Federation fisherman who has earned three Classic bids via the Wrangler/B.A.S.S. National Championship.

Although the B.A.S.S. general membership numbers dwarf the chapter member numbers, the formation of the federations was a milestone in the history of the Society.

Ray recalls how the audience snickered at a Classic Federation Awards Night when he enthusiastically called the Federation the "bowels of B.A.S.S." The snickers turned to roars of laughter. Ray grins at the memory. "I get carried away. My tongue frequently gets ahead of my brain. But everyone knew exactly what I was saying. I was looking for the word 'guts.' Because that's what the Federation is — the guts of B.A.S.S. I could say 'heart' and that would be real pretty. But the type of work — and play — these guys do just ain't pretty. Fishing your way to a Classic is back-breaking work. And not one of them is too proud to pick up the filthiest trash along a river bank or too macho to lift a handicapped kid into a fishing boat."

15

Bryan's Story

THE AFFECTION RAY feels for his tournament fishermen is unmistakable. He will tell anyone who listens that these fishermen are the "salt of the earth, the finest bunch of men under the sun. They'll clobber each other on the water. At the same time, they'll risk their lives to help a competitor in trouble . . . or at the very least, lose precious fishing time to lend a hand."

Every now and then, Ray would spot a rising star, starting with Bill Dance on Beaver Lake in 1967. They had a spark about them. Bryan Kerchal from Newtown, Connecticut, was one of those fishermen.

Young Bryan had twice fished the Classic as a Federation angler, one of five who had qualified through the gauntlet of local, state, and regional tournaments within the B.A.S.S. Federation system. In 1993, at age twenty-two, he finished last, but in 1994 he claimed the championship title. As Ray liked to say, "He went from worst to first."

Ray knew it would happen one day — an "amateur" from the ranks of the B.A.S.S. Federation would win the BASS Masters Classic. Tall, good-looking Bryan with the shy smile made the dream come true. He was the poster boy for every aspiring fisherman.

Ray cried when he found out Bryan Kerchal had been killed in a plane crash December 13, 1994, just four months after he had won the title.

He got the phone call from Federation Director Don Corkran the morning of December 14. Just the evening before, Ray was sitting in a sports grill with his sons Steve and Wilson. On a wall-mounted TV he saw a special news flash about a commuter plane that had crashed in Raleigh, North Carolina. He said a little prayer and returned to his Buffalo wings, little knowing what that news flash would mean.

Bass fishing was more than a hobby for Bryan. It was his passion — even his lifesaver. By his own admission, he was a very confused adolescent, painfully shy and nervous. At the age of eighteen, Bryan found his passion for bass fishing and it gave meaning to his life. It calmed him. He even wrote poetry about fishing:

> The reason I go fishin all by myself
> Is to sort out my problems.
> Put them up on the shelf...
> Sometimes I just sit there
> I sit there and cry.
> Sometimes I sit there
> And let time pass me by.

HE BEGAN FISHING at the age of seven when his grandfather took him fishing on the Fox River in Illinois. He was hooked after he caught a few catfish. When he returned to his Connecticut home, Bryan bought his first spincast rig and went after the bluegill and bass. By all accounts he was a natural.

The Kerchals moved to Newtown when Bryan was about ten. A few years later he started fishing Taunton Lake, a 350-acre pond owned by the Newtown Fish and Game Club. It was about that time that he saw Rick Clunn win the Classic on the Arkansas River on television. He was inspired by Clunn who would later become a friend and mentor. Bryan bought a baitcaster and crank baits and started fishing Lake Taunton from the shore. After his parents provided a small johnboat, he fished the lake almost daily through his middle and high school years. He gave college a try, but the whole semester he was there, according to Bryan, he would read *Bassmaster Magazine* into the night.

When he decided to drop out of college, he knew he needed to get involved in bass fishing on a serious level. Upon his return home, his longtime girlfriend, Suzanne Dignon, encouraged him to join a local bass club. The Housatonic Valley Bassmasters, a B.A.S.S.-affiliated club, had themselves a new member, and bass fishing would soon have a new legend.

In his very first year in the bass club, Bryan qualified for the State B.A.S.S. Federation Tournament as a non-boater. He loved tournament fishing and, to hone his skills, he fished every local tournament he could.

His work paid off. Bryan qualified for the B.A.S.S. Regional event, and, fishing from the back of the boat, he qualified for the Wrangler/B.A.S.S. Federation National Championship on the Arkansas River which would send five "amateurs" to the 1993 Classic. He made the cut by finishing fifth. The kid from Connecticut was on his way to the Classic on Alabama's Lake Logan Martin.

Bryan had a disastrous Classic. It was the first time he had fished an impoundment. His natural nervousness gripped him and he suffered heat exhaustion all three days of practice under the Alabama sun. He was self-conscious fishing among his own personal heroes and the weigh-in before twenty thousand people was an ordeal for a naturally shy person. Bryan told *Bassmaster Magazine* senior writer Tim Tucker, "I got no sleep during that tournament. I thought I was going to go crazy before it was over — the pressure was so great. I thought I was just going to snap."

Bryan finished last in the 1993 Classic.

But Bryan didn't give up. The next year, he fished his way through the grueling Federation system of elimination tournaments and again he qualified for the Classic. He was the first angler to qualify for two consecutive Classics in the Federation system, a remarkable feat, considering that more than thirty thousand amateur anglers compete for the five amateur slots in the Classic's forty-man field. It was a long shot to make it the first time.

Bryan was under a lot of pressure both on and off the water. He fished six Bassmaster Invitational Tournaments and other tournaments, all the while traveling the Federation trail. Money was a constant worry. He had only one significant money-paying sponsor — Greensboro-based Wrangler Rugged Wear. He flipped burgers at the Ground Round Restaurant in Danbury and babied his battered old truck. He concentrated on one thing — Classic XXIV on High Rock Lake near Greensboro.

A different Bryan attended the Classic in August 1994. Only twenty-three years old and still a little shy, he was nonetheless considerably more confident. Most important, he was more comfortable and decided to concentrate on one thing — having a good time. After finishing last in the previous Classic, he had only one way to go and that was up. He was genuinely relaxed.

Bryan's father, Ray Kerchal, told Tommy Tomlinson of the *Charlotte Observer*, "During the last year his personality just blossomed. None of us really knew what happened."

When he practically blanked on pre-practice several weeks before the Classic, he relaxed and took a nap in the boat. When he woke up, he proceeded to catch a five-pound bass on a plastic worm pitched next to a dock piling. He caught six more fish in an hour and a half. The fish were biting at the same place on each dock — he had found the pattern.

ON THE FIRST DAY of the '94 Classic Bryan caught fifteen bass. His total weight for the five he kept was eleven pounds, two ounces and it put him in fourth place. On the second day, he took the lead with another five-bass limit weighing fourteen pounds, one ounce.

On the final day, tournament officials checked the weight of each fisherman's catch as he came in and held back the top contenders for a grand finale. Hopefully the winner would — and usually did — weigh in last. The last two fishermen were Bryan and Tommy Biffle.

Bryan made his three-quarter lap in front of an excited crowd of some twenty-three thousand people. When his boat stopped at the weigh-in platform, he had another five-bass limit. The crowd roared as he pulled the last two up by the lip and held them high. He finished with thirty-six pounds, seven ounces, temporarily leading Biffle by just over nineteen pounds.

Biffle had a great last-day catch, including the tournament lunker of six pounds, eight ounces, Silence gripped the crowd as Biffle's catch was put on the scale. A nineteen on the scale meant Biffle would probably win; an eighteen meant Bryan would win.

The number finally flashed. It was eighteen! Federation angler Bryan Kerchal was officially the 1994 BASS Masters Classic Champion. His grin stretched from one end of Greensboro to the other. An enormous sense of relief swept over him.

But life after the Classic was overwhelming at times. Support from his family, from Suzanne, and from his friends helped him through the dizzying crush of business phone calls, well-wishers, and the press. Although his berth at next year's Classic was assured, Bryan wanted to do well on the Bassmaster Eastern Invitational Circuit and put to rest any whispers of "luck" in winning the Classic. With only one tournament remaining, he was in a good position to qualify for the Classic once again. But first, Bryan had to return to Greensboro to confront his own particular demons and what he considered a serious impediment to his professional success: his fear of public speaking.

Bryan came back to Greensboro for a day-long employee-oriented event for his faithful sponsor, Wrangler Rugged Wear. That afternoon he gave a speech to a large audience and his natural charm and enthusiasm carried the day and overwhelmed whatever jitters he may have felt. It was a good speech. That evening — December 13 — Bryan boarded American Eagle Flight 3379 for the short hop from Greensboro to Raleigh-Durham where he would make a connecting flight to New York LaGuardia Airport and meet Suzanne. He was a nervous flyer.

The plane crashed on its approach to the Raleigh Airport, killing all seventeen passengers and three crew members. An investigation would attribute the crash to a combination of mechanical failure and pilot error.

The fishing world was stunned, especially B.A.S.S. Federation members. Bryan was one of their own. Aspiring fishermen everywhere grieved. He represented the very essence of the impossible dream that comes true with hard work, sacrifice, and persistence.

ON A BRUTALLY COLD December day at a funeral home in Newtown, family, friends, and fishermen gathered. The memorial service turned into a celebration as friend after friend stepped up to speak. Speakers included Federation Director Don Corkran and Ray, who noted that Bryan "in two magical years had gone from worst to first."

Among the speakers at the funeral was one of Bryan's heroes — Rick Clunn. He was philosophical about Bryan's death, believing his contribution in the long run would far out-weigh the tragedy of the present loss. "He once said that I influenced him when he was thirteen years old. He did the same [for others], and he will continue to do so. Every time some kid reads about Bryan Kerchal, he's going to look at Bryan a lot faster than he would at me, and he'll say, 'If he can do it, then I can do it.'"

In his short life, Bryan had realized more dreams than many people achieve in a long lifetime. And he was grateful. Ironically, on the day of his death, a letter from Bryan had arrived and was sitting on Ray's desk. He had sent Bryan some chow-chow relish made from Ray's grandmother's recipe. The letter read:

Dear Ray,

Thank you very much for the gift. To be quite honest with you I've never heard it called Chow-Chow before but it taste great just the same.

Ray, it's always great receiving a gift out of the blue but this gift meant much more to me because it came from you. I watched you on TV and always imagined what a thrill it would be to weigh in fish in one of your tournaments. Not only did I get to weigh fish in but I actually got to hold the crown up by your side.

Ray, I'm just trying to say thanks for pursuing your dream to a reality. It's because of your vision that so many dreams have been spawned and captured. You're truly a great man and it's been one of the greatest thrills of my life just to shake your hand. Good luck with all your great new ideas.

Sincerely,
Bryan Kerchal

The Bryan Kerchal story did not end with the memorial service. His parents, Ray and Ronnie Kerchal, and girlfriend Suzanne, immediately turned mourning into motion. Together they founded and serve on the board of the Bryan V. Kerchal Memorial Fund, along with Don Corkran. The tax-exempt, non-profit corporation promotes activities that encourage young people to fish so they might find the passion and the joy and the peace that Bryan found in fishing.

16

Smart Bass and Smarter Tactics

RAY HAS ALWAYS believed that the largemouth bass has more "smarts" than other species, but he got proof of this from Elgin Ciampi, an award-winning cinematographer, author, and psychologist.

In 1964 Ciampi produced, directed, and filmed *Still Waters,* a classic short film on bass. It is a distillation of thousands of feet of film shot beneath the surface of a Florida largemouth lake. The film netted Ciampi twelve international awards and it enthralled audiences coast to coast on the B.A.S.S. Seminar Tour. Shot in color in totally natural light, the film showcases the incredible life-and-death drama in the natural world of the largemouth bass.

Earlier, in 1961, Ciampi conducted a study testing the intelligence of various fish for *Sports Illustrated.* He spent many hours in the Shedd Aquarium in Chicago ranking fish species as to their "intelligence." He defined intelligence as their wariness in striking a lure. In the process, he found out why different species — especially bass — attack different lures even when they are stuffed with food.

With the cooperation of the aquarium, Ciampi was able to control lighting and feeding conditions that tested the fish in environments that closely simulated their natural habitat. It would be impossible to do this in the wild, but the controlled aquarium habitat was the equivalent of virgin wilderness waters in that no one had ever worked the fish over with lures or flies.

Even so, some species, especially the largemouth and smallmouth bass, were immediately very suspicious of any artificial lures cast to them. By contrast, other species, notably the brook trout, were remarkably slow in learning the difference between real food and imitations. Between tests, Ciampi let the fish go without food for several days, but even then the reactions to the various lures stayed the same for the different species. The largemouth bass was always the most reluctant to go after lures.

Ciampi was convinced that the largemouth bass had a brain superior to those of the other species he tested at the Shedd Aquarium. After repeated tests, the largemouth showed the highest levels of discernment with the smallmouth close behind. As a matter of fact, both species of bass had many behavioral characteristics or traits in common. Along with muskies, the largemouth and smallmouth not only demonstrated the most suspicion but they were the only three species out of the eight tested that would not take an artificial lure after another fish in the tank had struck it. Ciampi's guess was that these species have a communication system of some sort that actually enables them to warn each other of danger.

In the other five species, this ability to communicate, if that is what it is, either did not exist or was not sufficiently developed to be of use. Certainly Ciampi found no indication of it with trout, bluegills or crappies. Ciampi was able to get largemouth and smallmouth bass to strike a lure in his tests, but only once. After that, they would charge the lure, but pull up short and back away, refusing to strike. He had to let the fish rest several days before trying a new lure. The same was true with muskies and northern pike. This may explain the sudden success of a new lure in bass waters. It is successful because the bass do not recognize it as a lure.

In contrast to the bass, several species would strike at anything cast their way, ranging from a bottle cap to a spoon, and they would often hit the same lure a second or third time. Again, the brook trout fell into this category. It took bass only one experience to learn that a lure was not food. The brook trout had to have this drummed into its head two or three times.

As Ciampi tested the fish, he scored their responses; and when the tests were concluded, he ranked their "intelligence." The largemouth was number one and the smallmouth number two. The muskie ranked third and the northern pike fourth. The brook trout was fifth, the bluegill sunfish sixth, the crappie seventh, and the gar eighth and last.

It became obvious to Ciampi that no matter how "smart" or "dumb" the various species were, certain lures definitely had more appeal than others and the appeal depended on three factors: color, the action, and the sound it made in the water.

As a general rule, all species tested showed a preference for lures that closely resembled natural food. But similarity of the color to the natural food was more important in getting a fish to strike than similarity of shape. For example, the keepers at the aquarium regularly fed the muskies goldfish. When Ciampi tested the muskies, they responded best to bright gold lures, even when the shape and size of the lures were not similar to a real goldfish. Although less discriminating feeders such as the brook trout and crappies would often strike at anything, they did show the greatest response to light-colored shiny lures, such as a small spinner. For all fish, the least effective colors were black and dark red. Lures in these colors did not reflect or pick up light, particularly in murky water.

Ciampi found that he could not simply drag a lure back through the water and expect to catch fish. The fish were not interested. But when he altered the retrieve with sharp sporadic jerks, the fish perked up. They really became interested when the sharp sporadic jerks were combined with a regular side-to-side action or flutter.

Sound was also enticing in a lure. If a lure had sound, it was usually an added plus. This was particularly true for largemouth and smallmouth bass. A noisy lure attracted attention because it was utterly foreign to the fish's environment. When a popping bug created a disturbance, fish apparently regarded it not just as a meal but as an annoyance or a threat. This would provoke a fish into striking, even when it was not interested in food. Largemouth and smallmouth bass were the hardest to trick into mistaking a lure for food, but they were the easiest to annoy into striking when a lure entered their territory.

Ray was not surprised. "I credit this reaction of a bass as an indication of his mean spirit and savage reaction to territory invasion by others, including artificial lures."

Ciampi also discovered that even during times of general maximum activity, all fish underwent dormant periods in which they neither moved nor fed. These dormant periods would last from two minutes to two hours. Whatever the duration, the dormant periods came and went with no definable pattern. One minute a bass or a pike might be feeding or on the prowl, and the next minute its fins would barely move and it would suspend near the bottom as though asleep. Not all the fish rested or became dormant at the same time during the day. A largemouth bass might suddenly decide to rest while the other fish in the tank moved about. The moving fish merely ignored the fish that was resting. Ciampi was fascinated to watch a dormant muskie. When a muskie was on the feed, a goldfish thrown into the tank barely had time to move a fin before it was struck. When dormant, however, this same muskie would appear almost oblivious to a goldfish.

The return to periods of activity came suddenly. There was no prolonged wake-up period. As though a bell had rung, activity abruptly resumed, and a lure which seconds before had no appeal, might very well be pursued and hit.

AS A RESULT OF both testing fish at the Shedd Aquarium and his own considerable time spent underwater in the wild observing largemouth bass, Ciampi has five tips to offer fishermen. In his words, they are:

1. Don't believe that a pond or a lake has necessarily been 'fished out.' I have been underwater in lakes and ponds so described, and I have seen bass in them. The fact is the bass have learned to be wary of fishermen and their lures, and the only way to take them is to try the unconventional.

2. Never rely on the built-in action of a lure to catch bass. The more

movement a fisherman gives to a lure by jerking, twitching or bobbing it, the more appealing it will be to the fish.

3. If not successful, use lures that are different from those ordinarily used. If you don't have anything unusual in your tackle box, alter the color or the action, no matter how wild or offbeat the new offering may look.

4. Although it has been said that God does not deduct fishing time from an angler's allotted span, and while it has also been said that you should fish whenever you get the chance, try to avoid the middle of the day with its direct, bright sunlight when fish are relatively inactive. And on overcast days particularly, make sure the lure you use is bright enough to be visible and noisy enough to be heard.

5. If a bass does not strike on the first three casts, change the lure. After three lures, try a different fishing spot. Nine times out of ten, an unproductive cast means the bass are not there or, if they are, they are wise to the fisherman. When they are wise, only a wiser fisherman will catch them.

Ray has always been fascinated with Ciampi's studies and the two have spent hours discussing the nature of the bass. When Ray recently discovered the film *Still Waters* had not been shown in over two decades, he asked Ciampi if he could make the classic available on video. Ciampi granted him the exclusive video rights and Ray has sold many copies especially in conjunction with his video series on creating bass lakes and ponds, *Ray Scott's Guide to Creating Great Small Waters.*

Ray will listen to anyone's philosophy about bass but he reserves the right to his own unique theories — Bass Psychology 101 — on why bass strike a lure. Indeed, he considers "psyching out" the bass just as important — probably more important — than tackle selection and presentation.

Ray's own theory on why a bass strikes a lure and a selection of his own favorite fishing tips and tactics are found in the Appendix.

17

Full Throttle

THE YEARS BETWEEN 1975 and 1985 are a blur to Ray. The decade would bring trials and triumphs, death and divorce. He would also make an important friend, George Bush, while serving as his state campaign chairman in his bid for the 1980 Republican presidential nomination.

B.A.S.S. was exploding, growing from 240,000 members to 420,000 in ten years. Everything grew apace — membership, the tournament trail, the Federation, the Classic, and catch-and-release, not to mention the entire fishing industry with new advances in boat technology and tackle. It was truly a bass boom as the media and Wall Street would proclaim.

In many ways 1975 to 1985 would be the decade of Martin and Clunn. Roland was the 1975 Angler of the Year, a title he had already won three times and would hold five more times in the next ten years. In 1976 Rick Clunn won his first BASS Masters Classic on Lake Guntersville, Alabama, and followed with a repeat win the next year at Lake Tohopekaliga in Florida. He took the title again in 1984 on the Arkansas River. His fourth Classic win was in 1990 on the James River in Virginia.

Classic fishing would prove extraordinarily tough as venues were chosen as much for crowd accommodations as for fishing. In 1983 Larry Nixon won the Classic on the Ohio River with a total weight of eighteen pounds, one ounce. By contrast, in 1984 Rick Clunn scored the highest

Classic total weight of seventy pounds, nine ounces in Pine Bluff, Arkansas.

"B.A.S.S. was like a child you couldn't keep in clothes," says Ray. "Every time we turned around, we needed a new pair of shoes. In 1972 we moved from Mt. Meigs Road in town to the absolute eastern edge of Montgomery — for a century the land had been a cotton field — into our beautiful new brick building on Bell Road. By the end of ten years we had doubled its size and then built another warehouse and office space out back across the parking lot."

Many ideas were born in the Bell Road building. And many ideas were buried as well. "If people think everything I touch turns to gold, they're mistaken," Rays says. "But I'd much rather try and fail than never try at all. And we tried everything. We were in the catalog business for a while in the early days and actually thought we were in competition — for about a minute — with Johnny Morris's Bass Pro Shops.

"We also successfully sold our own fully rigged Classic Ranger Boats and an aluminum boat for a number of years. That was when a fully factory-rigged boat was quite an innovation. We also started a franchise of hunting and fishing stores called The Outhouse, which did quite well for a while too, especially the one in Montgomery. Then I got real creative and built a beautiful catfish pond across the road so city folks and kids could fish. It was a real nice facility and a neat concept. People were charged for the pounds they caught. I'll never forget the mother who dropped off her ten-year-old boy while she went shopping — kind of cheap and convenient baby-sitting, she thought. Well, she had a whopping $90 bill and a big mess of catfish waiting when she came to pick him up. But the juices were always flowing and everyone was encouraged to have ideas."

Susan Scott recalls staff meetings in those years. "Ray's staff meetings were raucous. He did everything but buck dance on the conference table. You always left invigorated, motivated, full of ideas. He was very open to new ideas and didn't mind being challenged. I was always impressed that he was never afraid to take very strong political and environmental stands, even if it meant short-term losses. He was always aware, even on a subconscious level, that he was creating the very character of B.A.S.S."

Ray was not the easiest person to work with. He was impatient and could lose his temper. For many years he had a wonderful secretary named Jane Rudd. She was a highly competent and spirited lady from Oklahoma who could stand up to Ray most of the time. Sometimes, however, she would slam his office door and have to walk outside for a while. She told her successor, Genaé Jones, that Ray was the most aggravating, unreasonable, and infuriating man she had ever worked for — and also the finest. At five feet, two inches, the elegant Genaé had to look up to Ray, but she stood her ground as well.

"Boy, have I been lucky," says Ray. "I've had the greatest women to keep me straight. I've got another one now, named Jenny Olive. I can rant and rave and she stays calm and cool. She's raised three boys, so I guess she just considers me 'another one of her boys.'"

The year 1985 brought another milestone in the history of B.A.S.S., the creation of the successful television series, "The Bassmasters," which debuted on The Nashville Network and became its No. 1 fishing show. Bob Cobb was the producer. After fifteen years at the helm of *Bassmaster Magazine*, he brought the same quality to the television series for more than twelve years.

"We pried Bob's hands away from his manual typewriter," says Ray, "and changed the lock on his file-filled office. We put a video camera in his hand instead, and the rest is history. Fortunately, we already had Dave Precht on the B.A.S.S. staff to take over the *Bassmaster Magazine* responsibilities. He didn't miss a beat. Bob and Dave are the only two who have edited *Bassmaster* in all these years, except for my amateur efforts the first two years."

BY 1973 RAY AND his family had comfortably settled in a handsome, new house in an upscale area of ten-acre lots only a mile or so from B.A.S.S. headquarters. Eunice and the kids enjoyed their spacious new home. The three children completed high school in Montgomery and all went on to attend and graduate from Auburn University with degrees in business.

According to Ray, his family was resigned to his total dedication to his business.

"If you asked them today," he says ruefully, "they would say they had no choice. I lived and breathed B.A.S.S. I would come home late and then be back at work at 4:30 in the morning. I'd stop and have breakfast at an all-night Krystal with the same old group of insomniacs."

Naturally, Ray's new home was built on bass waters — a seven-acre lake he designed. And, according to his very exacting specifications, the house was literally at water's edge. "I wanted to lie in bed in the morning and watch the ducks swim by my window."

Built and stocked for bass and bluegill, the lake was not only his pride and joy but his classroom as well. "I learned about lake design and ecosystems on a firsthand basis," he says. "I made every mistake in the book. But I also did a lot of things right. And I sure found out nobody — I mean nobody — had put all the pieces together in building a proper bass lake. It was a good experience, because my frustration led me years later to produce my very own video series on how to build great small fishing waters."

Ray spent a lot of time and effort on his lake. So it was with horror when he woke up one morning and found his fish were dying. "They didn't just die all at once," says Ray, "like in an oxygen kill. They died that day, they died the next day and the day after. I noticed that every fish died with the pelvic fins straight out. I also remembered that the day before the dead fish began to show up, I had a very bad headache, a low-grade full-blown headache. My wife did, too. I don't know what possessed me to do it, but I got in touch with Dr. John Lawrence, a toxicologist at Auburn University, who asked that I bring a few of the fish to him in a cooler."

Dr. Lawrence ground up the fatty tissues in the fish, analyzed them, and determined that the cause of death was endrin, a pesticide sprayed on cotton and other crops and absolutely deadly to fish. In one of Ray's favorite books, *Silent Spring,* Rachel Carson wrote that, "In Louisiana thirty or more instances of heavy fish mortality occurred in one year alone (1960) because of the use of endrin on sugarcane fields. In

Pennsylvania, fish have been killed in number by endrin, used in orchards to combat mice."

It didn't take long for Ray to figure out the source of the endrin that killed his bass. There was a cotton field only half a mile away from the lake, and while sitting on the dock or out in his boat, Ray had often waved to the crop duster flying low over the lake. He had no idea who the crop duster was, or where he came from, but he asked Dave Newton to help him find out.

They didn't have long to wait. Three days later, about an hour before sunset, the crop duster appeared over the cotton field and began spraying. When the plane turned to leave, Dave jumped into his pickup truck and "followed him like I was following a honeybee back to the hive."

The chase ended five miles away. Just before the sun set, Dave watched the crop duster scoot the plane through an opening in the trees down onto a secluded dirt landing field with woods on three sides. Dave says, "There was no time to do anything that night, and so the next afternoon we went back. I'll be honest with you, I didn't want to go back out there, but Ray insisted. I thought, well, if they're going to kill somebody, I'll get behind Ray and they'll shoot him first, and maybe I can get away in the confusion."

The next day, late in the afternoon, the two of them went to the landing field. "We snuck in there with a camera," Ray says. "There were all these barrels, some of them empty, marked with a skull and crossbones and warning notices."

"It was a nasty looking area," says Dave, "a chemical nightmare with not only endrin, but all kinds of other herbicides and pesticides. It was a quagmire of chemicals. A lot of stuff had leaked out or been spilled on the ground, just what you might expect at a clandestine chemical site. There was no cover over any of it. He was very clearly not following federal regulations on chemicals, which even back then were very involved. I promise you that if we could go back today to that area of that field, it would still be barren."

Ray took pictures of the mess, and then he and Dave climbed onto the wing of the plane and began searching the cockpit for the certification papers. Federal Aviation Administration regulations require that the papers remain in the plane. They were going through the papers getting the owner's name — it was Lorenz Grubbs — and address when suddenly they heard a vehicle coming.

"It was Grubbs himself, and he looked like he'd been soaked in chemicals too long," Dave says. "He was about fifty-five years old, a big, burly guy, six feet, two hundred fifty pounds, with a splotchy red and white face and a crew cut with warts growing up inside the hairs. After years of inhaling endrin and whatever else he was spraying, you can imagine what that would do to your complexion. He was almost like a character out of *Deliverance,* really a menacing figure. And he threatened to kill us, literally, if we didn't get off his property. No bones about it. He didn't have a weapon visible, but he did have a wrench, and he cussed us out, and said, 'Get off of this property. You got no business here, and don't you ever come back.'"

"Listen, fella," Ray said, "we're here representing the newspaper, and we're gonna expose what you're doing." That set Grubbs off even more, but Ray and Newton got away safely.

"Dave Newton then had the wisdom to know that Grubbs had to have a log book that recorded when and where he sprayed." Ray says. "We later subpoenaed the flight records and then compared them to the day, hour, wind, and site. We found that the day before the bass started dying in my lake, the winds came straight toward my house." Never one to suffer in silence, Ray sent out news releases to the local press and started looking for a lawyer.

A powerful local family, the McLemores, owned the cotton field, and one law firm after another in Montgomery refused to take Ray's case. But he didn't give up. The crop duster had killed his fish, and he wanted compensation, he wanted justice. "Nobody wanted to touch the case. No one wanted to cross the McLemores." At the suggestion of his friend Morris Dees, Ray called Tommy Thagard, a local lawyer with a bulldog reputation.

"Ray," said Thagard, "let me tell you what happened two nights ago. I was at a party in Montgomery, and I overheard a guest ask Billy

McLemore, 'What are you going to do about killing Ray Scott's fish?" And McLemore said, 'I don't give a hoot about his fish. I've got a farm to run, cotton and cattle to raise.' After having heard that, I'll take the case."

Ray sued Billy McLemore, Ring-Around Products, the endrin manufacturer, and the crop duster for $100,000 and ended up settling for $10,000 and an agreement that McLemore would never have a crop duster fly near his property ever again. Ray says, "And I never saw one again." In January 1999, Ray ran into Billy McLemore at a restaurant, and they both had a quasi-laugh over the incident after McLemore was asked if he had ever used endrin again. Given all the chemicals that Grubbs was breathing every day, it was no surprise to learn from McLemore that the crop duster died of cancer.

RAY HAD ANOTHER interesting legal battle in this period that he likes to refer to as "the toilet wars."

From the beginning, Ray had excluded women from entering his tournaments, not out of chauvinism but for the highly specific reason relating to what he described as the "sanctity of the catch." Paranoia would be too mild a term to describe Ray's fear of cheating. That was why contestants, according to the rules, were not allowed to leave the boat for any reason other than a dire emergency. Nor could a contestant lose sight of his partner or his catch at any time. Therefore all bathroom functions had to take place from the boat. Going to the bathroom was definitely not, and never would be, considered a dire emergency. And all chivalrous notions on the part of the male angler had to be forgotten for the duration of the tournament. Ray decided early on to spare everyone the indignity of the "toilet situation" that could arise when a woman was paired with a man in a necessarily random draw of partners.

For years it was not much of a problem. However, it was only a matter of time before B.A.S.S. would be challenged, especially in the environment of the seventies. The challenge came from a female B.A.S.S. member in New York who wanted to fish the B.A.S.S. Invitational Tournament at Thousand Islands in Alexandria Bay, New York. The

ACLU filed for an injunction to stop the tournament unless she could fish. Just three days before the start of the event, an old Roosevelt-appointee judge on the New York Supreme Court heard the case. The ACLU had six lawyers; Ray Scott had one inexpensive one.

"The old judge listened to both sides," says Ray. "I made my case for tournament security and sexual privacy. Now the judge was no bass man. My lawyer showed an overview photo of a bass boat and the judge asked, 'Where's the head?' I said, 'There is no head, judge, it's just an open boat, eighteen feet long.' He was quiet and said, 'I'll give you my ruling tomorrow.'"

The next day the judge presented an envelope to each lawyer. We opened the envelopes and found the judge had ruled against the woman and the ACLU on the grounds of "sexual privacy."

In 1987, a year after Ray sold B.A.S.S., the Corps of Engineers threatened to ban B.A.S.S. from Corps lakes unless women were allowed to fish in B.A.S.S. Tournaments. The new B.A.S.S. management did not object or appeal the ruling. The gates were open for women contestants.

Surprisingly, or maybe not so surprisingly, the people who were most upset were the fishermen's wives. "They were in an uproar," recalls Ray. "Letters were flying and wives were calling me, begging me to do something. But the whole thing ended up being a tempest in a teapot. We worked out some simple guidelines whereby women would be paired with willing fishermen. And the women understood the rules of not leaving the boat. However, there was no pent-up demand on the part of women to participate in B.A.S.S. Tournaments. We have less than one-half woman per tournament. Of course, there are fantastic women anglers out there. There used to be a woman's tour and I wish there was one again, like there is a woman's tour for golf and tennis."

IT WAS ALSO DURING this decade (1975-1985) that Ray worked on the passage of the Wallop-Breaux amendments for the Sport Fishing Restoration Act. The amendments established a federal excise tax on fuel and an expanded universe of fishing tackle and related items, with the revenues "dedicated" and returned to the states for fisheries restoration and access programs. With passage of the amendments, Wallop-Breaux monies increased from $35 million annually to $102 million annually. The expansion program was the biggest boon ever for anglers and has allowed states to better protect and improve their fisheries.

Ray helped draft the legislation and took on the task of pushing the amendments on behalf of B.A.S.S. and fishermen everywhere. He was confident the task could be accomplished in a couple of visits to Washington — he wasn't called silver-tongued for nothing.

He was wrong and the experience has made him leery of red tape and bureaucrats to this day. "It took seven years," he says disbelievingly. "For seven years, I would fly up to Washington regularly, frequently with our Federation Director Bob Barker. He had the patience of Job, thank God. We also worked with a wonderful man named Carl Sullivan who was head of the American Fisheries Society. Sometimes he'd sleep in our hotel room on the sofa instead of making a late commute to the suburbs. I'd be cussing out every polite, pass-the-buck bureaucrat I'd talked to that day. Carl really helped me hang in there. Finally, things began to turn around when I had a friend in Vice President George Bush.

"I'll never know for sure what happened. Doors were slammed in my face again and again. For three weeks I tried to see Congressman John Breaux, of Louisiana, chairman of the House Subcommittee handling the legislation. I couldn't even make it through the secretary. It was a classic stonewall." Ray would later find out that the National Marine Manufacturers Association (NMMA), which he promptly dubbed "enema," was lobbying to block the legislation, fearful of additional taxes on marine products.

Out of frustration and in a last-ditch effort, Ray called his buddy George Bush and explained his dilemma. "Bush just said, 'Let me see what I can do.' The next day I called Congressman's Breaux's office and the secretary said, 'Oh, Mr. Scott, when can you come by?' I immediately went to the congressman's office and was cordially greeted. Over a cup of coffee in his private office, I started to explain the benefits of the proposed legislation, which was then called Dingell-Johnson, and Breaux said, 'I know all about it.' I asked, 'how do you know?' Breaux said,

'Because I was called out of a committee meeting yesterday by Vice President Bush. He told me all about the legislation. What can I do to help?' From then on it was downhill toward passage. President Reagan signed the legislation into law in 1984. Every fisherman in the country owes a debt of gratitude to George Bush. This is just one of hundreds of similar actions by George Bush that no one will ever know about."

RAY DOES NOT consider himself an internationalist but he did get into another interesting bass battle in the 1970s. And although it's hard to imagine that bass fishing could become an international political issue, it did after Ray came face to face with the grim realities of Soviet communism. Oddly enough, however, the actual battleground was an ocean away from Russia, in Cuba, a historical fishing mecca.

Cuba has long had the reputation of having the biggest largemouths on the planet, humongous fish that would top — even dwarf — the world record twenty-two pound, four ounce fish caught in 1932 by George Perry in Montgomery Lake, Georgia. Bass are not native to the balmy, tropical island, but were first brought from Florida in 1915 and then again in the 1930s, the latter time by the Texans who owned the King Ranch and had extensive landholdings in Cuba.

In 1959, after Fidel Castro took power, the Eisenhower administration imposed travel restrictions to Cuba but that didn't stop fishermen, among them Ray Scott, from dreaming about fishing there. In the early 1970s, Ray, Bob Cobb, Harold Sharp, Dave Newton, and biologist Sam Spencer got permission from the State Department to go to Cuba. Ray was eager to find and to identify the sub-species of bass in Treasure Lake — were they truly the Florida largemouth, *Micropterus salmoides floridanus?* And he had written to Cuba's National Institute of Sports about the possibility of breaking the world record. The Cuban government not only failed to give its okay, it never even bothered to answer.

In 1977, the Carter administration eased the travel restrictions, and Ray got a call from Dan Snow, who had been director of the short-lived B.A.S.S. tour enterprise in 1974-75 and who had since opened his own Latin American fishing tour business based in Houston. Snow asked his old boss if he would like to take part in a bass tournament in Cuba the following January. An American team would compete against a team of Cuban fishermen on fabled Treasure Lake.

"Man, put me down for that!" exclaimed Ray, who could hardly wait to finally fish in Cuba.

But before flying off to Cuba in February, Ray had another trip to make. He and Eunice joined bass pro Pete Nosser and his wife from Vicksburg, Mississippi, on a cruise of the Baltic Sea. After touching lively ports in Denmark, Sweden, and Finland, the ship dropped anchor in Leningrad where Ray arranged for the four of them to have a private dinner and an interpreter to take them on a tour of the city, which has since reverted to its pre-communist name of St. Petersburg.

"St. Petersburg is a beautiful city built by Peter the Great," Ray says, "but it was extraordinarily grim with no life, no spark, to it. All I saw on people's faces was despair and hopelessness, or just blankness. When we passed several churches that were covered with scaffolding, our interpreter said, 'Under restoration.' Finally, we came to another church, and after the interpreter said, 'Under restoration' again, I said, 'Stop the car.' We stopped.

"The church was covered with high scaffolding, like the kind I fell from when I was nineteen. I looked at it closely, and there were no signs of any building materials, and there were no workers running around. The pipes in the scaffolding were rusting, and rust was running down the stone walls. I said, 'This church is not under restoration. It's closed.' And the interpreter gave me a cold look and said, 'Churches are for old people.'

"That's when it all really hit me. It was another epiphany," Ray says. "To understand the communist economic system is one thing. But when you realize the government takes away God as well, that is another issue entirely. To imagine these people deprived of the comfort and hope of religious faith under a system that already crushes the human spirit is chilling.

"I realized on the way home, there was no way Ray Scott was going to fish in Cuba while Castro was a proxy for the Soviet Union, for this miserable system."

Back in Montgomery, Ray called Snow to say that after his visit to Leningrad, he could not in good conscience go to Communist Cuba. He apologized to Snow for canceling, but that was the way he felt. He also phoned Forrest Wood, Tom Mann, Bill Dance, Rayo Breckenridge, Hugh Massey, and Bobby Murray who were planning to fish the Treasure Lake tournament to explain why he had decided not to go. He told them Castro had thirty thousand troops in Angola, and the Cubans were plotting revolutions in Latin America. They cancelled out, but other pros went.

In the March-April 1978 issue of *Bassmaster Magazine*, under the headline of, "Are You Willing To Trade Bass For Communist Bullets," Ray appealed to all 270,000 members of B.A.S.S. by writing, "It may be difficult to imagine something as American as bass fishing being caught in the crossfire of international politics. But that's what's happening. The good old American bass, when caught in Cuba, may turn out to be a red herring served up with a topping of Russian dressing. American sport fishermen are being lured to Cuba to help bolster Fidel Castro's crumbling economy. An economy whose main purchase is bullets which will be used to further escalation of Communism, especially in Africa and Latin America."

With his usual zeal, Ray maintained his stand through the Reagan and Bush administrations, and indeed Reagan tightened restrictions on travel to Cuba.

He has grudgingly backed off the issue after the collapse of the Soviet Union in 1989. "I know Castro's a paper tiger now, but the Cubans are still suffering under his miserable system. Nobody can make me like the guy and I despise the philosophy he represents."

FOR AN ACTION-ORIENTED and often impatient man, Ray does have a profound sense of history, especially in unique areas that interest him. He will burrow into a subject with a single-minded intensity. He saves newspaper front pages of events he deems historical, and he'll pore over vintage photographs for hours, no matter whose they are.

He is passionately interested in documenting bass fishing history and one of the greatest pieces of bass fishing lore, he knew, was the story of George Perry and the still-standing world record bass of twenty-two pounds, four ounces he caught in Montgomery Lake, Georgia, on June 2, 1932. Every bass man knows the stats. The fish was weighed on a grocery scale and then, it being the depths of the Depression, the fish was promptly eaten.

After many interviews by many people, few doubted the veracity of the catch, not even a skeptical Ray. Nonetheless, for posterity's sake, before the aging Perry was gone, Ray wanted to verify the catch once and for all. To that end, he dispatched Bob Cobb's editorial assistant, Terry Drace, to interview Perry for the definitive story and, more important, to ask Perry to take a polygraph test to satisfy the naysayers. Drace made the trip and Ray couldn't wait to see if Perry would take the test.

Drace returned and told him, "Ray, I know that man is telling the truth. I just didn't think it was necessary to ask him to take the polygraph test." Ray was dumbfounded. Drace had missed the point entirely. Unfortunately the opportunity would never present itself again. George Perry died in a plane crash a little over a week later near Birmingham and Drace moved on to other pastures.

ON THE MORNING of February 16,1981, Ray got a call from his mother Matt. She was distraught but not hysterical. She had gone to check on Bud and he could not be roused. He had died peacefully in his sleep of heart failure at the age of seventy-four. Ray did not cry. "I've never cried over my father. I never had any unresolved issues with my Dad. He was the man I admired most in my life and I sure know where he is now. I just have no regrets. When I think of him, it is with such joy and gratitude."

Much more painful was Ray's divorce in 1983. "Maybe my Dad's death did have something to do with it. You realize how precious and fragile life is. The loss of a parent makes you take a long, hard look at what's important and what's left of your life. I think my father's death made me slow down for a minute. I realized my dedication to B.A.S.S. had taken its toll on my marriage. It's like I lost fifteen years somewhere. Eunice and I lived in two different worlds. I was blowin' and goin' with B.A.S.S. and she was blowin' and goin' with the house and kids and did a fantastic job. When my Dad died and all the kids were out of the nest and I stopped spinning for a minute, my world was so far away from hers. I guess it's a lesson a lot of men learn the hard way.

"I'm glad to see my kids stay so in touch with their spouses and children. I was from the generation where the man went out and did his thing rain or shine. Providing for your family was a very physical thing, not so much an emotional one. Plus, I have to say B.A.S.S. was a passion . . . an obsession. It wasn't just about bringing home the bacon, and it involved much more than making a lot of money. It had — and still has — facets that influence and direct my life. B.A.S.S. was indeed my 'calling' and in a way, I paid a price for that. I had a single-minded focus. I really don't know how to do things any other way. I never did."

The two years following his divorce were the most difficult of his life. He moved into a small town house surrounded by high brick walls. Many weekends, he never even left his "cave." His work was a welcome diversion. He had friends who were concerned about him. One was George Bush.

18

The Making of a Vice President

I N THE SPRING OF 1979, Charles Snider, a prominent Montgomery public relations man and political consultant, called Ray
and said, "I want you to have breakfast with George Bush."

"Who is George Bush?" Ray asked.

"Well, he's from Houston and thinking of running for President,"
Snider said.

"You better scratch me on this one," Ray said, suspecting the
breakfast was going to be a glorified fundraiser. "I'm sure I'm going to be
busy whenever breakfast is going to be."

A few weeks later, Snider called again and urged Ray to meet Bush
who was going to be in Montgomery in two weeks. Ray said he would do
it if he could have fifteen minutes to speak to Bush about environmental
issues, especially the Dingell-Johnson bill. After Snider checked with
Bush's campaign chairman, James Baker, he said it would be all right.

Ray then called Dave Precht, the B.A.S.S. News Service director, into
his office. Dave was formerly from Houston. "Tell me about this guy
George Bush," said Ray.

"Well, Bush has a lot going for him," Precht said. "He was a member
of Congress, the head of the CIA, a former chairman of the Republican
Party, and the first U.S. envoy to Red China. And he's a very honest man
who's well respected in Houston."

On the appointed day, Ray and Dave Precht went downtown to meet

Charles Snider at the Madison Hotel. They took the elevator to the fourth floor and met Bush in a small suite. "We visited for about thirty-five to forty minutes, during which time I dominated the conversation," Ray recalls. "I guess that was regrettable in one way, but in another way it wasn't, because I told him about the legislation I was trying to push — the Dingell-Johnson Bill, which later became the Wallop-Breaux Bill.

"We wanted nothing more than Congress to expand a dedicated excise tax on fishing tackle and boat-related products. We were having a terrible time trying to push this. In fact, we hadn't gotten anywhere with it. I told Bush that I had gone to Washington time and again, thinking that I could get Congress to enact this excise tax in a heartbeat, but instead it was a heartache.

"Bush looked at me and said, 'Well, as President I can support that because it is a user-pay tax. The fisherman is going to be paying the tax, and the tax benefits fishing.' Boy, I was glad to hear that."

Dave and Ray followed Bush downstairs where he stumbled through a sparsely attended news conference. Ray's eyes wandered around the room, and he noticed a dapper man who looked kind of out of place. "Who's that guy?" Ray whispered to Precht, nodding in the dapper Dan's direction. "I don't know," Precht said. "Well, go find out," Ray said.

Precht returned a minute later. "His name is Jim Baker. He's Bush's campaign chairman," he told Ray. Four days later, Baker called Charles Snider and Snider relayed an invitation from Baker: Would Ray consider being Bush's Alabama state chairman?

"Why Ray?" asks Snider, who knew Ray as a boy. "Second only to Bill France, Sr., of NASCAR, Ray is the greatest promoter I'd ever been around. He had tremendous energy and he had not been involved politically, so he was not tainted."

Bush says, "I selected Ray Scott because he's a go-getter. Others might know more about precinct politics, but none was more loyal or more energetic. Ray knows how to organize and how to take on the tough tasks."

Snider adds, "I also remember that when Ray was going to be

fourteen, he told Earl Murchison, a friend of his, that if Murchison could get Ray's mother to hold a surprise birthday party for him, he would split all the presents with him. About forty kids showed up at the party. That's what we wanted — people to show up.'"

RAY ACCEPTED THE chairmanship, and that October Bush came to campaign in Alabama. His trip coincided with the homecoming game at Auburn, and Ray and Bush attended, along with a plain-clothes highway patrolman. "We had private parking near the elevator in the stadium," he says, "and we went up and took our seats on the fifty-yard line. Unknown to Bush, I had employed the services of an airplane to fly above the stadium pulling a banner that said, 'George Bush for President.' The plane circled around and around, and I nudged Bush, who was sitting to my left, and said, 'Look up there.' He glanced up, saw the sign and said, 'Isn't that interesting. How did that happen?' I said, 'Well, just doing our job.' He got a chuckle and so did I. What was funny was when a lady sitting to my right in the next row down looked up at the plane and said to her husband, 'Who is George Bush?'

"Just after the second half got started, I saw George take his right hand and brush his neck, right above his necktie and collar. He said, 'Ray, do you see a bug or bee anywhere on me?' I looked closely and didn't see anything, all the time remembering that he was highly allergic to bee stings and that he always carried a little bee sting kit with him in the event he was stung. As fate would have it, that kit was in his suitcase back at my house in Montgomery. We went back to watching the game, but every now and then I'd glance to my left. After a few minutes I noticed a big round circle about the size of a silver dollar developing on the right side of his neck. I leaned over and whispered, 'George, we've got to go. You have a big circle developing on your neck. You've been bitten or stung.' I nudged the highway patrolman and we quietly got up, got in the car and went straight to East Alabama Hospital, about ten minutes away between Auburn and Opelika. They didn't know who George Bush was anymore than the lady sitting in front of me, but they took him in quickly.

"By now he had enormous welts, about the size of hen eggs, breaking out on his body, particularly his chest and the top of his shoulders. I had sense enough to realize that this could be a very serious experience if not treated immediately. They gave him a couple of shots, and in a matter of fifteen minutes the welts subsided. There's always the danger that if the welts develop in the throat, they can cause suffocation. Fortunately, it happened in the right place at the right time with a highway patrolman on hand, and we weren't caught in a traffic jam after the game. Nor did we have to stop for a flat tire.

"That night, back at our home in Montgomery, Eunice and I had a reception for a couple of hundred people to meet Bush. After they all left, Bush and I took a stroll out to the lakeside patio where he spotted my hot tub. He asked, 'What is that?' I said, 'That's a hot tub.' He said, 'You know, I've heard of them, but I've never been in one. Could we get in that hot tub before we go to bed?' I said, 'You bet.'

"It was a beautiful night with just a touch of fall in the air and the sky full of stars, as we slipped into the hot tub. I turned the eggbeaters on, and they churned us around for about fifteen minutes. It was highly relaxing, but we were soon medium rare. We climbed out and sat on the side of the tub with the agitator turned off, our feet dangling in the tub. Out of nowhere, I don't know what possessed me, but I said, 'George, I've decided what it is that I want after we get you in the Big House.' He asked, 'What do you want, to be ambassador to New Zealand where all that great fishing is?' With a straight face, I said, 'No, that's not what I want. What I want is something a lot more serious.' He became serious himself and said, 'Well, what do you have in mind?' I said, 'What I want, when you get in the White House as President, is for me to bring my wife up to the White House and sleep in Lincoln's bed.' He started laughing and said, 'I don't even know if Lincoln has a bed up there. I've never even been in that part of the White House.' We both laughed and that was the end of that for the time being."

JUGGERNAUT RONALD REAGAN won the 1980 Alabama primary, but Bush came second with a full third of the convention delegates.

When Ray got to Detroit for the Republican Convention, he quickly found that the best seats went to delegates from states that were historically faithful to the party. Yellow Dog Democrat Alabama was not in that category. As a result, the Alabama delegation found itself way in the back of the hall next to the toilets. Ray's seat was next to the ladies room, and every time the door swung open it obstructed his view of the podium. There was a constant parade of women. Ray says, "Some went in there two or three times an hour, and it got to the point where I knew them by name."

After Reagan won the nomination, Bush's advisors sent word to his state chairmen that they were not to stage any demonstrations or do anything to promote Bush for the vice presidency. Meanwhile, Jack Kemp's backers were doing all they could to promote their man for second place on the ticket. When Kemp spoke, his delegates waved placards that said, "Kemp for VP." Bush was to address the convention the next night and Ray says, "I thought to myself, why in the devil should we work a year and a half trying to get Bush elected and not even be able to promote him for the second spot?"

Ray got up and walked to the front of the podium next to the Michigan delegation. Henry Kissinger was speaking as Ray bent low and asked one of the Michigan delegates, "Who is the Bush chairman of your delegation?" "Lorette Ruppe," he said, pointing her out to Ray.

Ray edged his way toward her, and there just happened to be an empty seat next to her. Ray stepped over a couple of people, sat down in the empty seat and introduced himself by saying, "Mrs. Ruppe, my name is Ray Scott. I'm from Alabama."

"Oh, I know you," Mrs. Ruppe said. "You're the fisherman. George Bush told me about you. What's going on?"

Ray said, "Well, tomorrow night George Bush is supposed to be speaking. The last word I got, he didn't want us to demonstrate or do anything to promote his vice presidency."

"I know," she said. "I got the same message."

Ray said, "Well I don't know how you feel, but I have been working a year and a half and I'm not ready to quit without a heck of a celebration."

"I feel exactly the same way," she said. "Do you have any ideas?"

Ray said, "I've got the perfect idea. When can we talk about it?"

"How about right now? We can go backstage."

Mrs. Ruppe stood up, snapped her fingers at two young men in their late twenties, and tilted her head back. They got up and followed her and Ray into a corridor outside the back of the hall.

Turning to the two young men, Mrs. Ruppe said, "This is Ray Scott from Alabama, and he has an idea for tomorrow night — a demonstration on behalf of George Bush. Tell us about it, Ray."

Actually, Ray didn't have a clue, but he was inspired to start talking. "I know what will work," he said. "First we'll have to have 850 placards."

"No problem," said one of the young men. "We can handle that."

Ray went on, "Back and front, either way you look, the placards should have variations of 'Bush for Vice-President,' 'Bush for Veep,' 'Let's Go with Bush,' 'Bush for V President.' They all need to be creative and hand-painted, not printed like Kemp's. These need to be original-looking pieces."

"No problem," the young man said.

Ray said, "We need them finished by three o'clock tomorrow afternoon."

"No problem," the young man said.

"Ray, what else do you need?" asked Mrs. Ruppe.

Ray said, "We need thirteen men."

"No problem," the young man said. "What are they going to do?"

Ray said, "They are going to distribute the placards into the hands of all the delegates twenty minutes before Bush speaks. Everybody wants to play and have fun at a convention. Everybody wants to get in on the act. Give 'em all a placard, and they'll use it."

"What else do you need?" Mrs. Ruppe asked.

"Thirteen aerosol boat horns," Ray said. "You mash the little thing on top and they make an incredible sound."

"No problem," the young man said. "I know where I can get those."

"What in the world are those for?" asked Mrs. Ruppe, giving Ray a quizzical look.

Ray said, "I'm going to be way up in the balcony, in the nose bleed section, and I'm going to be watching and listening to everything that's going on. I want at least a dozen of these horns in different sections on the floor to be operated by our helpers. When the demonstration starts to calm down, I'm going to blow my horn up in the attic and that is the cue for everybody else to blow their horn. That'll get the delegates whoopin' and hollerin', jacking the signs up and down, and get them all juiced up again. The convention band will be playing, and we want this demonstration to last as long as it can."

"No problem," the young man said.

THE NEXT NIGHT, thirty minutes before Bush was introduced, placards were stuck under seats all around the hall and the boat horns strategically distributed.

"Bush got a glowing introduction," Ray says, "and when it was over, everybody screamed and hollered, and the signs went up in the air. The band played all these powerful songs, and everyone was cheering. We had our people rousing people, even the Reagan delegates. This is all documented by the TV commentators because I have footage of it. Cronkite and some of them were saying, 'This is certainly an impressive response from the attendees to the convention on behalf of George Bush.' The demonstration went on and on, and when it started dying down after about four minutes, I fired the boat horn up in the attic. When I did that, my buddies on the floor set theirs off. The band fired off again, and the crowd kept getting louder and louder.

"It became a game to see who could keep it going the longest. We had three or four times when we had to jack up the crowd with the boat horns but it worked every time. Finally, Bush was standing there, waving his arms, his palms down, begging the crowd to get serious. He was not embarrassed — well, knowing him, maybe a little embarrassed. But it was a wonderful demonstration and the longest one of the convention, maybe the longest one in history. It certainly impressed the media. Finally they got everybody quiet. But then the master of ceremonies, instead of yielding the mike to Bush, gave a new, brief introduction and said, 'Now, ladies and gentlemen, it is with great pleasure that I give you the Honorable George Bush.'"

Whereupon Ray sounded his horn in the attic, and the demonstration started all over again. It lasted for two more minutes, and then at last, Bush got to speak.

"It made an impact," Ray says, "and the moral of the story is that even if you are in the back of the convention hall sitting behind the swinging door to the ladies room, you can make things happen. Everything else was happy 'coincidence.'

"I happened to be watching television after the convention, and there was a one-on-one interview with Reagan who was asked, 'Why did you pick Bush?' He answered, 'Well, you know George is certainly a great American and a man who is very experienced by virtue of his service to his country. And you know, it was pretty obvious to anyone who watched television, that convention was certainly enthusiastic about George Bush, if you saw the demonstration preceding his speech.'"

Bush would later comment on his directive not to stage any demonstrations after Reagan's nomination. "We thought that it would look like I was trying to pressure Reagan into selecting me for Vice President. The staff was afraid that it would not look genuine, too contrived. But after the Kemp demonstration, Ray and others felt, the heck with it, let's show there is genuine grassroots support for George Bush. Our demonstration did have more 'feel' to it, more genuine enthusiasm. And I must confess to a certain happiness . . . exhilaration . . . appreciation for those who were out there showing support. And I do think the Reagan people took note of this and saw that it was a genuine manifestation of support. I have no recall of all the people who helped . . . but I know Ray was a mover and a shaker."

19

Endings and New Beginnings

I N 1986, RAY would have a year of milestones. It brought him industry accolades and, more important, it brought him re-marriage and several months later, the sale of B.A.S.S.

Ray Scott and Susan Chalfant Freeman were married on April 19 in an old wood-framed country church on the edge of their property in Pintlala. The Tabernacle Methodist Church had been built in 1846 and was maintained by the old families of the church and other interested parties as an historic site and cemetery.

The wedding was kept small and simple. Susan's twin brother, Barry Chalfant, and his family came from Atlanta and her old college room-mate, Karen (Casey) Cazavan, attended as well. Irish friends, Member of Parliament Liam Lawlor and his vivacious wife Hazel, flew in from Dublin. Zimbabwe B.A.S.S. pioneer Gerry Leach and his wife Bessie, who were in the states at the time, also attended. Orlando Wilson and his wife Carolyn represented the bass fishing community. And there were other friends and family.

The rehearsal dinner was held at Chantilly Plantation, an old "haunted" plantation home on the outskirts of Montgomery, where Ray and the witty Lawlors stood up and recounted raucous jokes after dinner, reducing many to tears. Hazel and Ray sang "The Rose of Tralee," and the restaurant owner recounted the plantation ghost story. It was indeed a magical Southern spring evening.

The wedding day was temperate and sunny. Bright pink azaleas bloomed outside the small church. Susan and Ray flanked tow-headed six-year-old "Little" Wilson and walked hand-in-hand down the aisle where the Reverend Gary Burton of Pintlala Baptist Church waited. Pintlala church member Beverly Williams played the old, slightly out-of-tune upright piano.

After the ceremony, guests boarded a borrowed yellow school bus to make the short trip to the Scotts' half-finished house and half-filled lake. There, amidst the concrete foundations and bare wooden framing, guests enjoyed a three-piece jazz band and an elegant buffet. It had all been arranged by Ray's gracious and efficient long-time secretary, Genaé Jones, who didn't blink an eye when her duties included planning a wedding. Chef Pooley Dawson and wife Mary not only attended the wedding but helped with the menu.

Susan and Ray had known each other for the fourteen years since she had come to work in 1972 at the recently completed B.A.S.S. Headquarters on Bell Road. She was the Creative Director for the booming company, working directly with Helen Sevier, then Vice President of Marketing.

Today Susan is still likely to be working on a promotional letter for Ray or creating a product brochure for the Whitetail Institute of North America, the business Ray started in 1988 out of his barn office. "Only now," she says, "I look out on a beautiful lake when I work, with two Dachshunds at my feet. It's great." Ray and Susan have an obvious compatibility though they are very different personalities. Susan is quiet, more reserved and scholarly, and Ray . . . is Ray. Nevertheless, they work together continuously as business and play weave together in one fabric.

Susan Chalfant had come to Montgomery in 1969 after graduating from Indiana University with degrees in Journalism and History of Fine Arts. Her father, a U.S. Air Force Colonel and World War II bomber pilot, had decided to retire in the area after his last tour of duty at Maxwell Air Force Base. Unfortunately, he was diagnosed with cancer immediately after he retired and died five years later at fifty-seven. Ray never met him, much to his disappointment.

Although Susan had lived in many places, including the Middle East, Southeast Asia, and Europe, she considered Montgomery more her home than any other place, having lived there in grades one through four while her father attended schools at Maxwell and served on the faculty of the Air War College.

Now, she and Ray and her young son Little Wilson (so called to avoid confusion with Ray's oldest son, also Wilson) were living in a small guest cabin while their home was being built on Ray's fifty-five-acre lake which was slowly filling through rain and natural run-off.

The property was situated twelve miles south of Montgomery in the historic community of Pintlala which is the Creek Indian word for "fish swamp." Both Aaron Burr and Andrew Jackson spent a night at Sam Manac's Tavern, a way station on the famous Federal Road from Washington to New Orleans, which had most probably been located on Ray's land. Manac's fifteen-year-old son David was the first Indian and Alabamian to attend and graduate from the United States Military Academy at West Point.

WHILE THEY WERE engaged, Ray and Susan had searched for a church home. They had made a conscious decision to make faith a part of their lives. Susan was a new Christian and although Ray was raised in a devout Baptist home, he had grown slack in his participation. They had visited churches in Montgomery and one Sunday decided to try the small Baptist Church in Pintlala.

"I remember thinking," says Susan, "that it would be too ideal to find a church in our own backyard. Well, we walked in and it was like we had come home. What an extraordinary feeling. We were just supposed to be there." An especially warm welcome came from red-headed Anne Malloy Bowles, who had known Ray as a childhood scamp in the Capitol Heights neighborhood.

"She looked at me with those big blue eyes," says Ray, "as if to say, 'Ray Scott, you've come to the place you need to be.' And it was."

A year later, upon her profession of faith, Susan was baptized by Reverend Gary Burton. A native of Birmingham, Gary had been pastor at Pintlala since 1972. He is a gentle man whose mild manner belies an irrepressible sense of humor and deep intellectual curiosity. He particularly delights in poking fun at his balding pate at opportune moments in the pulpit and out. And he never blinked an eye at Ray's vision for the church and his unorthodox manner of fund-raising five years down the road.

The Pintlala Baptist Church has grown steadily since the bass fishermen of America helped raise the funds to build a new sanctuary (Chapter 21). It draws many from the city of Montgomery who are attracted by its eclectic congregation and inclusive atmosphere. Recognizing Gary as an outstanding preacher and orator and knowing he had had other opportunities, Ray would ask Gary why he stayed at the little church. Gary simply says, Pintlala is "his calling." Both Gary and Ray believe their paths did not cross by mere coincidence. As Gary would say in a sermon, "Coincidence is just God's way of remaining anonymous." It was a concept Ray understood very well. His life had been laced together by such coincidences.

Ray and Susan settled down to country life. Little Wilson was enrolled near their home at the Pintlala Elementary School, an old public school built in 1923 and next to the church. It is a charming "U" shaped building constructed around an open courtyard. It has a southwestern look with stucco finish, and each classroom opens onto a colonnaded walkway. Little Wilson enjoyed an idyllic grade school experience with his rural classmates, both black and white.

Susan and Ray attended PTA meetings and school programs in the old-fashioned, high-ceilinged auditorium complete with a small wooden stage and well-worn green velvet curtains. "It smelled like the old schools I remembered," says Ray.

When word got out that there were plans to enclose the colonnades and make other major changes to the structure, Ray and Susan were appalled. It was the last intact school of its kind in the county. They got together with other community residents, notably local historian and preservationist Ethel Tankersley Todd, who had not only attended the school as a child but had also taught there until her retirement in 1978.

With characteristic determination, she obtained historic building status
for the school and it is now protected from future architectural changes.
A historical marker stands in front of the school by the side of the historic
old Federal Road.

In 1986 Ray received two prestigious awards for his accomplishments
in the bass fishing industry. The Living Legends Award was presented
after a vote by 102 writers, renowned anglers, lure manufacturers, and
other fishing personalities who had been featured in the 1985 book
Living Legends of American Sport Fishing. He also received the Ole
Evinrude Award from the Outboard Marine Corporation (OMC) for his
contributions to recreational boating.

IT WAS A YEAR OF NEW beginnings for Ray, and sometimes new
beginnings require endings as well. He had been building B.A.S.S. for
nearly twenty years and the child he conceived had grown into a healthy
adult. The frontier spirit he thrived on was being replaced by civilized
"systems" and he was too impatient for the day-to-day management of
the company. It was time to go on to other things.

He had many opportunities to sell B.A.S.S. over the years, but the
time and the buyers were never quite right. So it was with great
satisfaction that he sold the company in July of 1986 to his vice
president, Helen Sevier, and Jemison Investments of Birmingham,
Alabama. "Helen had been in charge of operations for so many years and
the Jemison people had an excellent reputation and were known not to
monkey with companies that were doing well. As a matter of fact, you
could not ask for better partners. It seemed like the ideal situation."

Ray sold the company and remained as the titular president of
B.A.S.S. and the company's visible spokesman and tournament emcee. It
was an arrangement that would continue for the next twelve years.

In a way, *both* Susan and Ray still worked for B.A.S.S. Although
Susan had worked with Ray for fourteen years at the company, she was
still not totally prepared for the full force of his personality. "I learned a
lot about him after we were married and I'm still learning," she says. "He
is really a complex man underneath his outgoing, straightforward per-

sonality. And yet at the same time, what you see is mostly what you get." Those who know Ray well will tell you he is the same whether he is in the presence of paupers or presidents. As a matter of fact, he is likely to treat a bellhop like a king and teasingly treat a king like a bellhop.

Susan laughs at one of her first "insights." "Ray has such an open mind — I would call it uninhibited — which is such a great strength. But occasionally he gets in trouble when his free spirit comes out his mouth. I never really appreciated how 'receptive' he was until our experience at a health spa in Arizona.

"We went to the Canyon Ranch Spa shortly after we were married. It was something I had always dreamed of doing and Ray indulged me. We were in a large yoga and relaxation class at the spa. Everyone was lying flat on their backs with their eyes closed, as this attractive instructor talked us softly through the relaxation of our bodies, starting with our toes. I was concentrating so hard, thinking about every little muscle. She was about to our knees, when I heard this strange sound next to me. I opened my eyes, turned my head, and looked at Ray. He was fast asleep, snoring loudly. He stayed that way throughout the entire forty-five-minute class. He woke up after everyone was gone and I was talking to the instructor. The man has no barriers in his brain. He's receptive to everything.

"I have to admit I had a hard time adjusting to his love of commerce. I am not competitive and grew up in a very uncommercial environment. So I was shocked when I would hear him say things like, 'I want to take the money from your pocket and put it into mine.' I soon realized, however, that he says these things with an implicit humor. Business is a game to him. A football player doesn't play for the exercise, he plays for the score on that big board in the end zone. And money is Ray's scoreboard. But anyone who thinks Ray sits around counting his gold is very mistaken. The man can't balance a checkbook."

Susan collects epigrams, little sayings that pack a punch, and many remind her of Ray. "I found one," she says "that describes his philosophy of business and life perfectly. It was in an in-flight catalog on a trip and I ordered a poster for his birthday. It's a picture of a sailboat in the middle of the ocean and says, 'Risk — you can't discover new oceans unless you have the courage to lose sight of the shore.' And that's Ray exactly. He has no fear of sailing into the unknown."

She found another saying she liked so well she had it engraved on a brass paperweight for Ray's desk. From one of her favorite writers, Oscar Wilde, it also captures an important aspect of Ray's personality. It reads, "Moderation is a fatal thing. Nothing succeeds like excess."

"I burst out laughing when I read it," says Susan. "It was vintage Ray. I tease him all the time about the philosophy 'less is more' which is totally alien to him. He grabs life with both hands. Moderation is simply not in his vocabulary. If he finds a good pepper sauce, he orders a case. He loves the sugar-roasted coffee he gets in Mexico. We have a freezer full of it. We've got four Red Rider BB guns in their original boxes. He found a wildlife lamp he liked at an outdoor show and he bought six. When I ask him 'Why?' he just smiles at me and says, 'you never know when you might run out.'"

Susan has learned to live with bad publicity as well as praise. Many of Ray's detractors accuse him of being a "con man." Such criticism does not faze him. He has heard such accusations, although made affection-ately, since childhood. He loves to point out that he is a promoter, not a con man, and that there is a very crucial difference. "A con man can get you once," he says "and then he's got to find someone else. A promoter can get you and you'll come back again and again." Ray Scott is proud to be a promoter and has been compared to P. T. Barnum in countless media reports. He takes it as a great compliment.

"I'm always amazed," says Susan, "at how philosophical he is about criticism and bad publicity, which I have to say is pretty rare considering how controversial he can be. Sometimes his storytelling and colorful speech can get him into a lot of trouble. And he does come across at times like a good ol' boy, which he loves. But there is so much more to him. There is no doubt he can be absolutely outrageous and I scold him. But it doesn't do much good."

However, Susan was totally baffled when she read about Ray in Howell Raines's best-selling book, *Fly Fishing Through the Midlife Crisis*. Raines is the editorial page editor of *The New York Times* and a fellow

Alabamian. Raines had grudgingly given Ray credit for popularizing catch-and-release in the sport of bass fishing. The title of his chapter about Ray was "Rerouting the Red Neck Way, or a Cracker Shall Lead Them." At the end of the chapter he pityingly portrayed Ray as a lonely bigot sitting in his big home in solitary grandeur.

"Good Lord," says Susan. "I didn't know whether to laugh or cry. But I was totally amazed at Howell's misperception. He was just so off the mark. Maybe it's a love-hate thing about being a Southerner. Ray's reaction was so calm. He was just pleased that Howell gave him credit for bringing catch-and-release into the mainstream. I was fussing and fuming and Ray teased me, "What do you expect from a trout fisherman?"

RAY CONTINUED TO BE honored in the fishing industry. In 1987 he was named to the National Freshwater Fishing Hall of Fame. In 1989 the Sport Fishing Institute named him Sport Fisherman of the Year, and President Bush presented the award to him in the Oval Office. That same year, he received the DuPont Outstanding Sport Fishing Achievement Award, and in 1994 he received the first Conservation Award given by the International Game Fish Association. He also "broke the jock barrier" when he was inducted into the Alabama Sports Hall of Fame, joining the likes of Bear Bryant, Joe Namath, Bo Jackson, Bart Starr, and Bobby Bowden. He was also inducted into the Montgomery Area Sports Hall of Fame in 1991.

Ray was uncharacteristically humble in 1995 when he was named by *Field and Stream Magazine* as one of twenty persons who have done the most to influence the outdoor sports in the past century, joining the likes of Fred Bear, Ole Evinrude, Theodore Roosevelt, Lee Wulff, and Ray's hero Rachel Carson. He was not aware of the Hundredth Anniversary feature until his brother Danny called him to congratulate him. "What article?" he asked.

He had much the same reaction in 1998 when *Outdoor Life Magazine* credited him with one of the top ten fishing innovations in the past hundred years — the bass boom.

Not long after he sold his business in 1986, a restless Ray fiddled with small projects "just for fun." He renovated part of an old horse barn on his property into an office area. A plaque behind Ray's desk reads, "If it ain't fun, we don't do it." He even bottled and sold his grandmother Ray's chow-chow (relish) under the label of "Ray Scott's Reel Good Recipes." He grins, "We had fun."

He is particularly proud of his three-volume video series on building small lakes and ponds, appropriately called *Ray Scott's Guide to Creating Great Small Waters*. He produced it with talented local videographer and producer Bill Schaum.

"I was amazed at how many people would ask me for advice about their lakes and ponds," says Ray. "And I knew from my own building experience how little information there is out there. So I put all my own know-how together and talked to experts, and then Bill and I documented the creation of a five-acre lake I built on some of my hunting property. We did the same thing with a small farm pond I renovated. It all took about two years.

"We've sold thousands of sets," he says. "I truly believe that small waters are the wave of the future. They enhance property values and allow total control over the fishing habitat and the water quality. It's incredible what proper management can do for the quality of fish. Building and managing a lake is a real lesson in the food chain and the importance of clean waters, underwater structure, and proper vegetation."

But Ray's biggest creation in this period sprang from his love of deer hunting, and again, his fascination with nutrition and managing for quality wildlife. In 1988, along with a friend, wildlife biologist Randall Rogers, he founded the Whitetail Institute of North America.

How does a man start a new business? It's easy for Ray Scott. One trip to the seed supply store literally provided the seed — no pun intended — of an idea that would bloom into a full-blown business.

Anticipating deer season in 1986, Ray went to the local seed supply store, Montgomery Seed, a venerable old establishment on the main street in Montgomery down from the Capitol building. He bought the

Bryan Kerchal, a 23-year-old from Newtown, Connecticut, was the first "amateur" to win the Classic from the B.A.S.S. Federation tournament trail. Only months after his 1994 triumph in Greensboro, he was killed in a commuter plane crash.

Larry Nixon was the first angler to break the million-dollar barrier on the B.A.S.S. Tournament Trail. By 1998 he had fished 21 Classics, was twice Angler of the Year, and had won 13 tournaments, including four Megabucks Tournaments (out of the first seven events), claiming a $100,000 first prize each time.

Politics and fishing make for strange bedfellows. Vice President George Bush joins Governor Bill Clinton on the weigh-in stand with Ray and Classic winner Rick Clunn at the 1984 BASS Masters Classic in Pine Bluff, Arkansas.

Ray talks to Dick Darman of the Office of Management and Budget (OMB) from the Lincoln bedroom at the White House during his and Susan's visit in March of 1989.

BELOW: A triumphant Barbara Bush shows off the big fish of the day in a New Year's Day visit to the Scotts' in 1990. She fished with Ray and her husband fished with Rick Clunn.

Ray and Forrest Wood in Mexico. Wood, the founder of Ranger Boats, sent Ray his first quality cowboy hat in 1968 after the Smith Lake Tournament. A prominent figure in the bass fishing industry, Wood, like Ray, sold his business in 1986.

Bob Cobb and Ray Scott enjoy sunrise coffee at Lake Novillo. The landmark Red Rock is in the background across the lake.

Rhodney Honeycutt and Ray share cooking duties in the "open air" kitchen at Lake Novillo in Sonora, Mexico. Rhodney grew up with fishing's greatest names.

Brother Danny, 11 years Ray's junior, bears an uncanny resemblance to his older brother and shares his love of pranks.

Noted pastor, author, and president of the Master's College and Seminary in California, John F. MacArthur receives a mounted lunker he caught in Ray's lake in 1998. It was MacArthur's first bass fishing experience.

Don Butler displays a largemouth taken from Ray's Pintlala lake on his own Gator Bug spinnerbait as Triton Boat President Earl Bentz looks on.

A promise fulfilled: In 1993 President Bush, Pastor Gary Burton, and Ray stand in the vestibule of the sanctuary that bass fishermen built with four fund-raising tournaments held on Ray's residential lake in Pintlala.

Branson, Missouri, music superstar and avid bass fisherman Shoji Tabuchi performs in the original Pintlala Baptist Church sanctuary. He would support the Eagles of Angling tournaments with both his talents and contributions.

Roland Martin cheers as Toyo Shimano and Orlando Wilson display two lunkers that were on the line at the same time at an Eagles of Angling Tournament. The team of Martin and Wilson was a two-time winner of the event.

Beverly Williams (L), Ministries Coordinator at the Pintlala Baptist Church, took over the Scott kitchen during the Eagles of Angling Tournaments. Volunteer helpers included Jerrie Burton, wife of Pastor Gary Burton.

Johnny Morris displays his big catch at an Eagles of Angling Tournament along with President Bush, Ray, and Morris's partner, pro angler Charlie Campbell. Morris's efforts as Tournament Chairman would add greatly to the success of the fund-raising tournaments.

ABOVE: Bill and Meredith Schroeder listen to Ray at the Eagles of Angling Friday night dinner with an amused George W. Bush in the background. Bill suggested building the new Pintlala Baptist Church sanctuary.

LEFT: Susan greets General Brent Scowcroft, President Bush's friend and National Security Advisor, and one of her favorite visitors. He fished as a guest contender in several Eagles of Angling Tournaments.

Ray enjoys sightseeing with Japanese bass fishing star and tackle shop entrepreneur Ken Suzuki in Japan in 1995. They were introduced by tackle manufacturer Bobby Dennis.

Texas Governor George W. Bush visits with Ray at the Governor's Mansion in Austin on the eve of the demonstration of a mechanical weed harvester at Lake Bastrop in 1998.

Susan and Ray in rare formal attire at the BASS Masters Classic awards banquet. In 1990 Ray decided to dress the fishermen up in tuxedos for the final night.

Ray reunites with old football teammates Bart Starr (L) and Bobby Bowden at Ray's 1990 induction into the Alabama Sports Hall of Fame.

Ray's sons Steve (L) and Wilson (R) bought into the Whitetail Institute in 1990 and took over the day-to-day running of the deer nutrition business. In 1998 it did $3 million worth of business out of a converted residence/office in Pintlala. (A curious doe in the back checks out the decoys.)

Ray taught youngest son "Little" Wilson to hunt when he was eight years old. This large atypical buck grew up on Ray's hunting grounds on supplemental plantings of his own Whitetail Institute clover formula.

To my sweet Jennifer
with all my love—
Daddy
Aug 1979

One of Ray's favorite pictures of his daughter Jennifer in 1979. She married Montgomery neurologist Dr. Larry Epperson and made Ray a first-time grandfather with the birth of daughter Jessica.

Ray and Susan and "Little" Wilson pause for a family photo with President Bush at the 1993 Eagles of Angling Tournament on a beautiful early spring day. Exactly one week later, a freak ice- and snowstorm paralyzed much of the Southeast. It was a date that had been seriously considered for the tournament.

Ray instructs his oldest grandson, Weston Epperson, on his first Zebco 33 baitcaster. According to his parents, Weston was trying to fish about the time he started walking.

Ray's seven grandchildren gather around the Christmas tree in 1997 in Pintlala. From left to right are Weston and Jessica Epperson, Ivey Scott, Jackson and Gates Scott, and Elisabeth and Sarah Epperson.

In the spring of 1999, Ray traveled to the Florida panhandle to meet 90-year-old G.H. Harris, the inventor of the foot-operated MotorGuide trolling motor. He displays the original foot-control patent as Ray holds one of the earliest prototypes for the MotorGuide.

usual rye grass and oats and on the recommendation of John Morgan, the proprietor, he also bought a bag of Regal Ladino clover.

As luck would have it — coincidence again — he was trying out new tractors at the time for his country property. The young man who delivered the John Deere tractor agreed to plant a two-acre plot with the demonstration tractor. "I'll never know why," says Ray, "but I had him plant all three seed types in strips. I was so tired of searching for the best deer forage planting and getting different advice from every person I asked. I decided to do my own 'taste test.' The results were amazing. The deer literally walked through the rye and oats to get to the clover. Then I really started to question why. Well, that one incident would lead to the creation of the Whitetail Institute of North America, which became the pioneer in the wildlife food plot industry. Nobody had paid much attention to it before."

Like a bloodhound, Ray tracked down the answers he needed. His search led him to wildlife biologist Randall Rogers who introduced him to Dr. Wiley C. Johnson, an agronomist and seed breeder with Auburn University, a school with a long and excellent reputation for its agricultural programs. Amazingly, Dr. Johnson was the inventor of the Regal Ladino Clover Ray had purchased in Montgomery. Ray promptly put him on the Whitetail staff full-time when he retired from Auburn. He also promised him a big bonus if he would develop a superior variety of clover for a wide variety of climates, exclusively for deer and other wildlife such as turkey.

A great relationship was born. Dr. Johnson worked on the clover improvements and tested and re-tested plantings. Ray and friends, including many deer-hunting fishing pros, put the clover to the ultimate test on their hunting grounds. It worked. Deer walked through other plantings to get to the Institute clover formulation. And the clover provided a high twenty-five to thirty percent protein for the entire year. It was exactly what Ray had been looking for. The more he researched deer management, the more he realized how critical it was to provide deer herds with protein the entire year, especially during the period of two hundred days when the bucks were growing their antlers and during the gestation period for does. "We took what used to be hit-or-miss planting solutions and turned them into a science."

The clover seed blend went on the market under the name of Imperial Whitetail Brand Clover. Susan helped with the promotional materials and a small staff was assembled. A major seed company executive who produced some of the early seed formulation told Ray he'd be lucky to sell a hundred thousand pounds. The Institute sold more than one million pounds the first year. Other products quickly followed, including a seed formula that did not require plowing, and a mineral/vitamin supplement specifically for whitetail deer.

WHEN THE BUSINESS got too big to handle on an informal basis, Ray approached his two older sons, both with successful careers, and asked if they would like to buy half the business and take over the day-to-day running of the Institute and develop new products. Steve and Wilson Scott agreed and since 1991 they have increased the business by 350 percent.

Their success has given Ray tremendous satisfaction. He had told his children when they were teenagers that although they might have summer jobs at B.A.S.S., he would never hire them as regular employees. Indeed his retired father had wanted to work at B.A.S.S. in the early days but Ray had gently turned him down. He would send his children to college and after that they would have to make their own way in the business world. All three did, including daughter Jennifer who became a star saleswoman with an office supply firm before she married.

Nonetheless, Ray had mixed emotions. "I remember the look on Wilson's face. He was sixteen and understood the implications of what I was saying. But it was the best thing I could have done for all of them. My boys came to Whitetail with a track record and money to invest. I couldn't be more proud."

Today the Whitetail Institute has more than 150,000 active customers and field testers and publishes a four-color tabloid three times a year. And the product line has expanded to include other seed formulas for different soil types, a plant growth stimulant, a nutritional attractant, and other products. "We really pioneered the deer nutrition industry," says Ray. "Everyone's jumping in now, but it started in little old Pintlala, Alabama."

Even Ray was amazed by the results of the products. "I don't know why I was surprised," he says. "I saw the same results in my fifty-five-acre lake. Nutrition and habitat are going to affect wildlife whether they have fins, feathers, or antlers. But we have harvested some incredible racks in our hundred-acre high-fenced area, where only our Imperial products are available along with normal, natural browse, of course. We found a naturally shed set of antlers that scored 215-5/8 points on the Boone and Crockett scale. The buck was four and a half years old so it had been born in the enclosure."

NOT EVERYTHING WAS coming up clover, however, in the 1990s. The decade brought a bizarre lawsuit that stunned Ray and Helen and other B.A.S.S. owners, as well as B.A.S.S. members. Headquarters had received a number of calls from members in Wichita, Kansas, telling of a lawyer — or lawyers — soliciting plaintiffs for a $75 million class-action lawsuit against the Society. All had refused to take part. Finally, two B.A.S.S. members were found. With the two plaintiffs, lawyers brought suit against Ray, Helen, Jemison Investments, and other B.A.S.S. owners.

"It's very complicated," says Ray "and I still find it difficult to explain. Basically they said I started a *non-profit* organization back in 1967, I guess because of my environmental activities. When I finally took the time to incorporate from a sole proprietorship in 1969, they claimed I did so fraudulently. In essence, they said the organization did not belong to me, but to the members. They accused me and current owners of 'looting and plundering' B.A.S.S. assets.

"What upset me and a lot of other people was that we paid — and I mean that literally — for voluntarily trying to do some good in environmental matters and we were penalized for it." He shakes his head wearily. "It's a heck of a note. I'm past anger. What's so ironic is that the year after I started B.A.S.S., my total income was slightly over $5,000, down from

$26,000 a year before when I sold insurance.

"It took seven years for the case to work its way through the courts. It started in February 1992 and we barely had a day in court," says Ray. "Meanwhile the lawyers' meters were running and the company was put in a straitjacket."

Finally, in early June 1999, U.S. District Judge Ira DeMent threw out the suit with prejudice, which means it cannot be filed again.

"It was an obscene abuse of our legal system," says Ray. "Here you have two fine companies [Jemison and B.A.S.S.] and a number of individuals held hostage for over seven years. One day the story will be told, and it will be about an unholy alliance between 'free-lance' lawyers and a so-called journalist and who knows who else. People always ask me, 'Why don't you sue?' Well, we have no one to fight except a lawyer or two who can file legal documents all day long while we have to pay expensive legal teams. It's a form of legal blackmail. As far as I'm concerned, every citizen in this country should get behind tort reform. No one is immune from frivolous lawsuits, and I mean no one."

ON A HAPPIER NOTE and to Ray's great satisfaction, the nineties also brought increased international activity. *Bassmaster Magazine* was being sent all over the world.

It became obvious even in the early years of B.A.S.S. that bass fishing was not exclusively an American phenomenon. Foreign countries began popping up on the membership rolls, notably Brazil, Spain, Portugal, Italy, Japan, Zimbabwe, and South Africa. There were even civilian members in Saudi Arabia and Malaysia.

In the early 1970s, Ray visited Spain with first Federation Director Bill McGehee. They discovered that years earlier, U.S. soldiers stationed in Spain brought over bass fingerlings on military transport planes and released them into the scores of impoundments built by dictator Francisco Franco. It didn't take long for King Bass to dominate the waters.

Later Ray started to hear from B.A.S.S. clubs in what was then Rhodesia, now known as Zimbabwe. He heard from one man in particular — Gerry Leach. Under Leach's determined leadership, the clubs became a federation in spite of a Civil War and tremendous political and economic upheaval. Ray and Gerry even managed to arrange for an aerated box of Florida bass to arrive in Zimbabwe. Lovingly nursed along the way, the fingerlings traveled from hatchery to hatchery in twenty hours.

Ray made a personal visit to Zimbabwe in 1980 as Gerry's guest and had an incredible experience that marked the beginning of a love affair with Africa. On that first trip, Ray fished for famous tiger fish on Lake Kariba. And in the Triangle Area of the country, Gerry also arranged for a Cape buffalo hunt. Ray returned twice to Zimbabwe on safari, notably to get "his leopard" which he stalked for two trips.

Bass fever ran high in Zimbabwe. The small country sent the very first international team to participate in the federation tournaments. The first group came over in 1980, led by Gerry Leach. In the wake of years of civil war, products were very scarce in the country and currency restrictions very tight. Each man was allowed to take only $600 hard currency out of the country for the two-week trip.

No one realized their plight until Ray found out during a dinner conversation one night. "Until that time they [eight men] were all sleeping in one hotel room. They never asked for help. Once we found out, we provided vehicles, extra rooms, and other assistance. They always looked sharp with their own kind of 'uniforms' — khaki shorts, knee socks, and coordinated shirts. They represented their country and the Federation very well."

Says Ray, "Seeing these guys in a sporting goods store was a sight to behold. Children in a candy shop couldn't match their excitement after years of deprivation and shortages. They especially loved plastic worms. Most of them threw their clothes away when they left and jammed their bags with tackle, choosing to meet airline weight restrictions with precious fishing gear."

In recent years the Zimbabwe Federation has been well represented by Gerry Jooste, a very talented fisherman from Banket in the northern part of the country. He would qualify for three Classics via the Federation in 1994, 1995, and 1997. Trim and poised, with a neatly cultivated mustache, Gerry would captivate listeners with his articulate British-accented English.

Years after his first contact with Africa, Ray made contact with another young go-getter, this time from Florence, Italy — Paolo Vannini. Like Gerry Leach, Paolo was a tireless crusader for B.A.S.S. In 1996 Ray visited Italy and met and fished with club members, including the reigning Bass Champ, Stefano Sammarchi. The tall, good-looking young man would become Italy's first representative at B.A.S.S. Federation finals in 1999.

"It was an emotional trip," says Ray. "Their passion is contagious." By the time Ray returned with Susan in 1997, Italy was federated, and the event was celebrated at dinner in a Tuscan restaurant with federation members traveling from all over Italy.

On the 1997 trip Ray and Susan also met with Portuguese B.A.S.S. members whom Ray had met on his trip the previous year. Under the enthusiastic leadership of yet another angler, Herminio Rodrigues, Portugal hopes to be federated one day. At a celebration dinner in a Lisbon restaurant, Ray and Susan were entertained by B.A.S.S. members and other bass fishermen. Ironically the revered "Godfather" of modern Portuguese bass fishing, Ventura Silva, who was present, had also been a founding father of bassing in Zimbabwe, where he emigrated and lived for nearly thirty years. It is indeed a small world for bass fishermen.

Bass mania is also alive and well in Japan. Ray fished there in 1995 as guest of mega bass star, Ken Suzuki, who has a popular TV show and owns the immense Johshuya chain of fishing tackle retail stores. Ray amused his hosts by eating every form of raw fish they placed before him and pretending that the potent warm sake drink was Japanese tea. He spent five whirlwind days in Japan filming two TV shows with Ken and visiting his stores. Ray was overwhelmed with the insatiable interest in all things bass. "They have their own bass universe, complete with heroes, slick-page magazines, products…and a B.A.S.S. federation."

By his own accounting, Ray has fished for bass in Canada, Mexico, Brazil, Spain, Portugal, Italy, South Africa, Zimbabwe, and Japan. He has also made many trips to northern Ontario's pristine Boundary

Waters area for smallmouth bass and deems it some of the most exciting light line fishing he has ever done. In Mexico he has fished Lakes Novillo, Dominguez, Hidalgo, Obregon, and Guerrero.

"It is truly amazing," he says, "how this critter crosses cultures and geography. The passion to catch this fish is the same, no matter where."

20

The White House Connection

T ISN'T EVERY DAY that a President-elect decides to go fishing a week before his inauguration, but that's what happened on December 29, 1988. Vice President George Bush, already a life member of B.A.S.S. for nearly ten years, landed in Air Force Two at Maxwell Air Force Base in Montgomery to go fishing at the Scotts.

It didn't surprise Ray because he knew Bush was an avid fisherman. During his years in the White House there were those, especially in the press, who were skeptical about Bush's professed love of fishing, considering it part of a public relations effort to portray him as an "average guy." They were wrong then and are still wrong. He is an authentic bass fanatic and general outdoorsman.

"Actually," says Bush, "I've been a fisherman for quite a few years, starting in Texas near Freeport in the early sixties. Ray's the one who got me interested in B.A.S.S. and I bought a life membership. I liked the magazine and I liked what the organization was doing for sound conservation practices and for the sport of bass fishing in general."

As a matter of fact, when Bush was campaigning for the presidency in 1988, he was asked in a *New York Times* interview about his reading habits, "Mr. Bush, what is your favorite magazine?" Without a blink, he said, "*Bassmaster.*" Ray loved it.

Bush confesses, "I don't get to fish nearly enough. On a scale of one to ten, I am probably a six in terms of skill. On the enthusiasm scale I am a ten."

Ray was willing and ready to give his friend a great fishing trip if the bass would cooperate. He, Susan, and Little Wilson rode to the air base to greet him. When they arrived back at the gate to the Scott property in the Presidential limousine, they were met by reporters, as well as Pastor Gary Burton, his wife Jerrie, and about thirty-five members of the Pintlala Baptist Church flock. They were holding signs and posters welcoming the President-elect. Bush got out of the limo, shook hands all around and said to Gary, "Thanks for the welcome, Reverend." Gary Burton couldn't have imagined then the impact this man would eventually have on his little country church.

A nasty cold front had passed through Pintlala the day before and fishing conditions were not good. Even so, in only a couple of hours on the lake, Ray and the President-elect caught and released seventeen bass, mainly on Bill Lewis Rat L Traps and Sugar Shads. "I am learning to be a better plastic worm man," says Bush, "and I always seem to have good luck with small Rebels and Rat L Traps. I especially love topwater plug fishing — that's where the action is really exciting."

The talk on the water was about fishing, not politics, except for the President-elect's assurance that he would continue to look after the interests of fishermen and hunters. They stopped fishing at dusk-dark and Bush joined the family and Ray's secretary, Genaé Jones, around the kitchen table for gumbo and Susan's special pecan pie before the return trip to Washington and the upcoming Inaugural activities.

"It was a very low-key visit," says Susan, "very intimate. He was a man who wanted to relax and go fishing after a long, hard campaign. We had no dignitaries or reception line at the house. With no other guests, the Secret Service didn't even have to be in the house, so everything seemed very normal."

ONLY THREE MONTHS later, in early March, Ray got an early morning call from a White House aide traveling with President Bush in Japan for the funeral of Emperor Hirohito. She said, "Mr. Scott, the

President and Mrs. Bush would like you and Mrs. Scott to be their guests in Washington. Can you come?" Without even consulting the calendar, Ray said yes.

The next morning a call from another White House aide firmed up the details. Ray and Susan would be met at Dulles Airport on the morning of March 19 and would fly home the following afternoon about two o'clock. When Ray asked where they would be staying, the aide replied, "Mr. Scott, you and Mrs. Scott will be sleeping in the Lincoln Bedroom."

Ray couldn't believe it. Nine years had passed since he made that impromptu request, half in jest, while he and George Bush dangled their feet in a hot tub, but it had stayed in the President's mind and now he was honoring it.

Shortly after Ray and Susan arrived at the White House, President and Mrs. Bush strolled outside in unseasonably mild weather with them as well as guests Crystal Gayle and her husband, Bill Gatzimo. A very pregnant Millie — the Bush's beloved English Springer spaniel — trotted at Barbara's feet. They came upon a horseshoe pit and the president said impulsively, "Come on Ray, let's play a game of eleven."

The President and Ray walked to the stake and began pitching. The President asked casually, "So, how are things in Pintlala?" giving it his own pronunciation of Pin-tala. Ray replied, "Mr. President, things are pretty fine in Pintlala, but the fishermen around Alabama are mad as hornets with me. And they tell me when they get me, they're coming after you."

President Bush stopped, horseshoe in hand, and looked at Ray with a bit of a frown, and asked, "What's that all about?"

Ray said, "Well, it seems somebody with your Office of Management and Budget (OMB) is trying to take the fishermen's money out of the Wallop-Breaux Fund. This somebody in the OMB is making a raid on the fund money and has his arm to up his elbow in the coffers. And the fishermen are mad as hell."

The President said, "The OMB can't do that — that's dedicated money."

"That's what I thought, too," Ray said. "You might want to remind somebody in OMB that's the case, because right now they're coming after our money."

So ended the brief conversation. They finished the match — the President won — and returned to the White House, Bush to the oval office, while Ray and Susan settled in the Lincoln Bedroom. They were in the room no more than ten minutes when the phone rang. It was the President's secretary, Patty Presock, saying that Richard Darman, the head of OMB, was on the phone. He asked, "Mr. Scott, what seems to be the problem?" Ray told him and Darman said, "I can assure you that is not going to happen. We'll report to the President no later than this afternoon with a solution to the problem."

The next morning over coffee, President Bush showed Ray the order that he had signed stopping the OMB from raiding the Wallop-Breaux Fund and told him firmly once again that the money was fishermen's money and was not to be tampered with. As the Scotts flew home that afternoon, Ray reflected on the series of coincidences that had occurred over the years. Dangling toes in the hot tub had led to having a chance to play a game of horseshoes that resulted in saving the Wallop-Breaux money. No matter how it came about, it was a multi-million dollar blessing to fishermen and state fisheries departments.

RAY AND SUSAN enjoy their relationship with the Bushes, and Ray says, "For some strange reason we seem to have an influence on their wardrobes." Ray and Susan had made a trip to Hong Kong and mainland China in 1987 while Bush was vice president. They were wandering through a maze of small tailor shops close to their Hong Kong hotel when Ray spotted a small picture of Bush in a window, obviously with the owner or an employee of the shop. After entering the shop and speaking with the manager, Ray discovered Bush had indeed bought shirts from the shop and that the shop had his exact measurements on file.

Ray couldn't resist. Pointing to Susan's shirt, an oversized, tailored uni-sex style, he asked, "Can you make this shirt in his size?" Ray had admired the shirt every time Susan wore it, with its epaulets and deep, vented front yokes on the front. The manager said they could. Ray and Susan picked out several fabrics for both the President and Ray.

As fate would have it, the shirts arrived shortly before Ray and Susan left for Jackson Hole, Wyoming, to spend the Fourth of July with the Bushes and other guests. At a small, casual dinner at the Yellowstone lodge where the President was staying, Ray presented a gift-wrapped box to Bush, telling him Susan had crocheted him some long underwear. The President opened the box, totally baffled that Ray had gotten shirts from his own Hong Kong tailor.

He immediately took the shirts into another room and returned wearing a full-cut, cream-colored twill that looked great on his tall, lanky frame. Ray recalls he wore the shirt at an outdoor church service the next morning and again that night at a barbecue dinner.

Ray and Susan later saw the shirts many times on TV and in magazines, especially during the Gulf War when the President was standing on a tank or greeting troops. Bush later called them "my Desert Storm shirts." "What was amusing," says Ray, "I found out later that his consultants had a devil of a time getting him to wear the clothing they wanted. I send shirts and he won't take them off."

Later, Susan managed to outfit Barbara with shoes.

At one of the Eagles of Angling Tournaments (see Chapter 21) everyone had left for the church weigh-in except President Bush and Susan. They brought up the rear in the Presidential limo with a stop at the Pintlala Elementary School where a crowd of students and teachers waited to greet the President.

And what does one talk about when riding alone in the Presidential limousine with the President? "Well," says Susan, "first of all we listened to a country music station which his security man automatically tuned in for him. Then while I was trying to think of something really profound to say, he looked down at my shoes — some Keds sneakers in a strange sort of khaki-green color — and said, 'Those are the kind of shoes Barbara wears all the time. I've never seen that color, though.'

"I said, 'Oh yes, I've got a whole collection of them. They come in all different colors.' I really had the man's attention now. 'You know,' he said, 'Barbara's birthday is coming up. I think I'll get her some of those.' I could tell he was making a mental note. I thought, a woman who appreciates sneakers for her birthday is my kind of woman.

"A month or two later, I was reading an account in a major news magazine about the President and Mrs. Bush's trip to Istanbul, Turkey. They were sightseeing and a reporter noted that Barbara was wearing two totally different colors of tennis shoes. Barbara told the reporters that they were a birthday gift from George. He had bought a whole 'wardrobe' of them for her in different colors. I got such a kick out of that. I thought I'm probably the only person in the whole, wide world who knows the real story behind those shoes."

Less than a year later, on December 1, 1989, Susan phoned Beverly Williams at the church with important news. Ray and she would be entertaining President and Mrs. Bush as their house guests on New Year's Day. Since Bev was not only a good friend but a catering Houdini as well, would she be willing to take charge of the event?

"Beverly is the church administrator," Ray says. "She is the number one woman who gets it done, whatever it is. She heads up the food, she heads up the music, she's the organist, she's the committee organizer, she's a one-woman everything who knows how to organize and get others to help. Every church can only pray for a Beverly Williams." Beverly happily agreed, little knowing, like everyone else what this presidential visit would eventually mean for the small church.

Susan had figured she would have at least four areas that would need food and beverages: The Secret Service would be headquartered in the guest cabin; the President's travel staff would be in a large game room with bath over the boat house; the President and Mrs. Bush and other guests would be in the main house; and local law enforcement would be at the barn where she wanted snacks and drinks available for them and any other souls who might pop out of the woods and the bushes.

"They might have dropped out the skies for all I knew," says Susan. "There were people everywhere, in the oddest places. An ambulance was in the driveway and a helicopter was parked over the hill near the barn.

Before the President arrived, I walked by a very plain black Suburban. The back panel doors swung open briefly and I got a glimpse of what seemed like dozens of men and machine guns packed into the cargo area."

Security people had started coming to the Scotts' house weeks before and were unfailingly polite and apologetic for the inconvenience. As one of the last precautions before the President arrived, Navy divers checked the docks and the lake. And finally a bomb-sniffing dog and his handler made a tour of the house. They sniffed everywhere — up the chimney, in the closets, around the houseplants. "I have no secrets," says Susan.

Susan says, "People often ask what it's like to have the President visit and it's hard to explain because it is almost surreal. The strangest thing to me was when they left. Within minutes of his departure — I mean minutes — everyone is gone. They just vanish. And it's so so quiet, so very quiet. You wonder if it really happened."

The Presidential visit on January 1, 1990, was a Pintlala exercise in hospitality from the start. Bill Carter, the manager of the airfield at Maxwell AFB was a Pintlala friend and neighbor of Gary Burton. He had the reception ready to run smoothly the second that Air Force One touched ground.

"It was a special moment," says Susan. "Here it was the first day of a new decade and there was Air Force One on the tarmac. It was one of those beautiful bright winter days and the plane just glistened in the sunshine. I'd look at the big Presidential seal on the plane and get goose bumps. Then down the steps came the President and Barbara as friendly and relaxed as ever, accompanied by National Security Advisor General Brent Scowcroft."

The Scotts rode with the President and Mrs. Bush to Pintlala. Once again, church members greeted the couple, and there were squeals of delight at seeing Barbara. At the house, Beverly Williams opened the front door and rushed to give the First Lady a spontaneous hug. Other special guests that day were Bill Schroeder, Forrest Wood, and Rick Clunn, a pro the President particularly admired.

Bev Williams had been in touch with White House staff and found out some of the President's favorite foods. For lunch, she served barbecue pork, beef stew, fresh black-eyed peas (a traditional Southern New Year's Day dish for good luck), cole slaw, corn muffins, banana pudding and other savories too numerous to mention. She was intrigued to watch General Scowcroft carefully put his cole slaw on top of his black-eyed peas after he saw Barbara Bush crumble muffins into her stew. Mrs. Bush asked for seconds, and afterwards when Beverly heard a noise in the kitchen, she looked in and saw the First Lady placing her dishes neatly in the dishwasher.

In the midst of all this, the phone rang. It was Orlando Wilson, one of Ray's buddies and host of a cable TV fishing show, "Fishing with Orlando Wilson." He told Ray, completely unaware of what was going on the Scott living room, "I have to tell you what happened last night. I was saved at a Baptist revival." He was very emotional. Ray was delighted and spoke to him for some time. Then, he said "Here, Orlando, tell George Bush your good news." The President got on the phone with a dumbfounded Orlando and offered his congratulations.

Although it was bright and sunny, it was still an unusually cold and windy day for Alabama. When the guests changed into fishing garb, Susan rounded up extra jackets for the Presidential party. "I knew all these product logo jackets would come in handy one day," she says. She was especially concerned for General Scowcroft who was small and slim and seemed somehow fragile to her.

"I fell in love with General Scowcroft," she says. "He's so quiet and unassuming and appreciates every thing you do. When you talk to him, you have his full attention and feel like what you're saying is of the utmost importance to him. He and George Bush both have a certain humility I think you find in most great men."

By his request, the President fished with Rick Clunn while Ray and Barbara laughed and joked in another boat. The angling honors of the day went to the First Lady who landed the biggest fish, a six pound, twelve ounce largemouth. To top it off, she took the bass in an area that had already been fished by both her husband and Clunn, a four-time winner of the BASS Masters Classic. She laughed with delight and teased her husband mercilessly. "Oh, George," she called out in a singsong voice, "look what I've got. Would you like to have your picture made with *my* fish?"

That evening, just minutes after President and Mrs. Bush departed, the remaining guests watched from the great room as the headlights of the procession of cars flickered across the lake.

It was a relaxing moment after all the excitement and exhilaration of the day. A fire crackled in the large fieldstone fireplace as everyone reflected and commented on the day's events. Bill Schroeder was silent and then, out of the blue, brought up a comment Ray had made earlier about the need to build a new sanctuary for the Pintlala Church. In his usual understated way, Bill said, "Ray, we ought to build that sanctuary for them."

Ray listened. He always listened to Bill's ideas. "You could have a tournament right on this lake," continued Bill. "It's probably the best bass lake in the world." A Pintlala tournament was an idea Ray had toyed with many times, but he never thought about it in conjunction with fund raising. The idea took flight. Over the next hour or so a plan evolved: Ray would get top bass fishermen to participate in a series of tournaments on his lake to raise half a million dollars for the new sanctuary. There would be ten two-man teams and each angler would pay an entry fee of $5,000. A total of $100,000 would go to the church sanctuary and Ray would donate $50,000 in prize money. The more Ray thought about it, the more excited he got. He would have been even more excited if he had known he would raise over a million dollars in the next four years.

21

The Eagles of Angling

SEVERAL WEEKS LATER, on January 21, 1990, during the Sunday morning worship at Pintlala Baptist Church, Ray, Bill Schroeder, Orlando Wilson, and Delta Airlines executive Tony Richards faced the congregation. No one had decided exactly what to say or who would say it. "We were kind of like the four stooges," says Ray. So Tony Richards stepped forward and simply announced their pledge to raise $500,000 for a new sanctuary with the help of the bass fishermen of America. Ray took a deep breath. It was done. He was committed.

The congregation in the small, cheerful blue and white sanctuary sat stunned for a few moments. There were audible gasps and then applause.

"We have been caught in a whirlwind of events which have left us transformed and breathless," Gary Burton wrote in the February issue of *Lamplighter*. "The visit of President Bush to Pintlala, capacity attendance at worship, the largest monthly average attendance in Sunday School in our church history, dramatic conversions and many other additions to the fellowship, the unanimous vote to build a new sanctuary and other facilities, and the pledge of $500,000 by the bass fishermen of America, have left us stunned and grateful."

Within three days, Ray had all his contestants for the first tournament as every fisherman called responded to his invitation. In later tournaments he did not even have to extend invitations; fishermen came forward. The church immediately swung into action; and by the end of March, architect David Payne presented the schematic drawing of the proposed new building. The week before the tournament on April 21, church members pitched in to get everything ready. They set up a special weigh-in platform in front of the church, volunteers picked up the tournament fishermen and their wives at the airport, and ten pickup truck owners agreed to pull the trailered boats carrying the fishermen and their catch to the weigh-in.

Most of the fishermen and their wives arrived the day before the tournament, but a few drove all night to make it by Saturday morning. All told, they came from ten states, ranging from Virginia to Texas.

On Friday evening before "The First Pintlala Invitational Tournament," Ray and Susan hosted a dinner at their home for the fishermen and their wives. After dinner Ray explained that the tournament was modeled on the ten-hole B.A.S.S. Megabucks format. Only trolling motors could be used by the ten two-angler teams, and the teams would rotate to a new hole every forty minutes, signaled by a shotgun blast, during the five hours of fishing. The limit was eight bass per boat, no culling allowed. Once a fish went into the livewell, it counted, period.

The ten teams consisted of Bill Schroeder and son Billy, Johnny Morris and Charlie Campbell, Orlando Wilson and Tony Richards, Ken Cook and David Gregg, Hank Parker and Junie Copley, Larry Nixon and Tommy Martin, Charlie Ingram and Guy Eaker, Paul Elias and Jack Chancellor, Woo Daves and Asa Godsey, and Rick Clunn and Gary Klein.

During the Saturday tournament Bev and church volunteers provided continuous refreshments at the house, quietly swapping out breakfast coffee and pastries for a buffet lunch. Meanwhile at the church, members put out folding chairs for the weigh-in, including a set reserved for the fishermen's wives. An easel near the weigh-in platform displayed the architectural rendering of the new building.

The day began horribly for Klein. The airlines had lost all his tackle, and a half-hour before the start, he had to borrow rods, reels, lines, and lures from other fishermen. But his luck would change dramatically.

Out on the lake, competition proved to be very keen, but what had begun as a nightmare for Klein turned into a dream day as he and Clunn took first place and a prize of $25,000 with an eight-bass limit that weighed thirty-six pounds, twelve ounces. The biggest bass, a thirteen pound, fifteen ounce bass caught by Clunn, was not only the biggest fish of the day, but also, to date, the biggest bass ever landed from the lake. It was also Clunn's personal best. Clunn's bass, as with all others, was returned to the lake. Second place, worth $15,000, went to David Gregg and Ken Cook; third place with a prize of $10,000 went to Johnny Morris and Charlie Campbell. Ray and Susan donated the $50,000 prize money to the church, as they were to do in the three succeeding tournaments.

Virtually all the contestants attended the Sunday morning service the following day, and at the invitation of Gary Burton a few fishermen and their wives came forward to make a spiritual commitment. "Landing the Big One" was the appropriate title of Burton's message, and it proved prophetic when it came to the amount raised by the tournament. After much head scratching and a recount by the deacons counting the money, the total came to $110,000. The "extra" $10,000 came from Johnny Morris and Charlie Campbell who had torn their prize-money check in half and returned it in an offering envelope.

The groundbreaking ceremony for the new building took place after the worship service. Bev had gifted each contender with a be-ribboned trowel. Ray announced that the wall of the vestibule of the new sanctuary would bear the inscription, "Dedicated to the Glory of God by the Bass Fishermen of America."

Not long after the tournament, Ray was talking to George Bush on the telephone. He complimented Ray on the fund-raising event and said that if there was anything he could do to help to let him know. It didn't take long for Ray to call him back and invite him to be a guest fishermen at the next event. The President agreed to take part in the second fund-raising tournament — now appropriately named "The Eagles of Angling Tournament" — scheduled for April 13, 1991.

A short time later, at the American Fishing Tackle Manufacturer's

Association (AFTMA) convention in New Orleans, Ray told Johnny Morris about the President's participation and Morris vowed to raise even more money for the church. He told Ray, "I want to be more involved. Let's get the industry involved."

"That's a great idea," said Ray, who quickly added, "You're the chairman."

Morris set out to get ten boosters who would pay $5,000 to get to fish in a boat with two world class bass pros. A week later he called Ray and said, "I've got a problem. I've got thirteen who want to come, and there's only room for ten."

Ray said, "Great. Try to get twenty. We'll let them change places after the fifth hole."

Two days later Morris called again. "I've got a problem again. I've got twenty-three, and there are only places for twenty. What do we do?"

Ray said, "Hey, boosters over twenty are lucky. They *don't* have to fish. They can sit on the porch and have tea and coffee with the wives and watch the *whole* tournament."

The sponsors and boosters included not only a who's who of the bass fishing industry but also other benefactors (See Appendix). One special booster who contributed his talent as well as money was violinist — and avid bass fisherman — Shoji Tabuchi. Shoji produces and performs in the top-rated show in the music town of Branson, Missouri. He packs them in for two shows a day at his own state-of-the-art theater.

With his big smile and the hymns he played during the worship service, Shoji, who is Christian, would capture the hearts of the Pintlala congregation.

Shoji began playing classical music at the age of seven in Japan. When he was seventeen he met Roy Acuff on tour in that country, who advised him to switch to country music. "If you ever come to the U.S. look me up," Acuff said. At age twenty, penniless and speaking little English, Shoji did just that in Kansas City. This time Acuff said, "When you get a chance and visit me in Nashville, I'll put you on the Grand Ol' Opry." And he did.

One $10,000 sponsor was Charles L. Brassell, a Montgomery asphalt contractor who felt compelled to get involved after a bizarre incident that coincided with a phone call from Ray.

A week earlier, Brassell and Ray had been talking on the phone about a $35,000 asphalt paving contract for the church parking lot. Just before they hung up, Ray asked him if he would like to be a sponsor for the tournament. Brassell said that he'd think it over and give him an answer.

A week later, Brassell called Ray and said that a strange thing had happened to him the day after they talked. He had been sitting in his office working on a highway bid that he didn't really want, but submitted out of courtesy. To make certain that he did not win, he had loaded up the bid on the high side, and he was nearly finished when he had an eerie feeling. He looked up from his desk and saw a man standing right in front of him, so close to the desk that his knees must have been touching it.

"This man was the nastiest, raunchiest, filthiest looking bum I have ever seen," Brassell said. "I don't think he'd shaved in at least ten days. He was looking right square in my eyes, and he had the bluest and clearest eyes I've ever seen. It was weird. He was weird. Then he said, 'Mr. Brassell, I need some work because I've got to make some money to get me to Oklahoma.' I said, 'Well, mister, we don't have any work,' and then, and I don't know why I did this, I reached in my left pocket and pulled out a hundred dollar bill. I wasn't even sure what I had it for, and I said to this bum, 'Mister, I don't have any work for you, but here's $100 and maybe this will help you get back to Oklahoma.' The fellow looked at me without even a smile and said, 'That will be more than enough to get me back to Oklahoma.' And with that the turned and walked out of my office."

Brassell totaled up the final figures for the highway job and then walked out of his office to have his secretary type the bid. He asked her, "Who was that guy who came into my office?" She said, "What guy?" That fellow who just left here two or three minutes ago," Brassell said. "I didn't see anybody leave," the secretary said. "I've been sitting here for an hour and nobody has been in your office that I'm aware of. And there's no other way anyone could have gotten in there."

Brassell was so startled that he walked out to the receptionist who sat right by the front door which faced the only gate to the building. He asked the receptionist, "Who was that grimy-looking fellow who came through here." She said, "Mr. Brassell, I didn't see any anybody come through here, and I've been here for an hour. I didn't even leave to get coffee." How bizarre, Brassell thought, how strange.

Four days later he was astounded to be told that his bid had won. "There was no way in this world that I was supposed to get that job," he told Ray, "and I'm going to make an enormous profit. But strangely enough I keep remembering the fellow with the blue eyes. Tell you what, I not only want to be a sponsor of your tournament, but I'll do all that church asphalt paving free."

Another benefactor was Ernie Maestranzi, owner of the Illinois Cutlery Works in Barrington, Illinois, near Chicago. Ray and Susan had met Maestranzi by chance at a seafood restaurant on the St. John's River in Florida. A bass fisherman, Ernie recognized Ray, and they started talking across the tables and became friends. Ernie made, donated, and presented specially engraved Bowie knives to President Bush, Ray, and all the fisherman in the 1991 tournament, and to all the fishermen, sponsors, and boosters in the 1992 and 1993 tournaments. Later on, when Ray mentioned to President Bush that Ernie's mother had just died, President Bush immediately called Ernie and his father to offer his condolences.

For the next three years Ray and Susan and Pintlala played host to the Eagles of Angling, President Bush, generous supporters and America's finest bass fishermen. Thanks to the combined resources of Ray's staff, notably personal secretary Jenny Olive and foreman Andy Dixon, the B.A.S.S. tournament staff, and the church congregation, the tournaments went off with hardly a hitch.

Miraculously, every early spring weekend brought beautiful weather and attendees were able to lounge around on the big covered porches and wide steps, or mill around on the lakeside lawns. Some peered through binoculars to watch the anglers. Every forty minutes a shotgun blast signaled the end of a round, and the fishermen rotated holes.

Some participants made themselves comfortable in the house. Because of space constraints, only contestants' spouses could attend besides the contestants and the sponsors and boosters. The only children allowed were literally nursing babies and yes, there were some. Jill Hibdon retired to the upstairs guest room to quietly nurse her newborn and Billy Schroeder's wife, Julie, did the same.

Once again, Beverly Williams was a dynamo, arranging everything from food to transportation and commanding an army of loyal volunteers. Each contestant, sponsor, and booster was picked up at the airport and delivered to the motels where they would enjoy a welcome basket of fruit and homebaked cookies. She and a small staff kept food and drinks out all day long on the veranda at the Scott's and the weigh-in was followed by a dinner at the church for all participants. Then, each Sunday following the tournament day, she and her volunteers would prepare a celebratory lunch in the church fellowship hall for the entire church as well as the tournament participants who were able to stay — and many did.

The Sunday sevices following the tournaments began in the tiny original sanctuary and ended in the open, spacious sanctuary the bass fishermen had built. "Each service was special," says Ray. "Gary always delivered a powerful sermon and we even kept the music in the family. Shoji Tabuchi gave mini concerts on his fiddle, and David Gregg, a pro fisherman from Houston, and his wife Linda and daughter Rachelle (Gregg) Fletcher gave professional performances. Dr. Rick Jones, son of my long-time secretary Genaé (Jones) Spinks, and Gary's daughter Dana (Burton) Brown also performed beautiful solos. There was a whole lot of spirit and talent in those services."

And once again, the Secret Service and the President's staff were treated to Pintlala hospitality. Indeed Bev became so friendly with the Secret Service they were on a firstname basis, and they presented her with a special plaque.

With the President's participation in the tournament, security was tight for the second tournament — and for the succeeding two tournaments as well. Secret Service agents flooded Pintlala the week before, checking the background of every volunteer, the church grounds and the church itself. Starting on Tuesday, there were no church activities until Sunday, and only designated "inside workers" were allowed in the building. Beverly Williams supervised all food preparation, and Secret Service agents later checked any food served to the President.

Bev was ready to please. Bill Schroeder had specifically requested the tiny, white "lady peas" she had served the first year at the Saturday tournament dinner. When she called her food wholesaler in Selma, she was told the peas were no longer available; the crop had been very small. Bev says, "When I finally broke down and told them they were for dinner for the President, the wholesaler lost all composure and promised he'd call all over the country to get me those peas. He found some a week later in Mobile and sent a truck down to get them. I had forty pounds of peas at the church door the day before the dinner."

The weigh-in platform was now bigger and higher so every spectator could see. Draped across the front was a white banner with red and blue letters proclaiming, "God Bless the U.S.A. and George Bush, America's #1 Bass Angler," while behind the platform a large sign declared, "Pintlala — Eagles of Angling Bass Tournament." There was nothing but the best for the President. Even the Pintlala Elementary School next door to the church got a fresh coat of paint.

To determine which team would get to fish with President Bush, the fishermen threw darts at a poster of Saddam Hussein before Friday night dinner at the Scotts. Roland Martin and Orlando Wilson won. The other teams were Johnny Morris and Charlie Campbell, Forrest Wood and Jerry McKinnis, Bill Schroeder and Billy Schroeder, Ken Cook and David Gregg, Denny Brauer and Gary Klein, Guy Eaker and Charlie Ingram, Jack Chancellor and Paul Elias, Larry Nixon and Tommy Martin, Junie Copley and Hank Parker, and Forrest Wood and Jerry McKinnis.

Halfway through the tournament day, President Bush came to shore for a lunch break. Little Wilson walked out of the woods to present lunch to him and his partners on a tray, followed by Tabuchi serenading the President with a medley of songs including "San Antonio Rose," "Cotton Eyed Joe," and "Presidents Prayer." The President shook his head in amazement and said, "What's going to happen next?" At the church, an Air Force band played while police, National Guardsmen, and the Secret Service kept about fifteen hundred on-lookers waiting to see the President behind ropes. The weigh-in was an hour behind schedule, and there were excited shouts when the Presidential limo finally arrived. President Bush mounted the platform where he good-naturedly called out the weights of the fish along with Ray.

Charlie Ingram and Guy Eaker won the first prize of $25,000 with thirty-four pounds, fourteen ounces. Second place and $15,000 went to the Schroeder father-and-son team, while third place and $10,000 went to Larry Nixon and Tommy Martin. The Schroeders endorsed their $15,000 check and put it in the offering plate on Sunday.

Before President Bush left to return to Washington, in a gesture of thanks on behalf of the congregation, Ray presented him with an honorary lifetime membership in the church which he graciously accepted. Ray also playfully presented the president with a one-year supply of dated offering envelopes. The President laughed and said "That's just like a Baptist church." Everyone cheered.

In church the next morning, Gary Burton asked the treasurer, Mary (Butch) Moseley to announce the total raised by the tournament. She opened an envelope and read aloud the sum of $310,000. Johnny Morris and George Bush had done the job. The congregation responded with an emotional standing ovation.

The third annual Eagles of Angling Bass Tournament took place on Saturday, March 7, 1992. Again security was tight and the national spotlight was on Pintlala because President Bush was paying yet another visit. The day before the tournament, George W. Bush, the President's older son and soon-to-be Governor of Texas, arrived to join his father and General Brent Scowcroft as guest contenders. Again thanks to Johnny Morris, even more sponsors and boosters contributed to the tournament. After dinner at the Scotts' house on Friday night, the 1991 winning team of Charlie Ingram and Guy Eaker, in a luck of the draw, got the President as a fishing partner. The other teams were Johnny Morris and Charlie Campbell, Bill Schroeder and Billy Schroeder,

Tommy Martin and Kevin VanDam, Jack Chancellor and Paul Elias, Hank Parker and Junie Copley, Ken Cook and David Gregg, Forrest Wood and Jerry McKinnis, Guido Hibdon and Dion Hibdon, and Roland Martin and Orlando Wilson, who drew General Scowcroft as their guest fisherman. As in the previous tournament, any fish caught by a fishing booster could count in the team total.

Ready for the weigh-in duties again, President Bush arrived in the boat with Ingram and Eaker. A good sport, the President didn't have his best day out on the water. To start off, he hooked himself in the thumb while removing his lure from a small bass (Eaker nervously removed the hook) — and his team finished fifth. First prize of $25,000 went to the team of Martin, Wilson, and Scowcroft, who set a tournament record with forty-seven pounds, one ounce. David Gregg and Ken Cook won the $15,000 second prize; and third place of $10,000 went to Bill and Billy Schroeder. Once again the Schroeders donated their check to the church.

That evening the President returned to Washington, and on Sunday Gary Burton presided over an unofficial dedication service of the new sanctuary. The six hundred-seat facility was not quite finished, but the main vestibule was. On the wall above the sanctuary entrance was the inscription, "Dedicated to the Glory of God by the Bass Fishermen of America," just as Ray had said it would be. Orlando Wilson gave the invocation and Shoji Tabuchi gave a mini concert, playing "Amazing Grace," "What A Friend We Have In Jesus," and "The Old Rugged Cross." Again a thundering, standing ovation greeted the announcement that this tournament had raised another $345,000.

The final dedication service of the completed sanctuary came three months later on June 14. The honored guests were Ray, Bill Schroeder, Tony Richards, and Orlando Wilson, the four who had made the original pledge to raise the funds. Gary Burton read a letter from President Bush who wrote, "Barbara and I are delighted to send our congratulations as you commemorate the thirty-second anniversary of the Pintlala Baptist Church and dedicate a new sanctuary. We join you in spirit as you give thanks for the sanctuary where you gather and for the congregation of families who have worshiped together for many years. May your community continue to grow in faith and friendship, and may the love that you share with each other be a witness to all. You have our best wishes for a joyous celebration."

The 1993 tournament, the fourth and final Eagles of Angling competition, took place on the weekend of March 6 and 7. Again George Bush attended, only no longer as a sitting President. Many repeat sponsors and boosters attended as well. For this final tournament there were twelve boats instead of ten, twelve holes, and the top five teams finished in the money. Johnny Morris had worked his magic again.

Susan and Ray particularly enjoyed the last tournament when Bush, now out of office, could come just as a good friend and fellow fisherman. Finally, he and son George W. were both able to spend the night in the guest cabin — an event that is marked by a tongue-in-cheek plaque on each bed. "Our other guests just love it," says Ray. "We ask them if they want the President's bed or the Governor's bed. One day, maybe they'll have the choice of two presidents."

The teams in the fourth annual Eagles of Angling Tournament were Johnny Morris and Charlie Campbell, Bill Schroeder and Billy Schroeder, Charlie Ingram and Guy Eaker, Jack Chancellor and Paul Elias, Hank Parker and Junie Copley, Forrest Wood and Jerry McKinnis, Jeff Barnes and Jay Yelas, Mike Folkestad and Tommy Biffle, Roland Martin and Orlando Wilson, Stan Mitchell and Steven Mitchell, Jim Eakins and Steve Lloyd, and Peter Thliveros and Kevin VanDam, who drew George Bush as their third man.

As in previous tournaments, President Bush emceed along with Ray. Roland Martin and Orlando Wilson finished first for the second straight time and won $25,000 with forty-five pounds, three ounces. Second prize of $15,000 went to Tommy Biffle and Mike Folkestad, and third place money of $10,000 went to Guy Eaker and Charlie Ingram. Johnny Morris and Charlie Campbell got $10,000 for fourth place, which they donated to the church. Hank Parker and Junie Copley also received

$10,000 for fifth place. When all four of the tournaments were over, eight of the pro contestants had caught the heaviest bass of their lives from Ray's lake.

Television crews from CNN, NBC, ABC, and local stations were on hand. After the weigh-in, everyone moved to the front of the church. The time had come to unveil the larger-than-life bronze group that commemorated the tournaments. The sixteen-foot high bronze had been brought in secretly at midnight Thursday so that it would come as a surprise on Saturday when President Bush unveiled it.

A cherry picker slowly lifted the huge cloth cover to reveal the monumental bronze, and sculptor Lincoln Fox stepped forward to eloquently explain the piece, which he entitled "The Strength of One." It depicts New Testament figures Peter and Timothy, an eagle clutching a bass, and water trickling down a bronze version of a rocky cliff. Peter is holding onto a sinking Timothy and the eagle appears almost as wings growing out of Peter's back.

Fox explained that Peter and Timothy represent the ongoing struggle we face while living and growing in our society where the strength of just one man can become the salvation of another. The Apostle Peter's strength and wisdom is exemplified through the art, while young Timothy represents the innocence and fears of youth. The eagle universally represents the highest aspirations of man, soaring far above physical limitations and opening new opportunities. Its fishing skill represents the abilities of great fishermen.

The bass — one of God's special fish — represents itself, for it is from this magnificent creature that sprang multiple industries, an improved environment, and a new level of outdoor recreation that both excites and soothes the soul of man. Running water reminds viewers of the relentless passing of time, forcing us all to count our days and seize our opportunities with enthusiasm and gratitude.

After the presentation of the bronze, everyone quietly moved into the sanctuary. Pastor Burton and Ray welcomed George Bush to the pulpit where he did a double take when he saw the sunburned fishermen filling the choir area behind him. "I sure hope they don't sing," he joked.

Ray presented him with the first maquette of the bronze, and Bush told the congregation, "I used to talk as President about the thousand points of light. Well, we're seeing many hundreds right here in this room . . . I was just privileged to fish with some of them. Some of my sophisticated friends in Washington, D.C., don't quite understand the feeling I have about friends and sports in life; and I've concluded, after having been President of the United States, that it is family, friends and faith that mean everything."

It was one of Bush's first public statements following his election loss to Bill Clinton.

Bush left Pintlala shortly afterwards to return to Houston, but a capacity crowd filled the new sanctuary on Sunday morning. Hank Parker gave the morning prayer, and once again baritone David Gregg led the singing of patriotic songs. Ray introduced all the fishermen to an extended standing ovation, and Gary Burton gave as his message, "A Surprise Catch." And indeed it proved to be that with the announcement that the tournament had raised $391,200 for the church. All told, the total from the four tournaments came to $1,060,000.

A week later, the phone rang at the church, and Beverly Williams answered. A man said, "This is George Bush." Beverly retorted, "Sure you are, and I'm Barbara." Then he said, "How are things in Pin-tala?" With that distinctive pronunciation, she knew that it was indeed George Bush.

22

Battle For Bass Waters

RAY HAD ALWAYS been interested in the environment, especially clean fishing waters. He had selfish reasons: good fishing waters and more of them meant better business. But emotionally, he knew he had a personal responsibility to be an environmental steward and his bully pulpit at B.A.S.S. gave him the perfect opportunity to be an activist.

In the full maturity of his life, he found himself wanting to do more. When he watched his seven grandchildren fish off his dock for bluegill and bass, he wondered what their fishing waters would be like as adults. He cringed when he thought about the endrin incident at his old lake in Montgomery.

In 1997, Robert F. Kennedy, Jr., sent him a copy of *The Riverkeepers,* the book he co-authored with John Cronin. It chronicled the successful cleanup of the Hudson River by the Hudson River Fishermen's Association, now Riverkeeper, in New York. Ray was so electrified by the book, he read it three times and personally sent copies to forty-six Federation presidents, as well as to Helen Sevier, Bruce Shupp, and Don Corkran. At Don's suggestion he also sent copies to the conservation directors.

"Sometimes you read a book that changes your life," says Ray. "*Silent Spring* by Rachel Carson did that. And more recently, *The Riverkeepers.* Everyone should read it."

In late 1997 he was alerted to two issues that hit his "hot button." The first alert was from his very own pastor in the church that the bass fishermen had built; the second came from the fishermen of Texas.

Ray's first battle began on December 7 — Pearl Harbor Day — in 1997 at Pintlala Baptist Church. After the morning service, Ray and Susan were greeting friends and neighbors beneath the large inscription in the vestibule: *"Dedicated To The Glory Of God By The Bass Fishermen Of America."*

In friendly chit-chat, Pastor Gary Burton suddenly asked Ray what he thought about the battery problem addressed in yesterday's paper. Ray drew a blank. "What paper?" he asked. "What batteries?"

"The Montgomery Advertiser," Gary said. He left and quickly returned with an editorial from the paper that soundly chastised the United States Coast Guard for dumping spent batteries — big, automotive type lead-acid batteries — during routine maintenance of navigation aids into Lake Guntersville, an 89,000-acre impoundment on the Tennessee River in north Alabama.

Inside the plastic casing of the batteries are such toxic contaminants as mercury and sulfuric acid. You didn't have to be an environmentalist to know these materials should not be dumped in waters used for fishing, water-skiing, swimming, and for municipal water supplies.

Back home, Ray traced the genesis of the editorial to a recent story in the *Birmingham News* by his friend Mike Bolton, that paper's very inquisitive outdoors editor. Bolton's story quoted divers as saying Guntersville is littered with hundreds — maybe thousands — of batteries.

Bolton had interviewed the man in charge of the navigation aids in the Coast Guard's Eighth District, Lieutenant Commander Byron Thompson, who told him the practice of battery dumping at navigation aid sites began in the mid-1950s and ended in 1973. But Bolton found strong evidence that disputed Thompson's claim.

Lieutenant John Clifton, chief investigator for the Alabama Marine Police, told Bolton that he dove on five sites in 1993 and had found batteries on four of them. As a matter of fact, he said, there were lots of batteries down there. He brought up three that were newer-type batteries (introduced in the 1980s). He didn't bring up the older batteries because they would crumble in his hands.

Ray also learned from Bolton's story that there was an eyewitness to the Coast Guard dumping. A Birmingham man, who insisted upon anonymity because of fear of reprisals, said he and his son, while camped on an island in Lake Guntersville, had seen the Coast Guard dump spent batteries. At dusk one evening, a Coast Guard maintenance boat approached a navigation aid just a few yards off the island. Coastguardsmen, unaware they were being observed, removed the spent batteries from the aid and tossed them into the lake. Lieutenant Clifton said the man identified the site for him and when he dove on it, he found the new-type batteries scattered in the muck of the lake bottom.

Bolton quoted Chris Cook, a mussel diver who had been working the lake more than ten years: "There's hundreds of batteries down there. . . . Some of these batteries are in big piles." Commander Thompson claimed the batteries posed no threat to the environment or to aquatic life although the EPA classifies lead as "a highly toxic" heavy metal and mercury contamination in the past has shut down some of the nation's best fishing waters. Mercury has the sinister ability to accumulate as it moves up the food chain. By the time a human eats a fish from contaminated waters, there may be enough mercury in the fish to damage the human central nervous system — damage thought to be irreversible. Ray could not believe a high Coast Guard official was saying in effect "not to worry, everything is okay."

Ray knew something needed to be done, and soon. He and Bob Boyle agreed to approach the problem from two directions. Ray would involve the Alabama B.A.S.S. Federation and pursue a more systematic investigation of the problem. Bob would contact the Environmental Litigation Clinic at the Pace University School of Law in White Plains, New York. The clinic represented Riverkeeper, the successor to the Hudson River Fishermen's Association, in pollution cases. Directed by Riverkeeper's John Cronin and professors Robert F. Kennedy, Jr., and Karl Coplan, the clinic assigns law students to investigate and help prosecute cases of environmental abuse. So far, they have won around a hundred cases in Federal Court without a single defeat.

The investigation soon began to reveal the scope of the problem. On-site dumping of spent batteries appears to have been a universal practice for at least fifty years. The toxic time bombs had been dumped from navigational aids coast to coast.

Ray and Bob realized that the Coast Guard, the agency responsible for preventing the pollution of navigable waters in the U.S. and its overseas territories and possessions, might turn out to be the biggest polluter of all.

The agency now admits it has dumped some 100.000 batteries into every waterway in the nation where lighted or audible navigational aids are located. However that figure may represent only a fraction of the problem, because with some 12,000 fixed sites, and another 12,000 floating navigation aids or buoys, there are bound to be more than 4.17 batteries per site. Ray considered it a laughably low estimate.

In his investigation at Guntersville, Ray, Al Redding, president of the Alabama B.A.S.S. Federation and Bob Fountain, conservation director of the federation, found twenty-nine batteries at just three sites in a search that lasted only a couple of hours. Ray's divers — Chris Cook, the mussel diver, and Allen Scott, a diver for the Jefferson County Sheriff's Department search and rescue team — said there were literally hundreds of batteries on the lake floor.

Beginning in 1994, the Coast Guard initiated its own cleanup effort very quietly and with virtually no public input or supervision by the EPA or any other governmental agency. They proposed to "clean up" only the fixed sites, claiming it would be too difficult to find and raise the batteries from the thousands of floating sites. And, it seemed to be official policy that since "most" of the batteries were concealed in bottom silt, they could be ignored. This approach may be what led to a bureaucratic fiasco on Lake Guntersville in February 1998.

Stung by the continuing reports of hundreds of batteries littering the bottom of Lake Guntersville and other lakes, the Coast Guard set out to prove the claim wrong. The agency, amid great fanfare and media coverage, imported a team of Navy divers who spent ten days inspecting fifty-five sites in the Alabama portion of the Tennessee River, including Lake Guntersville. They recovered twenty-four batteries. That trip cost the taxpayers $64,000 or $2,667 per battery.

That was just too much for Ray. He told the *Birmingham News*, "It wasn't the break-in at the Watergate that got Nixon in the end, it was lying about it. The Coast Guard came to the Tennessee River in their 'moon suits' and did their dog-and-pony show for ten days and said they found twenty-four batteries. Well, we spent a *couple of hours* out there and found five more than they did. The Coast Guard is not leveling with the public." To prove his point, Ray went back to Guntersville in March with divers Cook and Scott and in three days they found thirty-two more batteries at six sites.

In an attempt to calm, if not head off public outrage, the agency put out a slick brochure that played down the dumping. For example, the brochure stated "Most batteries were discarded before there was general environmental awareness or laws or regulations prohibiting this activity."

That statement is false. Laws on the books since 1899, not to mention the 1972 Clean Water Act, prohibited such dumping under penalty of a fine of up to $2,500 and a year in prison for each violation.

A group met in early January in Phoenix to assess the situation and plan strategy. Ray and Bob Boyle were going on to Lake Novillo in Mexico for a few days of fishing, but John Cronin of Riverkeeper, Al Redding, and Bob Fountain of the Alabama B.A.S.S. Federation flew out just for the day. Matt Vincent, the environmentally conscious editor of *B.A.S.S. Times* also attended.

It was agreed that if the Coast Guard were sued, the Alabama Federation would be lead plaintiff, followed by Ray and others. At Pace law school, Professors Coplan and Cronin soon finished their research and evidence gathering. They were ready to go. In addition to the federation, the plaintiffs were Ray, the National Association of River, Sound and Bay Keepers, Bob Boyle, Cronin, and a host of other Keeper organizations.

On August 30, 1998, Professor Coplan gave the Coast Guard commandant the required ninety-day notice of intent to sue in federal court. The notice cited several grounds for the suit, including failure to obtain the required permit before dumping hazardous waste; violation of federal open dumping laws; and in particular the "imminent and substantial endangerment to health or the environment" caused by the dumping of mercury into the nation's waterways.

With his usual finely tuned ability to grasp the moment, Ray returned to Lake Guntersville the day after the Coast Guard notice was mailed. This time he brought with him not only divers Cook and Scott but newspaper reporters and TV cameras. With the cameras rolling, the two divers recovered twenty-two batteries in only an hour and five minutes. "How many more do you want?" the divers asked. "They're not buried, they're easy to see," they reported.

To close the circle on the episode, Ray delivered the batteries to a Coast Guard station near Chattanooga. The Coast Guard chose to attack the messenger rather than confront the message.

"If they have taken batteries out of the water, that was a mistake," said Ed Wandelt, chief of the Coast Guard Environmental Management Division in Washington. "It's *our* program to deal with those batteries." Wandelt dug himself deeper into a hole by raising questions about the batteries themselves. "Can you prove in a court of law they are Coast Guard batteries?" he demanded, adding "How do I know that they didn't go to a junkyard and get those batteries?"

Ray calmly replied to reporters, "Why go to the junkyard to get batteries? There are more in the river than in the junkyards." The *Montgomery Advertiser* cut through the Coast Guard duplicity with a stinging editorial on September 6, 1998.

"The U.S. Coast Guard owes every Alabamian an apology for dumping obvious environmental hazards — used batteries from navigational aids — into the state's waterways," the editors wrote. "But it owes the critics of that reprehensible practice a special apology as well for suggesting that they planted some of the batteries to make the Coast Guard look bad . . . Such a suggestion, without evidence to back it up, is way out of line. Wandelt's superiors should see that he either backs up that statement with proof or retracts it with an apology."

If any proof was needed that the battery-dumping was a *national* scandal, it came the same day — September 6 — in the *New York Times*. In an editorial, following an article by correspondent Rick Bragg, the Great Gray Lady declared: "Until the raising of the nation's environmental consciousness in the 1970's, many Americans treated their bays, rivers and streams as little more than open sewers into which trash, sewage, and industrial waste could be cheaply and quickly dumped. Even so, it comes as a shock to be reminded that among the vandals was the official guardian of the nation's waterways — the United States Coast Guard."

AT THE SAME TIME RAY was searching for batteries on the cold, murky bottom of Lake Guntersville, loud noises were coming from Texas — the noisy, angry voices of bass fishermen.

The Texas Parks and Wildlife Department had declared a policy of eradicating all non-native aquatic plant species. To make things worse, Texas had virtually no regulation of aquatic herbicides, which meant, in essence, that just about anyone could buy their herbicide of choice and dump it into lakes and rivers, many of which serve as sources of drinking water. But what really had the fishermen upset was the decision by the Lower Colorado River Authority (LCRA) to chemically 'nuke' Lake Bastrop, a highly productive eight hundred-acre bass fishery in Texas. The fishermen knew what this meant — another destroyed fishery. Local lure maker Terry Oldham called Harold Sharp and Harold called Ray.

Terry had called the right person. Harold had been in this battle before. When he moved back to Chattanooga in 1990, he discovered his favorite bass lakes — Nickajack and Chickamauga — had been decimated by chemical weed control.

"Before TVA weed control it took twenty pounds of bass to win a one-day tournament," Sharp says. "But in 1991, only five pounds was a winning catch." That was not a scientific conclusion, but it was the language and logic of the fishermen.

"Let me say up front," explains Ray, "I used to hate hydrilla and milfoil and they must be managed very carefully. As a matter of fact, I would *never* introduce foreign vegetation into any public waters. *Bassmaster* used to run articles on the horrors of hydrilla, until the fish started disappearing when it was chemically eradicated, and people began to understand the intricate ecosystems that develop around this vegetation.

"And, it's not hard to understand once you start investigating. Very simply, this vegetation creates a rich but delicate ecosystem. Everything feeds on everything else. Poisons can devastate entire ecosystems in a lake beginning with the smallest micro-organism. It may take years to recover and in the meantime there is a crippled food chain to support a fish population. And that means there is no quality fishing.

"Can you imagine living in a world with no living plant material? No grass. No plants. No flowers. No trees. No birds or critters of any kind? When you virtually destroy aquatic vegetation and habitat, that is what you do to a fish's world.

"When you get down to it, aquatic vegetation is as much a natural resource as our forests. Fishermen say it's habitat for fish. Naturalists say it's habitat for waterfowl. Biologists say it's habitat for both game fish and waterfowl. Environmental scientists say it's a natural filtration system for lakes and rivers and that it's vital to clean waters.

"So how did we get in this predicament? It's simple" says Ray. "It's spelled M-O-N-E-Y. Chemicals are big business, like the drug industry. Some of these herbicides cost $2,000 a gallon. And a gallon doesn't go far on a big lake. And let's face it, it's a whole lot easier to put out herbicides than sweat under the sun on a mechanical harvester.

"Here's how it works. Let's say you are in charge of marketing a new aquatic weed killer produced by Toxidyne Solutions, a giant of the chemical industry. Where and how are you going to get the product introduced to the market?" he asks. "You're not going to get the results you need by advertising in *Outdoor Life*, or *The American Water-Skier*. You may sell a little here and there to people who want to clean out around the boat dock at their summer cabin, but that's not where the big bucks are. The really big money for chemical weed-killers comes from government, and quasi-government agencies and water resource authorities, and other agencies that control most of the nation's water-ways."

Chemical companies sponsor research by scientists who wind up endorsing the chemicals under study, points out Ray. Research dollars are always hard to find, especially in low-priority areas. The sponsor provides the dollars and has a good chance to influence the parameters of the research, and to get the label okay from the EPA: "This product is safe and effective when used according to the label instructions." That blessing from the EPA is worth millions, maybe billions of dollars to the company that gets it.

The connection between the chemical companies, research scientists, and government agencies has existed for decades. Without it, most chemical giants would be mom and pop operations, mixing up stuff on the kitchen stove. The chemical company, in this case Toxidyne, gets a good result from Professor Twitch at Kickapoo U., and this research leads — many millions of dollars and many more hoops later — to the official registration from EPA. The question now becomes how to sell it.

A chemical company doesn't necessarily call on the agency heads. It can send its "detail men" to call on employees on the front lines, the people who actually have to get out on the lake and get rid of the grass. They show them all the paperwork: "EPA-registered," "just use as directed," "spray it on and then go home."

Over the years, Toxidyne has learned just which buttons to push, just how to present its product in order to make the sale. It is worth it to them. Millions of dollars are at stake.

"There's no doubt," says Ray "that many times, surgical weed control is necessary, but that does not justify wiping out the entire vegetated eco-systems in a lake, down to the smallest micro-organism. When your grass at home gets too long, you cut it, you don't kill it. Do you have to make a choice of getting a trim or being bald? Of course not."

Ray thinks there is a better way, and he's giving this better way all the support he can muster. For many years mechanical weed control has been used. Lakeside cabin owners in the upper Midwest have employed mechanical cutters for decades to clear the shallows around their docks, and channels to open water.

The technology behind mechanical weed control is clean and simple. Visualize a wheat combine cutting through a wheat field, then imagine setting that cutter mechanism on a barge instead of a wheeled chassis and you've got the idea. Provide for raising and lowering the cutter head in the water and solve a few drive and lube problems, and you have a functioning aquatic grass cutter or harvester. The difference is that a cutter chops and drops the grass into the water while, if circumstances demand, a harvester brings the grass aboard a trailing barge for shore disposal.

By the time Ray decided to take up the Lake Bastrop issue, he was pretty well up to speed on the situation. He was amazed at the diversity of his allies: everything from bass clubs to a mainline church. The coalition called itself BAIT for "Better Aquatics in Texas." Oldham represented FISH (Fishermen Involved in Saving Habitat), which fittingly joined with BAIT to battle the threat to Lake Bastrop.

Ray decided there were at least two ways he could help the cause. With his experience in gathering crowds and in raising money, he took on those responsibilities. But more immediately he could also call on his friend, Texas Governor George W. Bush. Ray had come to know the governor well through his friendship with his father, the former President. Both Bushes are life members of B.A.S.S.

Ray called the Governor and said, "Governor, I'm calling to ask for a stay of execution on Lake Bastrop." He explained the situation and asked the governor to use his office to postpone the poisoning of Lake Bastrop. "We just want the chance to demonstrate the effectiveness of mechanical harvesting," Ray said. "This way the lake could be managed and trimmed with barber's clippers as opposed to being nuked."

Ray knew the evidence was mounting in support of mechanical control over toxic chemicals. A new study in the February 1998 issue of *Fisheries,* published by the American Fisheries Society, underscored his point. A team of scientists, led by Mark H. Olson of Cornell University and Stephen R. Carpenter of the University of Wisconsin, found that cutting a series of deep, evenly spaced channels in the near-shore grass of four experimental lakes — in contrast to nine control lakes — increased the growth rates of bluegill sunfish and largemouth bass.

Governor Bush contacted the river authority, which immediately granted the delay. With Harold Sharp's help, Ray borrowed a mechanical harvester and its operator from TVA. It cost $8,000 to haul the machine from Tennessee to Texas. With help from his friends in BAIT, Ray organized a phone tree that quickly raised the money in donations of $1 to $20 from hundreds of fishermen and others across the country.

In short order, the machine was afloat in Lake Bastrop. Fittingly, Governor Bush came over from Austin for the demonstration, climbed aboard, got in the driver's seat, and piloted the harvester across the lake clipping grass as he went. "It's very effective," he said, as the cameras rolled. "We cut a lot of hydrilla in a very short time."

Shortly after this demonstration, the LCRA placed an order for a $200,000 state-of-the-art harvester of its own. "As the governor said," Ray commented, "it's time for new thinking."

New thinking indeed. Sparky Anderson of Clean Water Action, a member of BAIT, says that as of January 31, 1999, "There has not been a chemical spray of significant size by any large river authority in the past year." Furthermore, a new organization has sprung up to take BAIT's message nationwide. It is called SMART, for "Sensible Management of Aquatic Resources Team."

Meanwhile, back home in Alabama, Ray staged a pre-emptive strike against any further poisoning in rivers and lakes across the country. He enlisted the help of Harold Sharp, who had organized a highly successful 1993 anti-herbicide parade in Chattanooga for the benefit of the TVA.

Ray and Harold organized a "Grass Parade" from Scottsboro to the shores of Lake Guntersville that drew 731 boats from fourteen states. It included a large contingent of Texans.

"The name of the game is education," Ray says. "We have to spread the word. As more and more people understand that there's no need risking destruction of fish habitat, drinking chemicals, swimming in chemicals, or eating fish from a chemical pool, there will be less and less spraying."

When all is said and done, Ray's position on aquatic herbicides is very simply stated: *"Chemical poison herbicides should not be used to control and manage aquatic vegetation in public waters until, or unless, every non-toxic mechanical or manual method has been completely exhausted, period."*

23

The Strength of One

"Never doubt that a small group of thoughtful, committed citizens can change the world. Indeed, it's the only thing that ever has."
— MARGARET MEAD

THIS QUOTE FROM famous anthropologist Margaret Mead hangs directly in front of Ray's desk in his small home study crowded with deer heads, fish mounts, and photos of friends, grandkids and celebrities.

"It's so simple and so true," says Ray. "But it still blows me away every time I read it. And I like to break it down even further. To paraphrase Ms. Mead, 'Never doubt that *one* thoughtful, committed citizen can change the world.'

"The older I get, the more I realize that's true. I talk to these 'world changers' every day from this desk." He thumps the desk and motions to the phone. "I am amazed and humbled by the people out there, especially all the 'Davids' — those bulldogs that have taken on the 'Goliaths.' Over the last couple of years, especially during this aquatic herbicide fight, I have come to have great respect and fear for the power and influence of the Big Money Goliaths. That may sound naïve, but as a dyed-in-the-wool capitalist, I don't find anything evil about money itself. What I do find evil is the suppression and/or manipulation of facts."

Oddly enough, a health issue precipitated Ray's newly found awareness. "I had a personal experience that lifted the blinders from my eyes," he says. "I found out about a treatment called chelation therapy, a simple intravenous medical treatment. My Uncle Sam had recently died of clogged arteries, arteriosclerosis. He couldn't even walk across a room without getting winded. But one of his good buddies, who had suffered from the same condition, was running around the block. My uncle was given a choice of by-pass surgery or do nothing. His buddy had found out about chelation therapy.

"Uncle Sam chose to do nothing because he had watched his brother, my Uncle Leo, develop a blood clot and suffer a stroke after 'successful' by-pass surgery. That's not uncommon at all. Leo died two years later in a nursing home, a very bitter man. Sam was a dentist and knew enough about the medical profession to know that a lot of surgeons bury their mistakes."

About this time Ray's old buddy Archie Phillips, a self-confessed "health nut," sent him two books — *By-Passing the By-Pass* and *Forty-Something Forever,* both about the chelation process. Ray learned that chelation had been around since World War II and is still used today to remove heavy metals, notably lead, from the human body. Hence, it is a bonafide medical treatment. It was observed over and over again that a side effect of the treatment was to remove plaque from arteries. In other words, it painlessly helped clear clogged arteries, and obviated the need for dangerous surgery.

After considerable research and talking to many people, Ray and Susan decided to undergo chelation on a preventive basis. However, they were to find the treatment was not readily available. As a matter of fact, it was downright difficult to find a provider.

"We had to track down a doctor who would do it," says Ray. "Thanks again to Archie, we found out that one of the pioneers of chelation therapy was right in our own backyard in Birmingham — Dr. Gus Prosch. He's a tough old country M.D. who has fought the government and the medical establishment tooth and nail to offer the treatment.

"Most doctors can't handle it. They're ostracized by their medical community and under constant scrutiny — some would say harassment

— by the government. But Dr. Prosch is just one of a growing number of physicians who had the strength to stand up to everyone."

While undergoing the simple I.V. treatment over a period of several months, Ray and Susan had the opportunity to meet dozens and dozens of chelation patients, many of whom traveled regularly from out of state. They heard recovery story after recovery story from survivors of by-pass surgery who did not want the surgery again. "Some had had two and three by-pass surgeries," says Susan. "The stories were incredible. And virtually all of them had to come to chelation without the blessing of their regular doctors."

Ray and Susan were amazed. How could this simple, inexpensive — compared to by-pass surgery — treatment be such a secret? Why wasn't it at least offered as a non-invasive alternative treatment as it was in other countries? It didn't take long for Ray to find out that the "By-Pass Surgery Industry" ($3 billion a year) and the Drug Industry (lifetimes on expensive medications) hate this process, which is simply a series of intravenous drips of a harmless enzyme.

"Why do they hate this process?" asks Ray rhetorically. "It's simple. The chemicals, the components in the I.V. drip, are out of patent. There is no money to be made. And because there is no money to be made, there are no fancy tests and double-blind studies done by the drug industry to prove how effective chelation is. And because drug companies have such an influence over the medical world and colleges and universities — scholarships, research grants and endowments — the doctors are not even educated about the treatment. Or they're told it's pure voodoo. Or more ironically, they're told it's dangerous, when in fact thousands die after by-pass surgery each year.

"Talk about voodoo. I remember when vitamins, physical therapy, RK surgery for myopia, acupuncture, and chiropractic were voodoo. Now they're mainstream and many are covered by insurance policies."

The moral of the story for Ray is that the drug and chemical industries are powerful and pervasive, and they're not going to tell you the whole story if it's not to their benefit. And frankly, he admits, they may not know the long-term effects of their products, which is even more frightening.

"One diet drink with aspartame isn't going to kill you," says Ray. "But I've never heard anyone say this is a good substance to put in your body. However, it makes lots of money. What happens after twenty years of using it? We sure found out what cigarette smoking does after twenty years."

Ray also cites DDT, the now banned highly toxic poison once lauded as the ultimate pesticide. Susan remembers as a child on Maxwell Air Force Base hearing the roar of trucks that regularly sprayed the residential areas late at night during the summer. The DDT killed mosquitoes. And she remembered the same smell on the cotton fields near their cabin on Lake Jordan.

"So, am I cynical about chemicals? You bet I am," says Ray. "I have been assured by experts that the herbicides they spray in our waters do show up in drinking water. Is one glass going to kill you? No. A lifetime? I guess we'll find out the hard way eventually. But if it kills and maims fish and wildlife, it's not a big jump to believe it might harm humans.

"Just remember, when it comes to chemicals, we are uninformed, misinformed and even dis-informed. I don't even think it's a conspiracy. It's a lot of groups of people 'doing their job' with the information they're provided. Frankly, that's even more frightening to me than a conspiracy. Because these people honestly don't know they don't know. One day we'll look at these herbicides in our waters and shake our heads, just like we did with cigarettes and DDT, and say, how could we have let this happen?"

Rachel Carson, the author of the history-making 1962 book *Silent Spring,* is another of Ray's conservation heroes. He keeps a copy close by on his book shelf and always has a supply of extras for the disbelievers.

Her research, Ray says, offered proof that certain pesticide residues — notably DDT — were killing our birds, fish and wildlife. "Remember," says Ray, "this was coming from a biologist with the U.S. Fish and Wildlife Service." The far-reaching influence of her book was instrumental in getting a ban on DDT in the late 1960s. Unfortunately the ban came after her death from cancer in 1964.

Something she said not long before her death spurs Ray on in his outspoken crusade against aquatic herbicides: "Man is part of nature and his war against nature is inevitably a war against himself."

"We just don't know what we're doing to ourselves. We just don't know what we're mixing together," says Ray. "Singly, a substance can be harmless. Ask any high school chemistry student and he'll tell you what can happen when you mix it with the wrong thing. It makes me sick to even think of dumping herbicides into our public waters. We have created a chemical soup. These are waters that we not only swim in, fish in, and ski in, but water that we drink.

"It's fine and noble to support things like the Clean Water Act and the Fishable Waters Act. And I have great respect for the lobbying process after my Wallop-Breaux experience. But supporting clean and fishable waters in the abstract is a little like supporting motherhood and apple pie. It's not nearly as much fun going up against vested interests and Big Money right down at the gritty, retail level. But if that's where the action is, that's where you go.

"And that's why I say 'God bless the bulldogs.' People like Harold Sharp and Dr. Prosch and Rachel Carson. And the Texans. And the Federation guys like Al Redding who won't be intimidated."

Ray continues to be awed and gratified by the environmental fervor and determination he encounters among everyday bass fishermen. He draws inspiration from them.

In 1998 he was discussing the anti-herbicide campaign with a young Florida fisherman who mentioned a book called *The Art of War* written by Chinese warrior/philosopher Sun Tzu twenty-five hundred years ago. Ray was so impressed with the young man's conversation that he immediately searched out the military classic at a local bookstore. He was electrified by one passage in particular that not only expressed his personal feelings but also the level of commitment necessary to win the "battle for bass waters."

"What Sun Tzu said," explains Ray "is when you cross the river with your troops in pursuit of the enemy, the first thing you do is burn your boats and smash your cooking pots. There is no turning back — you *can't* turn back."

A man who understands that philosophy is Harold Sharp, the long-time tournament director for B.A.S.S. Harold was involved in environmental issues in his Tennessee home before he ever came to B.A.S.S., and he has stood with Ray in his environmental battles ever since.

In the early nineties as Harold studied the herbicide problem on Lakes Nickajack and Chickamauga, he became an advocate of mechanical weed control. To help persuade the TVA to stop spraying chemicals in the river, he and his fellow anglers formed Operation SORE (Save Our River Environment) and took to the streets. Literally. In early 1993, he orchestrated a six hundred truck-car-boat funeral procession, complete with a fake human skeleton, that wound its way through the street of downtown Chattanooga and the TVA office complex. While reviewing the cortege, he told the media he wanted the TVA to convene a panel of experts to determine if it had the legal authority to use ratepayers' money to kill fish and wildlife habitat.

Three months later, after getting no response from TVA, the four hundred-member Chattanooga Bass Association, represented by Rick Parrish of the Southern Environmental Law Center, sued the agency in federal court to stop the use of herbicides in the entire Tennessee River system, not just the Chattanooga area lakes. The suit charged that TVA threatened the environment and public health, and that the agency had violated federal law by continuing to spray herbicides into the lakes before completing a detailed environmental impact statement that analyzed in full the effect of the herbicides.

The TVA began to wave the white flag. Beginning in 1993, it decided it did not need to apply herbicides to Nickajack and Chickamauga. Instead, it would use a mechanical harvester to achieve satisfactory control. Unfortunately, TVA did not surrender completely. It is again using herbicides in other Tennessee River lakes, including 89,000-acre

Lake Guntersville. It claims it is responding to local mayors and an area congressman who in turn are responding to real estate developers and lakefront property owners.

"It's amazing what a little 'citizen' input can do," says Ray. "But you gotta keep at it. Harold is the kind of guy who grinds it down to the bare metal. In the Old West, you wouldn't want Harold Sharp on your trail. He's a bulldog in a controversy. He's slow to form his position, but once it is fully formed, that's where he stands and nobody can budge him."

As part of his S.O.R.E. campaign, Harold put out a flyer for public distribution that compared the popular chemical herbicide SONAR with the mechanical harvester. It is pure Harold. And a grim description of SONAR.

> SONAR will not work in rain, wind, brackish or muddy water. A mechanical harvester will work anytime you crank it up.
>
> SONAR cannot be used within a quarter-mile of a potable water intake. A mechanical harvester will work within two inches of a potable water intake.
>
> SONAR eradicates aquatic plants and destroys the fish and waterfowl food chain. A mechanical harvester enhances the food chain by returning the harvested plants to the water in bite-size pieces.
>
> To use herbicides you should wear protective clothing such as coveralls, gloves, boots, goggles, hoods, face mask and respirators and cover your skin. You can operate a mechanical harvester in your bathing suit, or naked.

The Texans at Lake Bastrop displayed the same tenacity as Sharp. "They were so determined to protect their waters," says Ray. "But Lord knows, they're all such individuals and they had umpteen organizations going."

The Texans, however, did get their act together. They created a coalition of organizations called SMART for Sensible Management of Aquatic Resources Team (See Appendix). In Texas its members include everything from the Texas Audubon Society and the League of Women

Voters to the Rebel Bass Club and the Jeremiah Project: Presbyterian Church.

As Debra Dean, the outspoken managing editor of *Honey Hole Magazine*, wrote in the February 1999 issue, "We Texans have stirred up a hornet's nest on our home turf, but what you don't hear from the proponents of chemical use is that worldwide, there are millions like us in thousands of organizations."

Margaret Mead would be proud. So would Rachel Carson.

24

Sailing into the Sunrise

THE COVER OF the July/August 1998 issue of *Bassmaster Magazine* featured a painting (also on the jacket of this book) of Ray Scott by well-known portrait artist James E. Seward. The magazine was celebrating the thirtieth anniversary of Ray's founding of B.A.S.S. and the headline accompanying his portrait read: "The Man Who Woke the Sleeping Giant." The issue came out just before the BASS Masters Classic, but ironically the founder of B.A.S.S., the father of the bass fishing industry, and the man who conceived the Classic, would not be part of Classic for the first time in its history.

Ray's contract with B.A.S.S., the third he had signed with the company since he sold it in 1986, was due to expire on the last day of the 1998 Classic. Shortly before the Classic, B.A.S.S. and Ray began serious negotiations. Ray knew they would be difficult because he had already expressed his desire for more freedom and the opportunity to do some consulting within the industry that might not include Classic sponsors. In addition, he wanted to follow his own course in environmental issues.

He was well aware it was a situation B.A.S.S. might not accept, and ultimately B.A.S.S. made the decision it could not live with what it considered a conflict of interest. The official news release of Ray's departure came on January 19, 1999, stating that B.A.S.S. Inc. and its founder Ray Scott had ended their contractual relationship so that Scott could pursue other interests in the fishing and outdoor world. Helen

274

Sevier would say, "We truly regret Ray is leaving B.A.S.S. to pursue other interests in the fishing and boating industry. We wish him well in his endeavors."

Ray was quoted, "For a number of years, I've wanted to be free to do other things in the industry. But, I was restricted by my contract with B.A.S.S. I am proud of my work with B.A.S.S., but after thirty years, I'm also excited about developing a new career which will include continued involvement with environmental issues."

Indeed, Ray was increasingly uncomfortable with what he considered B.A.S.S.'s conservative, diplomatic stance on environmental issues, one it would call "cooperation versus confrontation." In fact, B.A.S.S. had been applauded for issuing "memorandums of understanding" with several Federal agencies and interfacing with other conservation groups.

But Ray had a different take. "That's not my style," he says. "I want to be able to take the gloves off and fight and not worry about who I might offend. Then I'll think about being diplomatic. I'd rather be a guerilla fighter and besides, some of my fishermen don't quite understand what a 'memo of understanding' is. I think history shows there's a need for both battle and diplomacy."

The media picked up on Ray's departure. "B.A.S.S. loses its master." "Ray Scott reels in his line." "Mr. Bass pursues bigger fish." Such were the headlines. Some reports expressed a "so-what" attitude to the announcement, but many lamented his departure.

Ray shrugs, "It was a three-day wonder, like an obituary. I sure hope I didn't create a company that couldn't survive without me. That's not what I intended. And I hope Helen is building a company that can survive without her as well. That's what good business is all about. That's what having good qualified people is all about. The show's got to go on and I know B.A.S.S. is going to go on." He pauses and smiles, "But it's going to be a whole lot better show with me." Modesty is not one of Ray's virtues.

WHEN THE CONTRACT negotiations fell apart, Ray went on with his life. He had been bored and restless for some time. He was only fifty-two when he sold B.A.S.S. Now he felt totally free and ideas churned in his head. He was wired, ready for yet another career. And within nine months, that's exactly what he had.

Many had speculated that Ray would start another fishing organization, host a TV show, publish a magazine, or organize a new tournament trail.

"I've heard all of the above and I've had offers on the table, but right now all I want to do is consult with a few top-notch companies and help the industry grow. There's a lot of work to be done," Ray says. "The truth is, the active fishing population is shrinking. There is so much to distract in our society, so many claims on our leisure time. Kids don't know a fishing pole from a hockey stick. And access to water is a real problem. Kids need a Taunton Lake like Bryan Kerchal had in Newtown, Connecticut. That's why I am such a proponent of both private and public 'small waters.' And that's why I encourage any and all fishing whether it's catfish or carp."

Ray looked forward to promoting fishing of all kinds, especially for kids and was ready and willing to take an unconventional approach. For example, in 1994, he was re-introduced to carp fishing. Charles Kelley, the Director of the Alabama Fish and Game Department for thirty-nine years, had introduced Ray and his sons to carp years ago at his cabin on Lake Jordan on the Coosa River. Now, Ray invited Bud Yancey, president of the U.S. based Carp Anglers Group (CAG), and Peter Clapperton, a successful English carp outfitter, to his home. And while he 'laid the grits and gravy' on them, they tutored him in the finer techniques of carp fishing.

Carp fishing is wildly popular in Europe, much like bass fishing in the U.S. "Catching a normal-sized ten-pound carp is very exciting," says Ray. "Carp have gotten a bad rap in this country. But as a sportfish, it is a real fighter." The more he thought about it, the more he realized carp fishing would be a great way to get kids involved in fishing. The common carp abound in virtually every river and lake in America, and fishing is done mostly from the bank.

He approached his old buddy, Alabama Federation President Al

Redding — "Ever-ready Al," Susan calls him. Al and wife Betty pitched in and Al enlisted the help of his Alabama Federation directors. Also helping were Bill Schroeder from Kentucky, Rhodney Honeycutt from North Carolina, and Oliver "Big O" Dunlap of Montgomery. Orlando Wilson brought his film crew in to film the event for one of his TV shows, "Fishing with Orlando Wilson."

While Yancey and Clapperton directed the operation, the volunteers treated twelve kids to a carp fishing expedition at Lake Jordan. They were joined by Charles Kelley who had always been interested in carp if for no other reason than it took some pressure off the bass. He, too, believed it to be a great way to introduce youngsters to fishing. The expedition yielded seventy-six carp that weighed in at 861 pounds. One of the participants was a wheelchair-bound eleven-year-old boy.

A week or two later when Ray mentioned the carp event to a friend, his friend said, "Don't you think it's a little demeaning for 'Mr. Bass' to fool around with carp?" Ray replied, "Hey, anytime Ray Scott or anyone else kneels down to help a kid catch a carp or any fish, he's not diminishing his reputation, he's enhancing it." He continues, "I have a simple philosophy about kids and fishing. Teach a kid to catch a fish — any fish — and he'll find his way to bass."

Conservation was also on his list of interests. "I know I sound like an evangelist preacher," he says, "but we've all got to be stewards of our waters and our fish habitat. Every single one of us. You know, bass fishing is unique as a sports industry. Unlike golf, tennis, NASCAR, and jock sports, we are ultimately involved with our environment. We need leaders in the industry who always keep that in mind because the recreation will die and our industry will die without the resource. It's that simple."

After his departure from B.A.S.S., Ray was particularly interested in building a "dream team" of top products that would allow him to promote his vision for the industry — a vision of "inclusion." "Bass fishing needs to be accessible and approachable," says Ray. "It's got to be user-friendly to all segments of society, young and old. We've got to go beyond tournaments and get back to the grass roots."

In the months following the expiration of his contract, Ray put his energies into the growing Whitetail Institute, appeared on numerous cable TV fishing shows, worked on his biography, traveled for speaking engagements, emceed Johnny Morris's Bass Pro Shops *Legends Tournament*, promoted his tape series on lakes and ponds design, and continued his environmental work, especially with his anti-herbicide campaign.

He was most proud of his growing "dream team." "I picked Triton Boats, Mercury Marine, and MotorGuide for my team and I have consulting contracts with all three. I couldn't be more excited and I couldn't be working with finer companies. They're tops in the industry." In fact, Ray had personal ties to all of them.

EARL BENTZ, FOUNDER of Triton boats, was the first to approach Ray. They had a long history of mutual respect. Ray had quietly watched Earl's career. He met him first as a young man after Bentz went to work for Hydra Sports in Nashville in 1975 as a performance consultant.

Then in 1983 at the age of thirty-one Bentz founded Stratos Boats. He sold the successful company to the Outboard Marine Corporation only four years later and at the same time became president of OMC's Fishing Boat Group which included not only Stratos but Javelin and Hydra Sports boats as well.

After his OMC contract expired, Bentz decided to start all over again in 1996 with a new company and a new boat — Triton Boats of Ashland City, Tennessee, just a short cast from Nashville. When he founded Triton, he also attracted a boatload of the best talent in the marine industry. "I don't know anyone who understands performance and safety better than Earl Bentz," says Ray. Indeed, Bentz literally grew up with boats. As a teenager, he worked on hundreds of tri-hull boats at his uncle's marine dealership in Charleston, South Carolina, modifying them for better performance. He'd sand the bottom and add a wedge to help soften the ride and minimize porpoising.

When Bentz wasn't playing with hydrodynamics, he was racing as a driver-member of the prestigious Mercury Driving Team. He would go on to win two world championships and nine national championships. But at age twenty-two, Bentz was in a horrific racing accident that broke his back and forever changed his perception of boating . . . and life.

In August 1973 Earl was racing at the American Power Boat Association Closed Course Nationals at Lake Eufaula in Alabama. On the second lap, with the first and second place boats in his cross hairs, he hit a big roller created by a spectator boat. "The boat came up level and flew level," recalls Bentz "because it was pretty well balanced. But I had air in my power trim line that we'd been working all week trying to get out.

"I backed off on the throttle so as not to over-rev the engine when the propeller came out of the water. As soon as the gear case re-entered the water, the engine shot out from the air in the power trim line and the boat went as high as a telephone pole."

Bentz flew out of the boat which hit the water at 115 miles per hour. When he came to, he was floating face down in the water. Another competitor, Bert Ross (now deceased), jumped out of his boat into the water and pulled Bentz's head out so he could breathe. Bentz knew immediately his back was broken from the numbness in his legs and the excruciating pain in his back.

Doctors were also concerned about swelling in Bentz's neck, thinking it might be broken because of the bucketing effect of the full-face helmet he wore. In the same race, one driver was killed at just sixty-five miles per hour when his helmet bucketed and broke his neck. Bentz recalls that in those days a broken neck with a full-face helmet was the way most race drivers lost their lives. Fortunately, however, he only had torn ligaments and tendons in his neck, although the second lumbar in his lower back was broken.

In December of 1973, just four months after the accident and a tremendous amount of physical therapy, Bentz, wearing a special back brace, won the Gator Bowl Boat Race Regatta in Jacksonville, Florida. It was that kind of determination and tenacity that attracted Ray.

As much as anything, Bentz had the horsepower to harness Ray's talents. He had successfully transplanted the steely discipline and calculated risk-taking of the race boat driver to the persona of a highly effective entrepreneur. He was Ray's kind of man — another individual who had taken his passion and built a business.

Environmental issues brought Ray and Bentz even closer. Bentz sat on the influential Tennessee Wildlife Resources Commission where he had taken a lead role in seeing that the TVA and the Army Corps of Engineers keep the commission informed of any habitat manipulation, be it control of aquatic vegetation or the raising and lowering of lake levels. Earl was well aware of the effects of herbicides not only on the fish population but waterfowl as well. He was a strong supporter and participant in the 1998 parade Ray organized at Guntersville Lake protesting the use of herbicides.

JUST AS IT WAS not a difficult decision to pick Triton Boats, it was not a difficult choice when Ray selected Mercury Marine for his dream team engine. Ray saw the same spirit in Mercury as he did in Triton Boats. Mercury, too, was carved out of the pioneer spirit of one man, Carl Kiekhaefer, and his legacy lives on.

"He was one tough guy," says Ray. "I met him in the sixties once when I was still wet behind the ears and the sheer force of his personality just radiated around him. He was like an energy field. His biography is called *Iron Fist*. That gives you a small clue as to what kind of guy he was — tough, strong willed, never satisfied with the status quo. Any intimidation by his competition only intensified his desire to be the best."

Ray signed a consulting agreement with Mercury in early 1999. The largest division of the Brunswick Corporation, Mercury is based in Fond du Lac, Wisconsin (Kiekhaefer's home state), with more than six thousand employees and seven thousand dealers worldwide. In spite of its size, or perhaps because of it, Mercury prides itself on staying keenly attuned to the demands of their consumers, whether bass fishermen or saltwater boaters.

"Mercury's been the leader of fishing boat outboards since the forties and still is today," says Ray. "You know, when I was a struggling insurance man with a wife and three small kids, and driving a little aluminum johnboat with a five-horsepower engine that worked when it wanted to, I dreamed of owning a 'black motor' [Mercury's famous Phantom Black color].

"I have always been impressed with their pro-active position in the industry, especially as it relates to the environment and safety," says Ray. "They put their money where their mouth is. Mercury was among the first to embrace clean-running engines and leads the world in its offering of low-emission engines. And they did it well in advance of the government-mandated deadlines, too.

"Not only that," continues Ray, "they also jumped on the ignition kill switch and made it a standard feature of their outboards before anyone else. When we were working to make boating safer, they were right there."

Ray also particularly admired their post-sales philosophy which was in keeping with his own Wheel of Fortune philosophy of continuing service. "They're working on a special MercuryCare program for service after the sale — a souped-up package of service, maintenance and boat upkeep. They found out that people were leaving boating because of hassles with the sport, notably marine service. So they're concentrating on fixing the problem and taking care of their current customers. That's the kind of thinking I like."

WITH THE COMPLETION of his agreement with MotorGuide Trolling Motor, Ray had finally established the core foundation of his own personal dream team — "Ray's rig" as he liked to call it.

As with Earl Bentz and Mercury Marine, Ray had a long and shared history with MotorGuide. A longtime sponsor of the BASS Masters Classic, this division of the Zebco Corporation is headquartered in Tulsa, Oklahoma, but its origin goes back to Starkville, Mississippi, where the units are still manufactured.

"I love the story of MotorGuide because it says so much about fishermen and all-American ingenuity," says Ray. "Once again, it's the story of one man with a better idea and the determination to make something happen."

The man in question was G. H. Harris, a building contractor from
Jackson, Mississippi, the site of Ray's inspiration for his very first bass
tournament. Harris liked to fish nearby Ross Barnett Reservoir. But he
got tired of sculling (or hiring someone to paddle) his small fishing boat
and didn't particularly like to use his noisy outboard when he wanted to
ease slowly into a fishing spot. He had a SilverTrol electric motor, but it
was awkward to use because it had to be turned on and steered by hand,
which distracted from fishing. Harris was certain he could develop a
trolling motor a fisherman could operate with his foot.

He obtained a field-wound electric motor used in the SilverTrol and
began tinkering with it. Within a few months, he had developed a motor
with a spring-loaded direction control that he could operate with his foot
to steer the boat. And when he took his foot off the pedal, the spring
would return the motor to its straight-ahead position.

Harris patented and trademarked MotorGuide, the first-ever foot
control system in 1951. But Harris found no ready market for his
invention in an economy coming out of the war years and producing
much-needed consumer goods.

Nine years and $30,000 later, as luck would have it, Harris made the
acquaintance of Dick Herschede, owner of the Herschede Hall Clock
Company of Starkville. (Ray owns three of their custom grandfather
clocks and another graced the White House when the Scotts visited in
1989.) While on a fishing trip with Harris, Herschede was fascinated
with Harris's MotorGuide trolling motor. Looking for other products to
produce in the clock factory "off season," Herschede became partners
with Harris in producing and marketing MotorGuide.

The rest is history. Harris patented five more MotorGuide improvements including rack-and-pinion steering that gave easy 360-degree
direction. The MotorGuide achieved growing popularity. By the time
Ray kicked off the bass boom in the late sixties, the improvements came
fast and furious, with smaller and more powerful variable speed motors,
the 12/24 volt motor, a retractable bow mount, stainless steel shaft and
the "clutch" bracket to protect the shaft from impacts. New power
thresholds were reached and better mounting systems were developed

that would not damage expensive boat gel coats. Improvements continued as MotorGuide developed trolling motors for all kinds and sizes of boats, both saltwater and freshwater.

When he signed his consulting agreement with MotorGuide, Ray discovered that G. H. Harris, now ninety, was living in the panhandle of Florida, a mere three hours away. Only days later, Ray jumped in his car and drove to Harris's home where the inventor produced the first foot-control patent and dug out the original prototype for Ray to see.

"He's sharp as a tack," says Ray. "He was interested in 'efficient fishing' back in the forties and I can't think of a single accessory that does that better than a foot-control trolling motor. All I can say is that every bass fisherman who wants to get into those out-of-the-way honey holes and keep his hands free for casting can say a little prayer of thanks for G. H. Harris and MotorGuide.

"WHEN I BUILT B.A.S.S. I knew the first sale was only the beginning. It's the repeat business that makes you successful. Triton Boats and Mercury Marine and MotorGuide understand that philosophy. I couldn't be more proud to be associated with them all. They represent what's right and good about American business."

Ray has other candidates for his product team and is enjoying the luxury of making his own choices in his own time. In the meantime, Susan tries to get him to relax, although, she says "I found out a long time ago work *is* his recreation. Let's just say I try to change the scenery a little bit."

Ray and Susan especially enjoy slipping away to two of their favorite places — Santa Fe and New Orleans. "They're both really unique cities," says Ray, "and similar in that when you visit, it's like stepping into another culture."

The Scotts often take off to New Orleans, an easy five-hour drive on the interstate from their home south of Montgomery. "We go just to eat. Our days revolve around meals," says Ray who loves Cajun and Creole cooking and is an unapologetic "pepperhead."

One of his favorite places, since 1963, is Tony Angelo's, a virtually unmarked restaurant that is a fifteen-minute cab ride from the French Quarter. Over the years, Ray has become friends with the owner, Tony Angelo, and his staff. Two of the restaurant staff, Dale Messina and Frankie Catalanotto, and two other New Orleans buddies, Steve Campo and Dr. Bob Rebert, form a group that comes to the Scotts during the deer season. "They come to hunt," says Ray, "but they also come to cook. They take over the kitchen. You can't imagine what it's like to have four Italian men in your kitchen who love to cook. Just stand back."

Another favorite restaurant is Brennan's in the heart of the historic French Quarter. One of the current owners, third generation Clark Brennan, is a B.A.S.S. member. When Ray walked into the restaurant several years ago, Clark instantly recognized him, and after a superb meal and warm hospitality, the two became friends. With Ray's encouragement, Clark was instrumental in getting the 1999 Classic to the New Orleans Super Dome. "He's another one of those men who has a passion for what he does," says Ray. "And because of that, he is very successful."

When Ray is not traveling or fishing, he's often at work "in the barn." Visitors are fascinated with Ray's "business in a barn," set among rolling hills and a pond just across the hill from his main residence and big lake. Even in the winter it is green with pines, magnolias and wax myrtles. His small staff bustles around in a warren of rooms that used to make up a little apartment carved out of a large horse barn by the previous owners.

The previous owner's house, a medium-size structure, is about one hundred yards from the barn and is headquarters for the Whitetail Institute, where a staff of ten pumps out more than $3 million worth of product a year. All around are huge wooded enclosures with experimental deer and test plot fields of Dr. Wiley Johnson's plantings. Not far away, Ray owns and leases some sixteen hundred hunting acres where he can personally field test all the Imperial Whitetail products.

His large, light-filled office (the only expansion of the original apartment) is loaded with southwestern relics and animal mounts. A near life-sized bronze by Lincoln Fox of an Indian warrior poised to throw a spear is in the corner and a pair of worn cowboy boots make up a lamp base. In contrast, two matching Louis XV style chairs are upholstered in rich jewel tones of antique Russian Caucasian tapestry. In soft, Southern accents his staff offers guests Coke or iced tea and run to D.J.'s — the only restaurant nearby — to pick up outstanding barbecue, beans and coleslaw from the old, converted, rural post office building.

Life at the Scott's house is very casual. Telescopes and binoculars (for wildlife viewing) litter the living room. Susan has a professional cleaning service come in once a week and does her own cooking. Visitors are likely to get a homecooked meal in the kitchen or Ray may take guests to Montgomery to Lek's, for the Thai food he loves. He orders half a dozen or more appetizers for his meal and insists that everyone else do the same, all the while adding fiery chili peppers to everything.

At lunch he relishes taking visitors, especially Yankees and foreigners, to Martin's for fried chicken, turnip greens and "the best corn muffins in the country." The restaurant is a long-time "soul food" tradition in Montgomery where one can rub shoulders with auto mechanics and construction workers as well as bank presidents and state senators. Ray is in his element, greeting familiar faces across the room. For a quick meal he still goes to Chris's Hot Dog Stand — a Montgomery main street landmark — as he has done since he was a child. He orders "by the foot or by the yard" (two six-inch hot dogs are a foot).

It is obvious that Montgomery holds many fond memories for Ray. "When I get too big for my britches," he says "I drive to the old duplex on Cottage Hill where I lived as a child. That puts everything back into perspective."

RAY COUNTS HIMSELF fortunate that all his children live in Montgomery and he is able to enjoy his seven grandchildren by his three oldest children.

Oldest son "Big Wilson" is a giant of a man — six feet, three inches tall and a former body builder with a calm and friendly demeanor. He is an excellent golfer and takes to the courses for a little rest from the booming Whitetail business. His petite wife Vicki is a registered nurse and they have one daughter, Ivey.

Son Steve is smaller at six feet, and darker, with nervous energy and a quick wit. He, too, loves to golf, but also has been a keen hunter and fisherman since childhood. Wife Kelly is a third-grade teacher who matches wits daily with her two young sons, Gates and Jackson.

Daughter Jennifer, like Wilson, was born in Auburn while Ray was in college. She is married to a Montgomery neurologist, Dr. Larry Epperson. They have an especially active household with four tow-headed children of stairstep ages — three girls, Jessica, Elisabeth and Sarah, and a son, Weston.

Youngest son "Little Wilson" is a student at Auburn University. The name belies his size; he is a strapping six-foot-plus former football player with a passion for weight training, animals, and the country life.

"When there were six grandchildren, before the youngest, Jackson, was born," says Susan "all the children were under the age of five. It was a sight to see Ray with all the kids in his lap, crawling on his shoulders, climbing over his head. He pranks with them constantly and tells them long, off-the-cuff stories that the kids make him repeat over and over."

The vanity tag on his truck reads "Granpap."

RAY STILL ENJOYS his Mexican fishing and more important, the trips to Mexico allow him to enjoy the company of old friends and bass pioneers like Forrest Wood and Bob Cobb.

Following his sale of B.A.S.S. in 1986, Ray renewed his connection with Lake Novillo in Mexico's Sierra Madres. Mexico had been a constant and pleasant part of Ray's life since 1969 when he discovered Lake Novillo in the northwestern state of Sonora. Die-hard bass fishermen and women had discovered it years earlier and formed a small expatriate community in the tiny village of San Pedro during the fishing months. Others resided lakeside in a small enclave at Batuc with the help of gasoline generators.

For many years Ray and his cohorts camped out on the shores right across from the big "Red Rock," a mini-mountain outcropping of iron ore that dominates the area. Reddish in color, it takes on the hue of glowing embers in the sunrise and twilight hours.

With the help of his good friend, John Nichols, Ray set up a first-class camp complete with sleeping tents, cooking tents, bathing tents and a dining cover. Young boys from the village twelve miles up the river helped with the chores including the fish cleaning. John, a weekend warrior and volunteer cook with the Alabama National Guard, whipped up incredible meals that included scratch biscuits and fruit cobblers. A day of fishing was punctuated by a shore lunch and a siesta on comfortable canvas cots under a canopy. Ray wanted the whole experience to be "safari quality," and it was. One guest quipped, "I was waiting for someone to whip out the sterling silver coffee service."

The trip to Novillo was a once-in-a-lifetime experience for many of Ray's guests that included writers, business acquaintances, fishing industry people, and family: "The peace and tranquility are hard for visitors to describe," says Ray. "A fisherman might see one or two boats the whole day or an occasional Mexican net fisherman. Time just stops. I've had some of my best ideas out there on those waters."

On one trip Ray was sitting under the dining canopy with guest John Smith, his personal life insurance agent in Montgomery. "John is a sharp three-piece-suit guy, intellectual, wire-rim glasses — the whole thing. We're sitting with our breakfast coffee looking at the big Red Rock and talking about the distance from the water's edge base to the tip top, which I knew to be very deceiving. It was much further than it looked. I said it would be a heck of a climb. John challenged me. He said he could climb it in forty-five minutes. I thought, no way. I accepted his challenge. And then, boys being boys, we made a bet. For $1,000."

"John takes a boat to the foot of the mountain. I'm sitting in the camp with my binoculars watching this guy start up Red Rock. I'm chuckling. There's no way this city boy is going to make it. The guy keeps going and going, up and up. I start to get nervous. He could have a heat stroke or a heart attack. Within forty minutes he's waving from the top of the rock. I couldn't believe it. I lost the bet big time. It was later that I found out John was a former Army Ranger. So much for the three-piece suit."

When Ray's friend and Novillo point man, Bill Curtis, drowned in a boat accident (without a life vest), Ray later moved his camp operation into the village where he and a group of friends bought a small house.

Ramon Silvas, a young man who had been one of Ray's camp boys years earlier, was now their official "get-it-done" man. A small, trim man with a twinkle in his eye and ready smile, Ramon looked after the house and bought supplies. And understood crazy Americans who loved to bass fish.

In 1995 Ray made a great discovery. He found a solitary little hacienda — obviously a weekend house — on the opposite side of the lake nestled among mesquite trees. *The power line side.* Not only was it totally isolated, but it had an electrical tap into the power line from the hydroelectric dam down the lake. Electricity right on the waterfront. Ray managed to make contact with the owner, a dam employee, and a type of "timesharing" was arranged between the owner and Ray's group of five gringo fishermen, including Ray, Bob Cobb, Forrest Wood, Bill Schroeder, and Rhodney Honeycutt, an electrical contractor from Hickory, North Carolina.

The fishing group enjoyed the house so much they dubbed it "la casa de los cinco amigos" or "house of the five friends." Ray had a belt buckle made with the faces of the five partners engraved "Rushmore style" on the brass. The set-up was ideal. The group financed some improvements and the camp eventually included a big stone patio overlooking Red Rock, indoor plumbing, and an "open air kitchen" with running water, a refrigerator and a dirt floor. "Susan has made two trips there and calls it the Robinson Crusoe house," says Ray. "It's a little primitive and makeshift in places, but very comfortable."

Before the group arrives, Ramon puts in supplies, always including a batch of home-made flour tortillas from his wife. Ray rolls his eyes, "My idea of heaven is sitting on the patio watching the sun rise on Red Rock. There is a stillness you can't comprehend. There's nothing like having a steaming cup of strong, sugar-roasted Mexican coffee in one hand and a fresh tortilla with honey and butter in the other. That's living. Don't tell Susan, but I've had some great business ideas too. Without phones, faxes and TV, you can let your mind 'out of the box.' The quiet is deafening and my mind runs free."

Ray has enjoyed many special moments with old buddies Bob Cobb and Forrest Wood in Mexico. Now that he is associated with Triton Boats, many have asked about his relationship with Forrest. There is no friction. "My friendship is with a man, not a boat. And I told Forrest up front what I was doing. You know, Forrest sold Ranger Boats in 1986, the same year I sold B.A.S.S. He and Nina are running cattle and making hay in Flippin and having a great time."

MEXICO FISHING also unites Ray with another of his closest friends, Bill Schroeder of Paducah, Kentucky. Bill not only shares Ray's interest in fishing but his philosophy of marketing as well. In fact, Ray's Wheel of Fortune helped Bill and his wife Meredith build a unique and highly successful business.

Ray met Schroeder in 1979 at a tournament on the St. Lawrence River in New York when Ray was working on George Bush's campaign for the presidential nomination. It was a meeting Schroeder would never forget. "Ray invited Merdie and me for an ice cream in the little village of Alexandria Bay," he says wryly, "and I ended up making a thousand dollar donation to the Bush campaign. We've had a good time ever since." Both Bill and his son Billy are formidable fishermen and have won many tournaments in and around their area of Paducah, Kentucky.

Like Ray, Schroeder is a self-made man and like Ray built his business on a personal interest and a shoestring. A pamphlet he wrote on collecting old Mason jars (and mailed out of his basement) turned into a multi-million dollar publishing empire specializing in books and price guides about collectible items on everything from barbed wire to Italian majolica ceramics. His company, Schroeder Publishing, is the world's largest publisher of books on collectibles.

Later Schroeder would quiz Ray intently on his B.A.S.S. marketing philosophy and techniques which he and Meredith applied to their fledgling concept for the American Quilter's Society (AQS). Today the Society has eighty thousand members, publishes a slick quarterly magazine, and has opened an impressive quilt museum in downtown Paducah. The museum and the Society's annual conventions are major tourist attractions in the Southeast. The museum draws more than seventy-five thousand visitors a year and the convention brings thirty-five thousand individuals from all over the U.S. and the world. The quilts — works of art — submitted to the show are juried in twelve categories and $100,000 in cash prizes are awarded, with a $20,000 best of show award.

"I picked Ray's brain at every opportunity," says Schroeder. "Even on fishing trips. I concentrated on his concept of marketing and philosophy of networking to build a brand-new organization. He gave me lots of free information. As a matter of fact, Ray loves to share his ideas and help people in their marketing. He doesn't hold back or hoard ideas. He gets as excited about your projects as he does his own."

ANOTHER BENEFACTOR of Ray's marketing concept was a young Montgomery man named Jackie Bushman, a successful tennis pro with a passion for deer hunting. He started calling Ray around 1985 with an idea he had to start an organization called Buckmasters. Ray encouraged him and shared his B.A.S.S. marketing philosophies and ideas. Bushman capitalized on his love of deer hunting as Ray did his bass fishing. Today Bushman has a highly successful national organization with a membership of more than three hundred thousand, a monthly *Buckmaster Magazine,* and even a Buckmasters Classic.

"Jackie made it happen" says Ray. "I couldn't be more proud. The Wheel of Fortune worked once again. I think it's remarkable that here in Montgomery, we have three national organizations that changed the face of the outdoors — B.A.S.S., Buckmasters, and the Whitetail Institute of North America. Wow!"

Rhodney Honeycutt, the fifth and youngest Cinco Amigo, exemplifies the continuity bass fishing has represented in Ray's life. A successful electrical contractor in Hickory, N.C., fishing and hunting around the world are his lifelong passions.

"I am seeing the second and even third generation of fishermen now," says Ray. "Here I am fishing with the son of one of my best friends [and early B.A.S.S. tournament champion], Blake Honeycutt."

Rhodney has a remarkable bassing pedigree. He literally grew up with B.A.S.S. As a matter of fact, at the ripe old age of fourteen he was paired with bass fishing pioneer John Powell at the Lake Eufaula National in Alabama in June 1968. He boated a nine-pound, six-ounce lunker that earned him the big bass award and a much-needed MotorGuide trolling motor.

Rhodney grew up around Ray, Forrest Wood, Tom Mann, Roland Martin, Hank Parker, and many other famous bassmen as he and his dad fished regular B.A.S.S. tournaments as well as Federation tournaments. He also had the privilege of knowing and learning from legendary Buck Perry, acknowledged by most experts as the father of modern structure fishing for bass. Indeed, Blake Honeycutt worked for Buck Perry for a time and helped him make his famous spoonplugs and develop the fishing method of spoonplugging. Today Rhodney happily continues his long-time association with Ray Scott, not only as a fishing partner but filling in as a popular chef at the Novillo hideaway.

RAY'S LAST YEAR at B.A.S.S. was particularly satisfying for him. One of the highlights was the inauguration of the Bassmaster Western Invitational Tournament Trail. B.A.S.S. had taken the tournament trail to the West in the 1980s with disappointing results. Response was lukewarm and it was hard to justify moving the tournaments from their strong base in the East and the Midwest and forcing the mainstay tournament fishermen to travel so far. With reluctance, B.A.S.S. turned away from the West and the estrangement further intensified when California and other Western states allowed 250-horsepower engines on boats while the B.A.S.S. tournaments were restricted to 150 horsepower.

In 1996, however, the ever-cautious Ray was finally convinced that boat and engine technology and safety precautions were such that it was time for B.A.S.S. to accept 250-horsepower engines as well. And the Western Invitational Trail debuted on the Sacramento River Delta near Stockton, California, in September 1997.

Ray attended and was overwhelmed at the personal reception he received. "At the big kick-off and pairings meeting, there were tears in the fishermen's eyes when they came up to welcome me; and there were tears in mine. It was like the prodigal son — me — coming home. I went home and told Susan what an incredible experience it was. I was so glad to be there."

It was a particularly emotional moment when California angler Mike Folkestad, a former Classic contender and Eagles of Angling participant, presented Ray with a plaque that read:

"With our deepest appreciation and warmest welcome to Ray Scott, Founder, Bass Anglers Sportsman Society. Your inspiration, creativity and leadership has brought America's finest fishermen into an arena of competition and camaraderie that is unparalleled — anywhere. We are forever grateful — forever loyal. From the bass fishermen of the West, presented at the B.A.S.S. California Delta Invitational, September 30, 1997."

B.A.S.S. was to discover not only avid fishermen in California, but outstanding fishing as well. In the April 1999 tournament, again at the Delta, tournament records were broken. The largest one-day, five-fish creel of thirty-four pounds, seven ounces was brought in by Mark Tyler and included the largest tournament bass ever of fourteen pounds, nine ounces.

California also claims another record bass — a twenty pound, fifteen ounce monster — caught by David Zimmerlee at San Diego's Lake Miramar in 1973. Ray has a mounted replica in his office and has had great fun with it. At one point he pulled it out of a boat while fishing with President Bush. Several non-fishing reporters excitedly snapped pictures and took notes. However, skeptical heads prevailed and it made the papers as a gag.

In 1997, Ray finally met Zimmerlee at a Triton Boat Show in Kansas City. Following an enjoyable conversation, Zimmerlee graciously sent Ray the Zebco 33 he caught the big fish with and it now sits in his office near the mount of the fish.

Another tribute came Ray's way in 1998 when he was in Texas for the weed harvester demonstration at Lake Bastrop. After Governor George W. Bush rode the harvester, he invited Ray to the Austin mansion for a private supper with him and his chief of staff, Joe Allbaugh.

Ray was struck by the unpretentious warmth of the Governor's mansion, but even more so by the wonderful irony that he was with the son of a man he so admired, twenty years after the elder Bush had made a run for the presidential nomination. And in 1999 his son was poised to do the same.

Governor Bush is an avid fisherman and a life member of B.A.S.S. In his study after dinner, he showed Ray a gubernatorial campaign video commercial that opened with him fishing in his bass boat. When it was over, Ray recounts, "George W. told me that outside his father and family, the two men who had had the most profound effect on his life were Billy Graham and Ray Scott. One had taught him about faith and the other about bass fishing.

"And they both mean a lot in his life," says Ray. "When you get down to it, fishing is a way of being close to God. It was one of the highest compliments I have ever been paid." Old friend Dave Newton says the accolade is well deserved. "How many men can say they touched millions of lives in such a positive way?"

And remarkably, it had all grown from Ray's rainy day vision, four precious names and a three-by-five metal file box of "hand-carved names."

"I had so much help along the way," says Ray. "There were many, many fine people who extended a helping hand."

One of those helping hands came from Homer Circle, the longtime much-honored angling editor of *Sports Afield*. He believed in Ray Scott and B.A.S.S. from the beginning. In 1967 Homer offered a benediction at the conclusion of the banquet at Ray's very first All-American Bass Tournament at Beaver Lake. It was a ritual that would become a tradition at the many Classics he attended through the years.

A copy of this prayer is one of Ray's favorite keepsakes. And it sums up much of his feelings for the sport and the men and the faith that has driven him since that rainy day in Mississippi. Here is what "Uncle Homer" prays:

> Almighty and all-loving Father, we fishermen thank Thee for
> blessings of Thy great outdoors, especially the privilege to pursue our

sport as free men and women in a free nation.

And we especially thank Thee for Thy son Christ, who so loved fishermen He chose four or more among his twelve apostles.

And in years to come, dear Lord, as each bassin' man comes to Thee, please remember these are a special breed. Their spirits would not be content to walk alabaster streets.

Grant them instead…clean waters with a quiet chop…with enough honey holes to last an eternity…and a bassin' buddy to share it with.

In Christ's name, Amen.

Appendix

APPENDIX 1

Ray's Fishing Tips

Why a Bass Strikes a Lure

A deeper understanding of the behavior attitude of a bass can make you a better fisherman, but accept the observations reported here as at best "almost fact." There are always exceptions, moods, and variations to the response character of a bass' reaction.

I have found the two most important stimuli that will trigger a bass' strike button are, very simply, hunger and territorial invasion.

Let's discuss the most basic of the two, hunger. A bass responds to hunger much like a human being. When you're hungry, you seek food. So does a bass. When very hungry, you will do most anything to hustle some grub, even eat something that is not on your list of favorite dishes. A bass is the same. When "starved" you will become almost hostile, do anything, pay any price, and even assault someone to provide any edible to assuage the pain of your empty belly. A bass is no different.

A ready example of the largemouth bass's varying degrees of hunger and corresponding reactions is an experience I had on a seven-acre lake located at my home on the edge of Montgomery, Alabama. This was a "test" lake I designed. When the lake filled, I stocked it with fingerling bass and bluegill.

No sooner had I completed the task than I became too impatient to wait a year or two to catch bass. To remedy this malady, I went on several fishing trips and brought the catch back and placed these larger bass in the lake. Over a period of a month, I released almost a hundred bass that weighed from two and a half to seven pounds. I added several hundred three- to four-inch bluegill taken from a neighbor's overstocked pond. The bluegill were to feed the larger bass.

After a few weeks, the largemouths were acting like bass always react.

I managed to catch a few on every trip. Then, something strange happened. Because of travel on a seminar schedule, I skipped fishing the lake for about three weeks. When I made the first cast later with a topwater lure, I saw several wakes speeding towards the lure from different directions at a high rate of speed. In a split second, the lure was inhaled by a speedy three-pounder. When the bass was brought into the boat, I observed that its belly was thin and the bass was obviously mighty hungry.

In an hour, I caught nineteen ravenously hungry bass on a variety of lures — topwaters, plastic worms, and diving baits. It just didn't matter; the bass were starving and would have hit anything. By adding a sufficient number of bluegill and large shiners, I remedied the "problem," and had a balanced fishing lake with a good crop of mature bass that acted as unpredictably as bass in most lakes or streams.

The point is that you can expect a different measure of aggressiveness from a bass in accordance with just how hungry the fish is. Seasons, weather, and water temperature have their effect on feeding habits, but those are other subjects.

Just as important as the stimuli of hunger to a bassin' man is his foe's attitude towards its "territory." A good example in nature is to observe birds. Many birds have a certain territory in the woods that they "claim" for themselves. Invaders are immediately made aware of this when the bird begins to raise cain. A naturalist could give you a better explanation for the bird's behavior, but put simply — it's his territory and he'd just as soon everybody stay the heck out.

A bass is no different. When Mr. Bass is not chasing dinner or on a migration, he is usually holding in one spot or relatively small area. There is usually some object that will give him some cover and protect his eyes from the sun. Theory holds that when the lake bottom is virtually bare, he can use cover as a reference point. I believe from observations that it's a resting or refuge area or simply a place to call home. A bass may stay in and under a bush for days, even months. It is his home, and the immediate area is his yard.

When you cast a lure through the bass' front yard, he gets provoked.

If you are exact with your cast and can get the lure to bump his bush, he's likely to come out fighting to nail your lure, and the battle is on. This reaction is more often than not a strike to drive the intruding lure away from his house. It is a strike of anger rather than a strike of hunger.

At times bass will vary their degree of aggravation. Sometimes a cast just close to the fish's bush will see the bass come out fighting mad. At another time, you have to really stick your lure in a bass' front door to get it mad enough to strike. Other times, a bass just won't strike with any offering.

Careful casts above or alongside a bass' refuge may be infuriating enough to make the fish slash savagely at the nuisance. I suspect that this bass, a largemouth especially, has no intention of eating the lure. He smashes at the lure to kill it or get it out of his territory.

Whatever the reason, you will discover that big bass are individuals. When you locate a lunker largemouth in a good bush or stump, you can expect to arouse the bass' reaction, time after time, if you stalk carefully and cast accurately. A bass usually remains in one of these refuges until he is taken. And, most likely when you have elected to remove one trophy size fish from its lair, another will be lurking there when you return again. A good refuge for one big fish will be a good spot for others, providing the season, water level, and the cover remain relatively unchanged.

A positive fishing attitude on your part is important. Remember the two basic instincts, hunger and territorial possessiveness. When you observe a certain structural setting that should hold bass, believe that a bass is there. Be patient, vary your lure selection, and the manipulations of the bait. In most cases, there is a lure and a means of working it that will provoke the strike.

Lures — Versatility vs. Specialization

It has been said on many occasions that B.A.S.S. tournaments became known early on as the proving ground for new ideas and innovations. That premise still holds true today. Modern technology has accelerated the growth of the sport in terms of lures, rods, reels, line and other equipment. While a lot of the techniques pros use today are mainly adaptations of old Bassmaster tricks, bass fishing has become a complicated sport.

In the early days, we mainly fished with a few types of lures: topwaters, spinnerbaits, crankbaits, soft plastic bait and leadheaded jigs. Within those categories today are innumerable subgroups. For example, there is a crankbait designed for every depth and fishing condition imaginable — from the surface to 30 feet and from thick brush to broad, open flats.

In similar fashion, the techniques used to present and work those lures have grown dramatically. Formerly, a well-rounded angler needed to be proficient in fishing practically every lure available. That's difficult today, with so many options available. But it is possible for an angler to master one category of lures, such as crankbaits or spinnerbaits, and be well-equipped for any fishing situation.

Years ago on the pro circuit, versatility was defined as how many patterns a fisherman could master using a dozen different lures. Rick Clunn was considered versatile because he could win a tournament in Florida by catching fish on a weedless spoon in lily pads, and win again the following month in Arizona using a jig for bass suspended against a steep canyon wall.

Today versatility can be defined by the number of different techniques a fisherman can master within the same lure category.

Clunn still fits the bill as a versatile angler, and he's been good at it for the past three decades. Crankbaits have been responsible for three of his four BASS Masters Classic championships and a host of top finishes on the tournament trail. In each situation, the crankbait was applied in a different way, despite the fact it seemed out of place at the time. Clunn is proficient in many different techniques using a variety of lures, but his identity as a legendary bass pro is connected to his crankbait prowess. It's his style. And you can develop your own trademark style.

This doesn't mean spreading your lures out on the floor, picking the one that "looks" the best and leaving the rest at home. Instead, you could select a type of lure that has proved reliable for you over the years — your confidence lure — and master its use. If you consider yourself a novice, so much the better. You have the advantage of trying a host of different lures until finding the one that instills in you the most confidence.

Once you find the best combination of tackle, the next step is to develop an effective and accurate lure presentation. And make up your mind to apply the lure or technique in any angling situation for which it is suited. And some for which it isn't. Case in point: Oklahoma pro Jim Morton once won a tournament in November on a buzzbait in shallow water. The contest, held on Grand Lake, Oklahoma, took place during a week when Arctic cold fronts blasted through the area. The key to his win was the ability to adapt a favorite technique, topwater fishing, to a difficult situation.

Develop your angling style and stick with it. You'll be pleasantly surprised at the results, and your fishing trips should become less frustrating and more fun.

My Favorite Bassin' Tips

1. The Gator Bug Flutter

Former BASS Master Classic winner Don Butler has been building spinnerbaits since the 1960s, but none excites me more than his recent "double jointed" Gator Bug creation. Named for its raised, alligator-imitating eyes, the lure is hinged on each side between its head and upper wire and between the head and the hook.

On the fall, this bait's incredible undulation makes it flutter like a dead shad falling slowly to the bottom, making it irresistible to a temperamental bass. Cast this bait along a creek ledge, let it fall to the bottom and retrieve it slowly, making short, intermittent lifts with the rod. The Gator Bug is most effective in cool water seasons.

2. One Stop Shopping

Have at least one spinnerbait rigged up inside your boat's rod locker, regardless of the season. This versatile lure can be fished deep or shallow, through brush and grass, and burned near the surface. Use lightweight spinnerbaits for shallow water, heavyweight models for finessing fish from the deep structure.

3. Cure for the Common Backlash

If you're still dealing with backlashes by using the old pick-and-pull method, there is a better way. Press your thumbnail firmly against the snarled line and make a couple of cranks of the reel to flatten out the coils. Then, it's simply a matter of releasing the spool, pulling free the offending snarl and reeling back up for another cast.

4. Make Contact with Cranks

When casting crankbaits, contact is everything. The goal is not to dredge the bottom, but to make contact with the cover. This creates a more erratic, disjointed action that is often simply irresistible to the bass. Too often, crankbait fishermen don't apply baits to match the conditions, as in too deep for a shallow-runner or too shallow for a deep-diver.

5. Double Skirted Spinnerbait

Add a second skirt to a spinnerbait and you'll have a bait with three different looks and actions. Doing this will make the lure run slower, give it a bulkier appearance, and provide more lift.

6. Run and Gun

Older impoundments generally lack an abundance of visible shore-line cover, or what I like to call "mile markers" during the springtime spawning migration. And that means you have to burn a lot of boat gas by covering a lot of territory.

When you idle up to a lone stick-up, first make a cast with a buzzbait to tempt a "killing" strike. If you fail to get hooked, pick up a rod rigged with a plastic worm and follow up with an "eating" strike. Keep trying the same approach using different combinations of "reaction" and "finesse" bait.

7. Bait-less Trolling

Before you tie a lure to your open-faced spinning rig, open the bail and let out a hundred yards of line as you idle from the boat ramp. Close the bail and "troll" it for a couple of minutes. The drag created by the water and motion of the boat will straighten out any coils left on the bail, wet and soak the line thereby reducing the chance of the proverbial "birds nest."

8. The Highs and Lows

Flood-controlled, power-generating river systems can be tough to pattern, since the water typically fluctuates frequently according to the generation schedule. During high water periods the bass move up to feed on shallow flats. In these conditions, it's best to use baitfish imitators such as crankbaits fished in the shallows.

When the current is "off," the bass move off the flats and down to a deep water sanctuary such as a rockpile, stump or laydown at the bottom of the original creek channel, then it's time to just fish heavy jigs, Texas-rigged worms, or deep-diving crankbaits.

9. Play Hooky

When fishing big impoundments that generate power, I've found the best bite on weekdays when the workings of industry demand a flood of electricity. The increased power generation strengthens the lake's current and triggers bass to move to structure and feed. Power requirements fall off on weekend. This reduces the current and slows bass activity.

10. Cure for Chine Walking

Contrary to popular belief, you cannot "drive through" chine walking, a boat handling characteristic that occurs at high speeds with many of today's high performance bass boats. Instead, you can make steering adjustments to control chine walking and keep the boat balanced at high speeds.

As the boat starts to roll to the right, simply pick it up by turning the wheel an inch or less to the left. And if it rolls left, turn it slightly to the right. All you want to do is counteract the prop rotation and keep the boat on pad. If you oversteer, you're going to pull it off pad and the front end will start swaying drastically from side to side. It's really a balancing act.

11. Short Arm

Use a short-arm spinnerbait in muddy-to-murky water, and at night in deep, clear reservoirs. This design is ideal for ledge-hopping; pull the lure off the edge and stair-step ledges and let it "helicopter" or fall straight down on a tight line.

12. Sock It to 'em

Fish an in-line buzzer on a long pole with a few feet of stout line tied to the end rather than a conventional rod and reel. Move slowly through shallow cover, sloshing the buzzer back and forth repeatedly over every likely spot you encounter. Eventually a lunker bass will be aggravated

into blasting the lure. Old timers call this tried-and-true technique
"jigger fishin'". I was introduced to this technique at age fourteen.
Nothing could be more exciting when a strike occurs. This technique is
not allowed in tournament competition.

13. Do Nothing

Fish a do-nothing worm (a short, stubby worm popularized by BASS
Masters Classic winner Jack Chancellor) on a Carolina rig. Position the
boat in deep water and cast the rig to the shallow part of a ledge or point.
Once the heavy sinker hits bottom, reel slowly and steadily, more like
you'd fish a crankbait than a worm.

The tiny worm will dart and settle as the sinker moves along the
bottom. When a bass strikes, don't set the hook — merely reel faster and
tighten down on the fish. Then set the hook.

14. Finesse

When bass aren't biting your usual worm offerings, switch to a finesse
worm, downsizing your line and tackle accordingly. You may not catch
many big bass on it, but you'll get good action and plenty of keepers.

15. Dive Shallow in Spring

In early spring, the extreme shallows will warm up the quickest. A
small shallow-diving crankbait fished in as little as a foot of water may
produce a lunker bass. If the water is muddy, use chartreuse or fire tiger.
In stained water, try red or crawfish.

16. Cranks without Lips

A lipless crankbait can be fished effectively over the tops of submerged milfoil, hydrilla, and coontail grass beds. Try a high-visibility
color such as chartreuse and clip the leading hooks from each treble so
you can scrape the tops of the weeds without hanging up.

17. The Old Reliable

I still like to use the old Hellbender or Mudbug, metal-lipped crankbaits introduced more than three decades ago. Back then, they were trolled across humps and flats because high-ratio gear reels hadn't been created to make cranking these arm-breakers easy.

Few crankbaits are more effective when fished around stumps, logs and rocks, the bill makes a sharp, bass-attracting clicking sound upon impact. Use heavy, abrasion-resistant line and a slow retrieve baitcasting reel and "feel" the lure over cover.

18. Cold Water Jerks

Jerkbaits are dynamite in cold water. Many pros fish these lures in clear lakes during the transition period from winter to spring, when bass stage prior to spawning. Use Storm's SuspendDots (stick-on weights) to give the bait neutral buoyancy. Twitch, pause, twitch — a big fish will inhale the lure.

19. Walleye Baits for Bass

On a highly pressured lake, bass may become conditioned to avoid popular bass crankbait designs, but they may have not seen a walleye crankbait before. Walleye anglers often prefer superhot colors, but stick with the more natural finishes like shad and perch for largemouths and smallmouths.

20. Limber Up with Buzzers

Don't use a rod that's too stiff when fishing a buzzbait. If you do, you may overreact and pull the lure away from the bass when it strikes the lure. A medium-action rod has enough give to the tip to allow the bass to inhale the buzzer before you can react.

21. Stop-and-Go Topwaters

Most artificial lures work best when retrieved in a stop-and-go manner, but not a surface wobbler. Retrieve it slowly and steadily. This gives the lure the profile of a swimming terrestrial creature such as a mouse and allows the bass to track it down easily in low-visibility conditions. If this technique doesn't work, try the stop and rest method of letting the lure "rest." Sometimes this method works.

22. Chugging on Top

Chuggers are at their best when large schools of baitfish are in shallow water, such as when shad school on flats in the fall. Watch for signs of baitfish flipping on the surface and bass swirling on them, then break out a chugger. If you see a bass flash on the lure but refuse to take it, immediately pick up another rod rigged with a soft jerkbait and cast where you saw the bass.

23. Props on Top

Many savvy bass anglers are convinced the pitch and volume of a prop bait's noise can dramatically affect its productivity. If you aren't getting strikes, "tune" the prop on the bait's nose by bending it slightly inward or outward. Experiment with lures having small as well as big propellers, on some days the loud, deep gurgle of a big propeller works best; at other times the quieter, higher-pitched "slush" of a small prop draws more strikes. Don't get locked into any offering.

24. Rats on Top

Dense surface weeds are low-visibility conditions for bass, and many missed strikes occur when you're fishing weedless topwaters such as a plastic rat. Use a slow, steady retrieve, allowing the bass every opportunity to track down your lure. When a bass blows up on the bait and the lure disappears from view, don't set the hook immediately. Instead, lower the rod tip, count to three and set the hook hard. If the hooked bass tangles itself in thick pad stems or grass, don't try to force it out with rod pressure, or you may rip out the hook. Instead, keep a tight line and move your boat to the fish; a push pole may be necessary in the thickest grassbeds.

25. Backseat Bonus

Being confined to the backseat of your buddy's bass boat isn't necessarily a handicap. The door is open to you on days when the bass are hitting short, especially when your disgruntled partner has just missed a strike. Aim true, be confident, use opposite lures and you might out-fish the man in the front. Harold Sharp beat me from the back seat for fifteen years before I figured out his scheme of letting me make the bass mad, and he would come from behind and catch the bass.

26. First Fish of the Day

It's easy to get excited when you've caught your first bass of the day. After you get settled down, make a mental note of the depth, structure, retrieve, lure and water conditions where you broke the ice. That first fish might give you all the information you need to add more of his relatives to your livewell, all day long.

27. Hit 'em on the Nose

In extremely hot or cold weather, and especially just after a front, bass will hug cover and not range far for a meal. This is where casting accuracy pays off for savvy bass anglers.

On bright days, drop your bait along the shady side of the cover. Where there is current, bass will hide in the eddy on the downstream side of a stump or other object. And whenever bass are hiding in submerged brush or trees, they'll likely be in the very center of the brush with noses almost touching the main stems or trunks and they'll be facing upstream.

APPENDIX 2

Resources

Ray Scott
Route 1, Box 3006
Pintlala, Alabama 36043
Tel.: 334-281-3661
E-mail: rayscott.net

American College for Advancement in
Medicine (ACAM) (Chelation Therapy)
23121 Verdugo Drive
Laguna Hills, California 92653
Tel.: 800-532-3688
E-mail: acam.org

B.A.S.S.
5845 Carmichael Road
Montgomery, Alabama 36117
Tel.: 334-272-9530
E-mail: bassmaster.com

B.A.S.S. Federation
5845 Carmichael Road
Montgomery, Alabama 36117
Tel.: 334-272-9530

Buckmasters
10350 Highway 80 East

Montgomery, Alabama 36117
Tel.: 334-215-3337
E-mail: buckmasters.com

Carp Anglers Group
P O Box 69
Groveland, Illinois 61535
Tel.: 309-387-2277
E-mail: carp.net/cag/index.htm

Homer Circle
1900 South West 55th Lane
Ocala, Florida 34473
Tel.: 352-237-4210

Fishin' Talents
Harold Sharp
6710 West Point Drive
Hixson, Tennessee 37343
Tel.: 423-843-9016

Great Small Waters
Route 1, Box 3006
Pintlala, Alabama 36043
Tel.: 800-518-7222
E-mail: bassboss.com

Honey Hole Magazine
Debra and Jerry Dean
124 Koldine Lane
Fort Worth, Texas 76114
Tel.: 817-738-5596
E-mail: honeyholemagazine.com

Bryan V. Kerchal Memorial Fund, Inc.
Suzanne Dignon
Ray and Ronnie Kerchal
9 Pocono Road
Newton, Connecticut 06470
Tel.: 203-426-1837
E-mail: rkerchal@freewwweb.com

Mercury Marine
W6250 Pioneer Road
Fond du Lac, Wisconsin 54936
Tel.: 920-929-5000
E-mail: mercurymarine.com

MotorGuide
6101 East Apache Drive
Tulsa, OK 74115-3300
Tel: 800-999-7335
E-mail: motorguide.com

Riverkeeper Association
25 Wing and Wing
Garrison, New York 10524
Tel.: 800-217-4837
E-mail: info@riverkeeper.org

Sensible Management of Aquatic Resources Team (S.M.A.R.T.)
David Stewart
3415 Shenandoah Drive
Cedar Park, Texas 78613
Tel.: 512-258-2414

Sporting Lives, Inc.
SOSpenders
1510 North West 17ᵗʰ Street
Fruitland, Idaho 83619
Tel.: 800-858-5876
E-mail: sospfd@primenet.com

Triton Boats
Earl Bentz
15 Bluegrass Drive
Ashland City, Tennessee 37015
Tel.: 615-792-6767
E-mail: tritonboats.com

United States Coast Guard
Commandant (G-MOR-3)
2100 Second Street, South West
Washington, D.C. 20593-0001
Tel.: 800-424-8802
E-mail: nrc.uscg.mil

Whitetail Institute of North America
Route 1, Box 3006
Pintlala, Alabama 36043
Tel.: 800-688-3030
E-mail: deernutrition.com

Eagles of Angling Contenders

1990 Fishermen

Charlie Campbell

Jack Chancellor

Rick Clunn

Ken Cook

Junie Copley

Woo Daves

Guy Eaker

Paul Elias

Asa Godsey

David Gregg

Charlie Ingram

Gary Klein

Tommy Martin

Johnny Morris

Larry Nixon

Hank Parker

Tony Richards

Bill Schroeder

Billy Schroeder

Orlando Wilson

1991 Fishermen

Denny Brauer

Charlie Campbell

Jack Chancellor

Ken Cook

Junie Copley

Guy Eaker

Paul Elias

David Gregg

Charlie Ingram

Gary Klein

Roland Martin

Tommy Martin

Jerry McKinnis

Johnny Morris

Larry Nixon

Hank Parker

Bill Schroeder

Billy Schroeder

Orlando Wilson

Forrest Wood

1992 Fishermen

Charlie Campbell
Jack Chancellor
Ken Cook
Junie Copley
Guy Eaker
Paul Elias
David Gregg
Dion Hibdon
Guido Hibdon
Charlie Ingram

Roland Martin
Tommy Martin
Jerry McKinnis
Johnny Morris
Hank Parker
Bill Schroeder
Billy Schroeder
Kevin VanDam
Orlando Wilson
Forrest Wood

1993 Fishermen

Jeff Barnes
Tommy Biffle
Charlie Campbell
Jack Chancellor
Junie Copley
Guy Eaker
Jim Eakins
Paul Elias
Mike Folkestad
Charlie Ingram
Steve Lloyd
Roland Martin

Stanley Mitchell
Steven Mitchell
Johnny Morris
Jerry McKinnis
Hank Parker
Bill Schroeder
Billy Schroeder
Peter Thliveros
Kevin VanDam
Orlando Wilson
Forrest Wood
Jay Yelas

APPENDIX 4

Eagles of Angling
Boosters and Sponsors

1991 Boosters

ABU GARCIA
Niels Stenhoj

BAGLEY'S SILVER THREAD LINE
Jim Bagley

BILL LEWIS LURES
Bill Lewis

BILL NORMAN LURES
Bobby Dennis

BRUNSWICK CORPORATION
John Charvat

DAIWA
Terry Flynn

JOHNSON WORLDWIDE
Terry Malone

LUCKY STRIKE LURE CO.
John Hendricks

MANN'S BAIT CO.
Frank Oelerich

NORMARK CORPORATION
Jarmo Rapala

OMC (OUTBOARD MARINE CORPORATION)
Jim Chapman

PLANO MOLDING CO.
Peter Henning

PRADCO
William H. Wilson

SHOJI ENTERTAINMENT
Shoji Tabuchi

TECHSONIC INDUSTRIES
Jim Balkcom

WELLINGTON LEISURE PRODUCTS
Chuck Hurney

WRIGHT-McGILL
Lee McGill

ZEBCO – QUANTUM – MOTORGUIDE
Jim Dawson

1991 Sponsors

ALFA
Goodwyn Myrick

ASPHALT CONTRACTORS
Charles Brassell

BASS PRO SHOPS
Johnny Morris

CHEVROLET
Jim Perkins
Dora Lyne Nowicki

DELCO VOYAGER
John Fuhrmann

ILLINOIS CUTLERY WORKS
Ernie Maestranzi

RANGER BOATS
Forrest Wood

RUBBERMAID
William Smith

ZEBCO – QUANTUM – MOTOR GUIDE
Jim Dawson

1992 Boosters

ABU GARCIA
Niels Stenhoj

BILL NORMAN LURES
Bobby Dennis

BLAKEMORE LURE COMPANY
Joe Hall

BRUNSWICK CORPORATION
John Charvat

CHEVROLET MOTOR DIVISION
Jim Perkins

DUPONT COMPANIES
Al Russo

EBSCO INDUSTRIES
Dixon Brooks

FLAMBEAU
Bill Sauey

JOHNSON WORLDWIDE
Terry Malone

LOWRANCE ELECTRONICS
Darrell Lowrance

MANN'S BAIT COMPANY
Frank Oelerich

NORMARK CORPORATION
Ron Weber

OUTBOARD MARINE CORPORATION
Jim Chapman

PLANO MOLDING COMPANY
Peter Henning

SHIMANO OF AMERICA
Toyo Shimano

SHOJI ENTERTAINMENT
Shoji Tabuchi

TECHSONIC INDUSTRIES
Tom Dyer

WELLINGTON LEISURE PRODUCTS
Bill O'Dell

WRIGHT-MCGILL
Lee McGill

ZEBCO – QUANTUM – MOTORGUIDE
Jim Dawson

1992 Sponsors

ALFA
Goodwyn Myrick

ASPHALT CONTRACTORS
Charles Brassell

BASS PRO SHOPS
Johnny Morris

DELCO VOYAGER
John Fuhrmann

ILLINOIS CUTLERY WORKS
Ernie Maestranzi

JEMISON INVESTMENT COMPANY
Jim Davis & Corbin Day

RANGER BOATS
Forrest Wood

REDFIELD SCOPE
Charles Dunkin

ROYAL OAK ENTERPRISES
James Keeter

RUBBERMAID
Pam Carestia

SELMA GRAVEL COMPANY
Willie Hamilton

TRACKER MARINE
Johnny Morris

TRACTOR AND EQUIPMENT COMPANY
Bill Bixby

WRANGLER
Mackey McDonald

1993 Boosters

ABU GARCIA
Jim McIntosh

BILL NORMAN LURES
Bobby Dennis & Jim Howe

DUPONT
Neil Oldridge

JOHNSON WORLDWIDE ASSOCIATES
Terry Malone

MANN'S BAIT CO.
Frank Oelerich

MARINE DYNAMICS
Jon Templeman & Art Templeman

MERCURY MARINE
Carl Scheel

NORMARK CORPORATION
Craig Weber

REALTREE
Steve Lamboy

SHIMANO OF AMERICA
Toyo Shimano

SPORTING LIVES
Scott Swanby

TRACKER MARINE
Johnny Morris

WRIGHT-MCGILL
Lee McGill

ZEBCO – QUANTUM – MOTORGUIDE
Denny Jackson

1993 Sponsors

ASPHALT CONTRACTORS
Charles Brassell

BASS PRO SHOPS
Johnny Morris

DELCO VOYAGER
John Fuhrmann

FARMERS FURNITURE
Ron Payne

ILLINOIS CUTLERY WORKS
Ernie Maestranzi

JEMISON INVESTMENT COMPANY
Jim Davis & Corbin Day

LOWRANCE ELECTRONICS
Darrell Lowrance

MITCHELL BROTHERS TIMBER
Harry Mitchell

OMC/STRATOS
Earl Bentz

RANGER BOATS
Forrest Wood

ROYAL OAK ENTERPRISES
James Keeter

TRACKER MARINE
Johnny Morris

Special Supporters

AMERICAN SPORT FISH HATCHERY
Barry Smith & Don Keller

B.A.S.S.

KYSER FURNISHINGS
Kyle Kyser

MIDSTATE ADVERTISING
Hugh Parks

TONY RICHARDS

WELLS PRINTING
Irvin Wells

APPENDIX 5

S.M.A.R.T.

(Sensible Management of Aquatic Resources Team)

Board of Directors

PRESIDENT
David Stewart

VICE PRESIDENT
Ed Parten

TREASURER
Lindy Ellison

SECRETARY
Bill Bales

ASSISTANT SEC-TREAS.
Pat McCarty

SARGEANT AT ARMS
John Alexander

PARLIAMENTARIAN
Jerry Gold

BOARD MEMBERS AT LARGE
Mike Woehst
Mike Hastings
Randy Kindler

Ray Scott
B.A.S.S. FOUNDER

Jack Allen
SOUTH EAST TEXAS OILMAN'S BASS CLASSIC

Duane "Sparky" Anderson
CLEAN WATER ACTION – TEXAS CHAIRPERSON

Earl Bentz
TRITON BOAT COMPANY

Neil Carmen
SIERRA CLUB OF TEXAS

Ed Churchman
T.A.B.C.

Johnnie Davis
ANGLERS CHOICE TOURNAMENT CIRCUIT

Jerry Dean
HONEY HOLE MAGAZINE

Bruce Goss
FISHING TACKLE MANUFACTURER

Bob Hood
STAR TELEGRAM

Ray Murski
FISHING INDUSTRY LEADER

Terry Oldham
F.I.S.H., OLDHAM LURES

Sue Pittman
THE CHEMICAL CONNECTION

Robin Richardson
H.A.W.K.

Bob Sealy
SEALY OUTDOORS

Harold Sharp
FISHIN' TALENTS, FIRST B.A.S.S. TOURNAMENT DIRECTOR

Bruce Shuler
T.A.B.C.

Ron Werner
APRIL PLAZA MARINA

S.M.A.R.T. Member Organizations

ANGLER'S CHOICE, INC
Johnnie Davis

B.A.I.T. (BETTER AQUATICS IN TEXAS)
Terry Oldham

BASTROP ENVIRONMENTAL ASSOCIATION
Dr. Gary Rasner

CATFISH & CRAPPIE ASSOCIATION
A. B. Gartman

CENTRAL TEXAS ASSOCIATION OF BASS CLUBS
David Stewart

CLEAN WATER ACTION
Sparky Anderson

CONSUMERS UNION
Reggie James

H.A.W.K. (HEALTH AWARENESS AND WATER KNOWLEDGE)
Robin Richardson

HENRY, LOWERRE, JOHNSON, BOSS & FREDERICK
Rick Lowerre

F.I.S.H. (FISHERMEN INVOLVED IN SAVING HABITAT)
Mike Hastings

HONEY HOLE MAGAZINE
Jerry Dean

L.C.M.A. (LAKE CONROE MARINA ASSOCIATION)
Ron Werner

LONE STAR CHAPTER OF THE SIERRA CLUBS OF TEXAS
Dr. Neil Carmen

METRO LEAGUES OF BASS CLUBS
Harvey Holmes

PRO TEAM TOURNAMENT TRAIL INC.
Jerry /John Nichols

RAYBURN BASS CLASSIC
Byron Gianfala

S.C.O.T. (SPORTSMANS CONSERVATIONISTS OF TEXAS)
Alan Allen

SEALY OUTDOORS
Bob Sealy

SOUTHEAST TEXAS OILMEN'S BASS CLASSIC
Jack Allen

T.A.B.C. (TEXAS ASSOCIATION OF BASS CLUBS)
Bill Bales/Jerry Gold

T.B.B.U. (TEXAS BLACK BASS UNLIMITED)
Ed Parten

TEXAS B.A.S.S. FEDERATION
Randy Kindler

TEXAS CENTER FOR POLICY STUDIES
Mary Kelly

THE CHEMICAL CONNECTIONS
Sue Pittman

TEXAS OILMEN'S BASS INVITATIONAL
John Alexander

TEXAS SPORTSGUIDE
Pat McCarty

INDEX

(Page references beginning with P1- or P2- are to the two photo sections.)